Taxpayer's Comprehensive Guide to LLCs and S Corps

2018 Edition
(last updated on January 7, 2018)

Includes the Tax Cuts & Jobs Act of 2017 and Section 199A Business Deduction

by   Jason Watson

and

The Watson CPA Group
Certified Public Accountants
Business Consultants

Copyright 2018 by Watson CPA Group
9475 Briar Village Point Suite 325
Colorado Springs, Colorado 80920

719-387-9800

www.watsoncpagroup.com

ISBN-13: 978-0692279649 (Watson CPA Group)
ISBN-10: 0692279644

About the Author

Jason Watson
Managing Member

Jason Watson is the Managing Member for the Watson CPA Group, a Colorado Springs tax, accounting and consultation firm. His main focus as Managing Member is small business consultation, and financial, investment and estate planning.

Jason has owned two small businesses in the past and holds both a Bachelor's and Master's in Business Administration from the University of Wisconsin – Madison. He also became an Enrolled Agent with the IRS in 2013 and passed the Series 7 General Securities test in 2015.

Note, he is a not a CPA. During college he migrated towards finance, economics and statistics, and not towards accounting. However, he obtained 15 more credits in accounting, and is trying to knock the CPA exam out by spring of 2018. Three parts down. One to go.

So, if he's a bit grumpy please understand why. Debits and credits. Yuck. Why do they have to equal? What a crummy system.

Aside from carrying the one in accounting class, his desire is speaking with small business owners and creating a dynamic map for the future. Jason enjoys talking about business planning, corporate structures, self-employment taxes, health insurance issues and retirement planning. He is quick to point out that while 70% of the all situations can be covered with the basics, every business and person is truly unique.

Ask a question and have a dry erase board handy, and you'll see the true passion of a person who not only wants to educate but also wants to see small business owners thrive. While this book is on LLCs and S Corporations can be labeled as shameless self-promotion, at the same time it truly came from Jason's heart to help small business owners everywhere.

Jason is also a Certified Divorce Financial Analyst and business valuator, and offers mediation support for divorcing couples. He also appears as a financial expert witness, and volunteers for the National Institute of Trial Advocacy in Boulder, Colorado.

While not speaking to a group of business owners, chatting it up with Colorado Springs CPAs or reading the latest thrilling IRS Publication, Jason likes dirt biking, boating in Wisconsin, watching the Packers beat the Bears (it never gets old), and running trails in Colorado. He used to also be a pilot for SkyWest Airlines, a United Express airline, but resigned in March 2015 to focus on small business owners and financial planning. This seems like an odd dichotomy, being an airline pilot and a small business consultant, but it is what it is.

Lastly and most importantly, he is a father of three numbskulls (Brendan, Corinne and AJ) and married to the Watson CPA Group's founder and Senior Partner, Tina Watson, CPA.

You contact Jason at 719-428-3261 (direct) or **jason@watsoncpagroup.com**.

The Watson CPA Group
9475 Briar Village Point Suite 325
Colorado Springs CO 80920

Team Profile

While Jason Watson is the primary author of this book, the Watson CPA Group's entire professional team is utilized to ensure accuracy and comprehensiveness. Here is a quick outline of our team members.

Tina Watson, CPA, MBA
Senior Partner

Tina Watson became a Certified Public Accountant in 2003. Tina has both a Bachelor's and Master's in Business Administration and consults with a variety of small businesses including Defense Contractors.

Tina takes pride in helping her client understand how the numbers come together. She believes that the extra time spent with a client illustrating the mathematical nuances helps everyone better understand their business. Tina manages Pod A.

As a mother of three and avid tennis player, Tina still finds time to enjoy traveling, exercise and the occasional moment of downtime (which is like a unicorn).

Sally Rhoades, CPA
Tax Manager

Sally began her tax career in 1988 with Ernst and Young (never heard of them, are they big?) in Nashville and became a CPA licensed in Tennessee in 1989. For 10 years, she followed her Air Force husband all other the world and was a full-time mother of two and a volunteer at various Air Force tax assistance offices.

She has lived in Belgium and Germany and has deep experience with expat and military residency issues. Sally joined Watson CPA Group in early 2014 and became a licensed CPA in Colorado shortly thereafter. Sally manages Pod C.

In her spare time, she enjoys camping, tailgating at USAFA football games, and spending time with her family.

Michelle Day, EA, CFE
Tax Manager

Michelle began her career in the United States Air Force where she was a Command Lead and Manager of Computer Operations. From there she's worked for a handful of tax and accounting firms culminating 25 years of cross-functional expertise in business consultation, financial analysis, strategic planning and tax preparation. Michelle manages Pod D.

She is an Enrolled Agent with IRS and a Certified Fraud Examiner. She assists Jason in divorce litigation support and financial analysis. Instead of "show me the money" it becomes "where'd the money go?"

When she's not a work, Michelle enjoys reading, spending time with her loved ones including her four-legged family member, cooking, watching movies, and dark chocolate.

Amanda Rowles
Business Development

Amanda will be the first to tell you she loves organization, efficiency and a fast-paced environment. This brought her to Watson CPA Group during tax season and she never left! Amanda has become an addition to the year-round team as an onboarding liaison and a business development team member. During her day she wears many hats and enjoys moving from one project to another.

In her personal life Amanda loves to spend time with her family, friends and animals. She also loves to curl up with a good book and her cat, usually with some kind of snack nearby. Seriously, during snow storms we all raid Amanda's desk drawers. Peach Rings, Yum!

Others currently not pictured are Lana Rollins, Jon Neilson, CPA, Theresa Eggen, CPA, Brian Baum, Trevor Patten, Keegan Patterson, Karen Pleshek and Shelby O'Donnell.

Progressive Updates

The tax law is continuously changing from the acts of our government, to the decisions by the tax court and federal courts, and through notices and private letter rulings from the IRS. In addition to changes, other topics of interest pop up in various trade journals such as Journal of Accountancy and Kiplinger's Tax Letter. As we discover other issues concerning LLCs, S Corporations and self-employment taxes, we want to get the word out right away.

More importantly, the frequent business consultations we perform and the questions we field provide a steady stream of new ideas that are worthy of being wormed into this book. So here's to you- the curious small business owner helping others. Please don't be like Mr. Collins who could have offered constructive criticism but rather chose to be unprofessional in his commentary. It is a shame when an intelligent person has the ability to educate others yet fails on delivery. No one is perfect. Opinions will differ.

Currently this book is in the middle of a 2018 Edition makeover due to the Tax Cuts & Jobs Act of 2017, and specifically the Section 199A Qualified Business Income deduction. This is a major departure from the way things used to be. However, two things remain critically important- S corporations remain a viable tool for reducing self-employment taxes and the Section 199A deduction is simply an add-on component to the S Corp advantages.

We have not updated Chapter 8 on Tax Deductions and Fringe Benefits. Frankly we have been a bit busy with the Section 199A deduction which is much more of a needle-push than other changes. And... we are a tiny 20-person firm gearing up for tax season. Two big notables- meals and entertainment has shriveled under the new laws, and automobile depreciation has increased. There are some other minor things and we'll update as soon as we can.

As big chunks get updated, we are pushing out the versions on Amazon and PDFs within our website. However, having purchased this book and expecting it to be complete, you can get the final version of the 2018 Edition at no cost to you. Please write us with your order number from Amazon, Nook, iTunes, etc., and we will mail a copy to you at no charge.

We encourage you to visit our website for information on updates-

www.watsoncpagroup.com/book

Disclaimer

The information materials and opinions contained on the Watson CPA Group website and this book are for general information purposes only, are not intended to constitute legal or other professional advice and should not be relied on or treated as a substitute for specific advice relevant to particular circumstances.

The Watson CPA Group and Jason Watson make no warranties, representations or undertakings about any of the content of our website and this book (including, without limitation, any as to the quality, accuracy, completeness or fitness for any particular purpose of such content), or any content of any other website referred to or accessed by hyperlinks through our website and this book. Although we make reasonable efforts to update the information on our site and this book, we make no representations, warranties or guarantees, whether express or implied, that the content on our site is accurate, complete or up-to-date.

Shameless Self-Promotion

This book originally was a collection of KnowledgeBase articles that were written to help small business owners and to help our own small business through educational marketing.

Since you probably paid some money for the privilege of being bombarded with shameless self-promotion, we hope you take our comments with a grain of salt. Our primary focus is to educate you, minimize your tax consequence, maximize your wealth and keep you out of trouble. If you read this, arm yourself with knowledge and then ask pointed questions to your accountant, we are completely happy. We have done our job with this book.

Having said that, if you want the Watson CPA Group's assistance in whatever capacity necessary, from quick second opinions to full-time service, we are also happy to provide that. Want more information? The Epilogue in the back of this book has all kinds.

Introduction

How can I avoid self-employment taxes? This simple question was the inspiration for creating an article describing the benefits of an S Corporation. That original article, which was about four pages long, quickly became a series of KnowledgeBase articles on the Watson CPA Group website. The articles touched on basic topics such as how to elect S Corp status, shareholder payroll, reasonable salary determination, retirement planning, health care, fringe benefits and liability protection.

Those broad topics demanded much more information, both horizontally by spanning into more related issues, and vertically by digging deeper into the granular yet riveting levels of the tax code. The articles were grouped and relabeled as the **Taxpayer's Comprehensive Guide to LLCs and S Corps** which grew to 39 pages in its first edition. Sorry, all the good titles were taken (remember, the longer the title the less important the material is. Bible, Beowulf, Caddyshack... short and sweet). The Hunt for Red October is one exception, yet we digress.

Time marched on, and more information was added to the first edition such as expanded retirement planning concerns, health care options after the Affordable Care Act and business valuations including exit strategies. Boom, we now had our second edition at over 100 pages. At that point it was suggested by some clients and colleagues to convert the PDF into an eBook as well as paperback. So here we are on our sixth edition which is now called the 2018 edition, and the changes are primarily focused on the Section 199A small business tax deduction.

Each week we receive several phone calls and emails from small business owners and other CPAs across the country who have read our **Taxpayer's Comprehensive Guide to LLCs and S Corps** and praised the wealth of information. Regardless of your current situation, whether you are considering starting your own business or entertaining a contracting gig, or you are an experienced business owner, the contents of this book are for you.

This book will show you how to <u>reduce your self-employment taxes</u> through an S Corporation election and how to use your corporation to your retirement and fringe benefit advantage. You will also learn the operational considerations of an S Corp plus the 185 reasons you should NOT elect S Corp status. Want to buy or sell a business? That's in here too.

This book is written with the general taxpayer in mind. Too many resources simply regurgitate complex tax code without explanation. While in some cases tax code and court opinions are duplicated verbatim because of precision of the words, this book strives to explain many technical concepts in layperson terms with some added humor and opinions. We believe you will find this book educational as well as amusing.

Table of Contents

There is a lot of information here. Over 300 pages- whoa! And not a lot of picture pages. Put it on your bedside table and work through it over the next few days. Or use your handy tablet. You'll be glad you did (or so we think). Happy reading!

[Rest of page intentionally left blank]

Chapter 1
Business Entities and LLCs
(updated December 23, 2017)

Basic Business Entities

There are three basic business entities with variations within. The three basic are-

▲ Limited Liability Company (LLC)

▲ Limited Liability Partnership (LLP) or General Partnership (GP)

▲ C Corporation including Professional Corporation (some states require doctors, for example, to be a Professional Corporation)

Two notables missing from the list. First, sole proprietors are not an entity nor is the variant "Doing Business As" (DBA). If you wake up and want to sell used copiers, you can, right now, without any formalized structure. It is not smart, but certainly permissible. At times sole proprietors are interchanged with single-member limited liability companies (SMLLC) since the IRS and most states consider a SMLLC to be a disregarded entity for taxation, and both a sole proprietorship and a SMLLC will end up on Schedule C of your Form 1040. However, they are truly different in several underlying ways.

Also note how an S corporation is not listed. It is not an entity. It is a taxation election. The underlying entity has to be one of the above, and usually it is an LLC (either single-member or multi-member) for the ease of formation. Let's chat about each in turn. Here we go...

Sole Proprietorship

We don't want to spend too much time on sole proprietorships since most people reading this book don't want this arrangement. It also behooves us to say that you cannot elect a sole proprietorship to be taxed as an S corporation. Therefore, if you been in business for several years without an underlying entity, such as an LLC, then you must first create one and file an S Corp election to enjoy the benefits of an S corporation.

As a sole proprietor you might still need a state registration or some licensing for your particular line of work (such as real estate agent), but it is easy to do without needing to form an LLC. Additional downsides to sole proprietorships include zero financial liability protection, poor transfer of ownership and self-employment taxes. Income is reported on Schedule C and your Form 1040, a separate business tax return is not necessary.

Single-Member Limited Liability Company (SMLLC)

Single member limited liability companies (what we abbreviate as SMLLC) are treated the same way as a sole proprietorship since in the eyes of most taxing agencies SMLLCs are considered a disregarded entity. Just as the name suggests, the entity is disregarded and all business activities are reported on Schedule C and your Form 1040. SMLLC equals sole proprietor from a taxation perspective. However a SMLLC enjoys more liability protection than a sole proprietor, and technically has improved transfer of ownership through its Operating Agreement.

Multi-Member Limited Liability Company (MMLLC)

Once you take your single-member LLC and add a member, you are now a multi-member LLC (MMLLC). The IRS will simply call you a partnership since you will file a Form 1065 Partnership Tax Return. However, you are technically not a partnership, you are a multi-member LLC with an Operating Agreement as opposed to a partnership with a Partnership Agreement. Adding your spouse typically counts as a MMLLC unless you are in a community property state which is explained a bit later in this chapter.

MMLLCs are similar to sole proprietorships and SMLLCs in terms of self-employment taxes, but enjoy a bit more financial protection through the concept of Charging Orders (more on that later in this chapter as well). Transfer of ownership is the same as a SMLLC since you have a member interest that can be gifted, sold, inherited, etc. However, most MMLLCs will have an Operating Agreement governing the transaction of each members' interest.

Operating Agreements will also define the sharing of expenses and income. For example, you could be an angel investor at 20% injection but demand 50% of the income. Operating Agreements also become critical when the entity has value- issues like death, divorce, incapacitation and exit strategies must be handled within the agreement, and perhaps a separate Buy-Sell Agreement (usually funded with life insurance- we can help navigate on this). You and your business partner are besties today, but our job at the Watson CPA Group is to not unnecessarily complicate things, but to protect your future. See Chapter 10 for more on Exit Strategies.

In terms of self-employment taxes, the taxation of a MMLLC is very similar to a sole proprietorship or SMLLC as alluded to earlier. However, since a MMLLC's business activities are reported on Form 1065 Partnership Tax Return (with an exception for those living in community property states), there are additional tax pitfalls involving basis and capital accounts. Push pause on this concern for now; it is something to consider down the road.

Partnerships and those mimicking partnerships (MMLLC) commonly require a separate partnership tax return, Form 1065, which create K-1s for each member or partner. This might be your first brush with the term K-1. A K-1 is similar to a W-2 since it reports income and other items for each member / partner / shareholder / owner / beneficiary, and is coded to tell the IRS how that income should be treated.

A K-1 is generated by an entity since the entity is passing along the tax obligation to the K-1 recipient. There are three basic sources for a K-1, and the source dictates how the income and other items on the K-1 are handled on your personal tax return. Here they are-

▲   Partnerships (Form 1065)

▲   S Corporations (Form 1120S)

▲   Estates and Trusts (Form 1041)

All of these are pass-through entities with the exception of a trust, which might or might not be depending on the purpose of the trust. A K-1 is usually electronically filed as a part of the tax return that is generating the K-1. So the IRS will be expecting the recipient of the K-1 to report the information on his or her individual tax return.

A K-1 from a Form 1065 Partnership Tax Return and a K-1 from a Form 1120S S Corporation Tax Return are scarily similar. We could hold two K-1s about two feet from your face and you couldn't tell the difference- heck, we couldn't either. What makes matters worse, is that they both are reported on Page 2 of your Schedule E, and ultimately on line 17 of your Form 1040.

But here is the crux of the matter- one is subjected to self-employment taxes and the other is not simply based on which form created it (1065 versus 1120S). There is another subtle difference. Expenses associated with K-1 income from Form 1065 are deducted immediately on Page 2 of Schedule E as Unreimbursed Partnership Expenses (UPE) while shareholders of S corporations do not have a place to deduct shareholder expenses. Having said that, most shareholders are also employees so they would deduct unreimbursed employee business expenses on Form 2106 and Schedule A. We'll talk about why this is bad in Chapter 6 (hint: don't deduct expenses, silly rabbit, get them reimbursed to you, tax-free).

Partnerships do not pay Federal tax as an entity- the partners or the members of a MMLLC do as individuals. Note the word Federal. States can do a lot of crazy things, and there is a whole chapter about the 185 reasons not to elect S corporation taxation that touches on state related issues.

Limited Liability Partnerships (LLP) and General Partnerships (GP)

General Partnerships (GP) have unlimited liability exposure whereas Limited Liability Partnerships (LLP) have as the name would suggest limited exposure for the limited partners. Remember, this is financial exposure not necessarily other perils such as tort liability. More about that later.

We won't discuss these much either since they have fallen out of favor lately. Many attorneys are now creating two classes of memberships within a MMLLC to mimic the different groups that a true partnership would create. So it walks and smells like an LLP but it is actually a MMLLC, without the burden of complication and cumbersome ordering rules. Most of the attorneys we work with don't create partnerships anymore, including family limited partnerships (FLPs), opting instead for the use of MMLLCs.

Throughout this book we will refer to partners. More often than not we are referring to a member of your multi-member LLC. While partner and member are technically different, and that the entity type will ultimately decide member or partner, these words are often interchanged.

C Corporations

Messy. Wyoming was the first state allowing LLCs in 1970, but most states did not follow suit until the 1990's. Therefore if you wanted to avoid self-employment taxes you had to first create a C corporation and then elect S corporation taxation. Again, messy since LLCs are simple structures that provide the same tax benefits (and some argue the same protection as well).

C corporations are required in certain situations such as more exotic retirement planning and foreign investors, but typically not the best choice for small businesses. The double taxation issue is the biggest thing- a C corporation will be taxed on its net income **before** dividends. So, dividends do not reduce taxable income. Thanks to recent tax law changes, corporations now enjoy a 21% income tax rate. Then, dividends are taxable to you up to 23.8% (which is 15% to 20% capital gains plus 3.8% of Medicare surtax potentially). Therefore, your effective tax rate for using a C Corp as your entity choice ranges from 36% to 44.8% where the top individual rate is 37%.

If you think you are clever and drive corporate profits down to zero with high officer salaries, this too unnecessarily pays more in overall taxes ultimately. You will discover in Chapter 6 that reasonable salaries must be paid in an S corporation; however, the same is true in a C corporation where too high of a salary is a target for the IRS. Seems odd, but true.

In other words, C corporation plus high salary, Bad. S Corporation plus low salary, Bad. Like Goldilocks, it needs to be just right to the IRS.

If you are even more clever, and attempt to split up your $400,000 income into eight $50,000 corporations and attempt to pay a small corporate tax rate, think again- this IRS forces you to reduce the tax rate break points into smaller chunks, which in essence combines all your income and catapults you into the tax stratosphere regardless. Sorry. If there was some silver bullet tax avoidance technique, you aren't the first to think of it. Yes, you are a smart person, but you are not special nor unique (wow, that was harsh).

C corporations enjoy better financial liability protection however, and have much easier transfer of ownership. Taxes are paid at the corporate level both to the IRS and states (either through an income tax or a business tax) on Form 1120. Notice the subtle difference; 1120 and 1120S.

C corporations are also required for any type of self-directed IRA or 401k, and in some cases where a life insurance policy is being paid for by the corporation (and where the beneficiary is the corporation). For example, if you wanted to open a business with a rolled over IRA it would need to be a C corporation. However, some providers are creating LLCs and funding it with a self-directed IRA. The jury is out on the legality of this, and there are enough attorneys and legal professionals on either side to warrant concern.

If you wanted a life insurance policy on your best sales producer, these are sometimes restricted to C corporations only (essentially, it cannot be a pass-thru entity such as a multi-member LLC or partnership, or any entity taxed as an S corporation). C corporations might also be necessary for exotic stock options, vesting schedules, different classes of voting stock (one share equals ten votes, Class A or one share equals one vote, Class B) and initial public offerings. If you have these needs, seek an attorney. A smart one.

How does the recent changes from the Tax Cuts & Jobs Act of 2017 play into this? As stated earlier the highest tax rate is now 21%. With the elimination of several deductions available to individuals, there might be some arbitrage with corporations where their use makes sense. We'll have to wait until some of the dust settles on this.

Professional Corporations or Limited Liability Company

Several states require certain professions such as accounting, law, medicine, architecture and engineering to be a Professional Corporation (PC). These have the same housekeeping and corporate governance as a C corporation, and they can also elect S corporation status. Other states only require these professions to create a Professional Limited Liability Company

(PLLC) which is what the Watson CPA Group is in Colorado. Again, PLLCs can also elect S Corp taxation.

S Corporations

This book is all about S corporations so we saved the best for last. The benefits include corporate financial liability protection and easier ownership transfer yet the big benefit is the reduction of payroll taxes. Read that again. Payroll taxes. There is very little difference between a garden-variety LLC and an S corporation from an income tax perspective; the savings is from the reduction of payroll taxes which comprise of Social Security and Medicare. Recall that Social Security taxes stop at $128,700 (for the 2018 tax year) but Medicare continues into perpetuity. Other payroll taxes such as Unemployment, State Disability Insurance, etc. actually increase by electing S Corp taxation, but they are minor.

S Corporations are a pass through entity and therefore do not pay Federal income taxes, and the shareholders do not pay Social Security nor Medicare taxes on distributions from an S corp. Having said that, S corporations have a various sweet spots in terms of income versus payroll tax savings. In a later chapter, we'll demonstrate the savings from $30,000 to $2 million, between sole proprietorships, LLCs, partnerships and entities taxed as an S corporation.

S corporations are never formed contrary to popular belief. They are spawned from a limited liability company, partnership or C corporation that elects to be taxed as an S corporation. After the election is made on Form 2553, you are treated as an S corporation for taxation purposes only yet all future governance such as minutes and adoptions should follow the corporate structure. Some attorneys argue that this bolsters your corporate shield however you remain a closely-held corporation where veils are pierced every day during Jerry Springer commercials. Most junior associates can do this left-handed so don't think you have this impervious shield.

All kidding aside, the equity section in your balance sheet should also have a Capital Stock account and an Additional Paid-In Capital account. We can help with the journal entry to populate these accounts correctly so your equity section resembles that of a corporation. This is necessary for tracking basis in your S corporation. Chapter 4 has some examples.

You are in a weird limbo with electing to be taxed as an S corporation. You need to walk and talk like a corporation, but the underlying entity and what the secretary of state will have on file is going to be an LLC, partnership or C corporation. More on the election, and the behind the scenes stuff in a later chapter plus our thoughts on corporate governance such as meetings and minutes.

Section 199A Pass-Pass Thru Tax Deduction

Section 199A deduction also known as the Qualified Business Income deduction arises from the Tax Cuts & Jobs Act of 2017. This is a significant tax break for small business owners but there are rules and limits of course.

Section 199, without the A, is the section covering Domestic Production Activities Deduction. Section 199A is seemingly modeled after this (or at least a portion was ripped off by legislators) since the mathematics and reporting is similar between Section 199A and Section 199. Recall that Domestic Production Activities Deduction was reported on Form 8903 and eventually deducted on line 35 of Form 1040 (rumor is it's now dead).

However, it appears that Section 199A Qualified Business Income deduction is a deduction from adjusted gross income to arrive at taxable income (what we nerds call a below-the-line deduction, from AGI). This is contrasted with an adjustment to gross income to arrive at adjusted gross income (what we nerds call an above-the-line deduction, for AGI).

It is unclear how Form 1040 will be modified to accommodate this new deduction- personal exemptions no longer exist so there is room to replace one deduction with another. We'd all despise seeing Form 1040 move to three pages. Yuck.

"The line" is essentially lines 37 and 38 of the Form 1040 which represent adjusted gross income (AGI).

As with any major revision to the tax code, there will be modifications and interpretations which will change how Section 199A can be used for pass-through businesses. Stay tuned to updates.

Defining Terms

Pass-thru entities and structures include-

▲ Sole proprietorships (no entity, Schedule C).

▲ Real estate investors (no entity, Schedule E).

▲ Disregarded entities (single member LLCs).

▲ Multi-member LLCs.

▲ Any entity taxed as an S corporation.

▲ Trusts and estates, REITs and qualified cooperatives.

Specified Service Trade or Business is defined as-

▲ Traditional service professions such as doctors, attorneys, accountants, actuaries and consultants.

▲ Performing artists who perform on stage or in a studio.

▲ Paid athletes.

▲ Anyone who works in the financial services or brokerage industry.

▲ And now the hammer... "any trade or business where the principal asset is the reputation or skill" of the owner. Why didn't they just start with this since everything else would have been moot. Oh well...

Interestingly, removed from the traditional service profession are engineers and architects. But an engineer operating a business based on his or her reputation or skill is still a specified service trade.

Sit on the ledge, sure, but don't jump off a bridge just yet. The specified service trade or business problem only comes up when your taxable income exceeds the limits. So, a financial advisor making $150,000 might still enjoy the Section 199A deduction. Keep reading!

Income Limits

▲ Based on taxable income including all sources (not just business income). Also limited to 20% of taxable income.

See Line 43 of 2017's Form 1040 to assess your 2018 taxable income using 2017 as a proxy, adjusted for itemized deductions and exemptions (or lack thereof).

▲ Single is $157,500 completely phased out by $207,500 (adjusted for inflation)

▲ Married filing jointly is $315,000 completely phased out by $415,000 (adjusted for inflation)

Calculating the Qualified Business Income Deduction

The basic Section 199A pass-through deduction is 20% of net qualified business income which is huge. If you make $200,000, the deduction is $40,000 times your marginal tax rate of 24% which equals $9,600 in your pocket. Who says Obamacare isn't affordable now?

Here is the exact code-

(2) DETERMINATION OF DEDUCTIBLE AMOUNT FOR EACH TRADE OR BUSINESS. The amount determined under this paragraph with respect to any qualified trade or business is the lesser of-

(A) 20 percent of the taxpayer's qualified business income with respect to the qualified trade or business, or

(B) the greater of-

   (i) 50 percent of the W-2 wages with respect to the qualified trade or business, or

   (ii) the sum of 25 percent of the W-2 wages with respect to the qualified trade or business, plus 2.5 percent of the unadjusted basis immediately after acquisition of all qualified property.

There are some devils in the details of course. The best way is to show some examples-

▲ Wilma makes $100,000 in net business income from her sole proprietorship but also deducts $5,000 for self-employed health insurance, $7,065 for self-employment taxes and $10,000 for a SEP IRA. These are not business deductions- they are adjustments on Form 1040 to calculate adjusted gross income. Her deduction is the lessor of 20% of $100,000 (net business income) or 20% of her taxable income, which could be less (see Pebbles below). This might change as the IRS clarifies.

▲ Barney owns three rentals with net incomes of $20,000 and $5,000, with one losing $8,000 annually. These are aggregated to be $17,000. He would deduct 20% of $17,000.

▲ Barney has passive losses that carried forward and are "released" because he now has net rental income, those passive losses are taken first. With using the same example above with $10,000 in passive loss carried forward, Brian's deduction would equal $17,000 less $10,000 or 20% of $7,000.

▲ Pebbles earns $100,000 from her pass-thru business but reports $80,000 of taxable income on her tax return due to other deductions such as her itemized deductions. Her Section 199A deduction would be $16,000 since it limited by the lessor of 20 % of $100,000 or $80,000.

▲ Mr. Slate operates an online retailer S corporation which pays $100,000 in W-2 wages and earns $400,000 in net qualified business income. Because he is considered a "high earner" by exceeding the income limits, his deduction is limited to 50% of the W-2 or $50,000 which is less than 20% of $400,000.

▲ If Mr. Slate instead operates as a sole proprietor and earns $500,000 but does not pay any W-2 wages, his deduction is the lessor of 50% of the W-2 wages (or $0 in this example) or 20% of the $500,000. If he paid out $200,000 in wages and had $300,000 in net business income, his Section 199A deduction would be the lessor of 50% of $200,000 or 20% of $300,000.

In other words, he would deduct $60,000 ($60,000 is less than $100,000, even in Canada). He would want to create an LLC, tax it as an S corporation and pay out W-2 wages to maximize his Section 199A deduction.

▲ If Mr. Slate instead operates as a specified service trade as defined previously, he would completely phase out of the Section 199A deduction by exceeding the income limit of $207,500 and $415,000. This is the specified service trade "gotchya."

▲ If Mr. Slate was married and operated a specified service trade, and the taxable income considering all income sources (spouse, investments, etc.) exceeded $315,000 but was less than $415,000, there would be a sliding scale of deduction eligibility. Silly rabbit, tax reform doesn't mean tax simplification.

▲ Fred... yes, we can't neglect Fred... is single and operates an S Corp as an accountant. Days of busting up rocks for Mr. Slate are in the rear-view mirror. He earns $100,000 in net qualified business income after paying $50,000 in W-2 wages to himself.

He is a clearly a specified service trade but because he earns less than $157,500 total ($150,000 in this example) he can take advantage of the full Section 199A deduction of 20% of $100,000. The question of reasonable salary is not being entertained here... focus on the W-2 to income relationship.

▲ Betty becomes a slumlord and earns $500,000 in rental income. No W-2 since she is operating the properties as an individual (and converting passive income into earned income vis a vis a W-2 would be silly). Let's say she purchased the properties for a $1,000,000 (unadjusted basis). The math would go like this-

- 20% x $500,000 is $100,000 (straight calculation).
- 50% of $0 is $0 (W-2 limit calculation).
- 2.5% of $1,000,000 is $25,000 (depreciable asset limit calculation).

Section 199A is limited to the lessor of $100,000 as compared to the greater of $0 (W-2) and $25,000 (depreciable assets).

Takeaways

No entity is penalized under the new tax law. Some entities and situations might not qualify or be limited in some fashion, but the high-water mark in terms of taxation is the old crummy 2017 tax law.

Taxable income becomes a big deal for two reasons! First, $1 over $157,500 or $315,000 starts the specified service business disqualification and W-2 limitation (and there is also a depreciation component that we are glossing over in this summary). Second, the Section 199A deduction is limited by 20% of taxable income from all sources (what would be reported on your tax returns).

W-2 wages include all W-2 wages, not just those paid to the owner(s). Converting a 1099 contractor to a W-2 employee might be beneficial.

It appears that self-employment taxes will still be calculated on the net business income before the Section 199A deduction since the deduction is taken "below the line" on Form 1040. Therefore, you could earn $100,000 and deduct $20,000 under Section 199A, but still pay self-employment taxes on $100,000. This remains unclear however and we will await further IRS guidance.

S corporations remain a critical tax saving tool for two reasons. First, the usual self-employment tax savings remains intact for all business owners including specified service trades or businesses. Second, a business owner might need to pay W-2 wages to himself or herself to not be limited by income, and only corporations can pay W-2 wages to owners (in other words, an LLC cannot without an S Corp election).

Section 199A Pass-Thru Optimization

As you can see, there is some optimization that is necessary for a small business owner to get the most from the Section 199A deduction. On one hand we want to reduce W-2 salaries to shareholders to minimize self-employment taxes. On the other hand, we want to increase W-2 salaries so they do not limit the amount of Section 199A that is deducted.

This seems straightforward since payroll taxes are 15.3% plus some unemployment and other insidious stuff and the Section 199A Qualified Business Income deduction is 20%. However, the 20% Section 199A deduction must be multiplied by the marginal tax rate to obtain the true tax benefit. Even at a 37% marginal tax rate, the additional payroll taxes might exceed the Section 199A deduction tax benefit. Again, optimization is important.

We go over the math in Chapter 6 with examples of qualified business income, W-2 salaries paid, the Section 199A pass-thru calculation and the net benefit of an S Corp as compared to non-S Corp situations.

Section 199A Deduction Decision Tree

Remember that taxable income is all income for the household.

Specified Service Trade or Business

▲ If taxable income is less than $157,500 (single) / $315,000 (married) then the 20% deduction for your pass-thru entity is fully available.

▲ If taxable income is greater than $157,500 / $315,000 but less than $207,500 / $415,000 then a partial deduction is available. The phase-in of the limit is linear.

▲ If taxable income is greater than $207,500 / $415,000 then you are hosed. Sorry.

All Others

▲ If taxable income is less than $157,500 / $315,000 then the 20% deduction is fully available.

▲ If taxable income is greater than $157,500 / $315,000 but less than $207,500 / $415,000 then a partial deduction is available with the W-2 and depreciable asset limit calculations phase in.

▲ If taxable income is greater than $207,500 / $415,000 then the 20% deduction is compared to the full W-2 and depreciable asset limit calculations (see Betty above).

LLC Popularity (Hype)

The power of advertising, the ease and the hype have created this fervor surrounding the limited liability company. Note the word company. An LLC is not a limited liability corporation. An LLC is a company and a corporation is a corporation. Woefully different.

Some people think they must create an LLC just to operate a business- not true, you can be considered a sole proprietor the day you woke up, decided to ruin your life and started operating a business. Some people also think they save taxes by creating an LLC- not automatically true unless you take the additional steps to either elect S Corp status and / or implement executive benefits that are otherwise unavailable.

While there are benefits as explained throughout this book, there are also many misconceptions and downright pitfalls to forming and operating an LLC. Don't be fooled, or at least keep it to yourself if you are.

The Formation of an LLC or S Corp

It is very easy to form an LLC and have it be taxed as an S corporation. It is also very easy to screw it up. The Watson CPA Group can assist with all the filings with the Secretary of State (for any state), and our fee is $425 plus the state filing fees ($50 to $200ish, some states are even $500). Some states such as Nevada require an initial report, and that will typically add $100 to our fee plus the initial report fee. As an aside, Nevada might have good corporate laws but it is an expensive state to form a business entity. More on the Nevada hype in a bit.

Sure, you can do it on your own or through LegalZoom, but we will provide consultation and advice during the startup process. You can also use an attorney. Be careful however since not all attorneys are the same. If you were an idiot before law school getting a law degree doesn't suddenly make you smart. We have seen many things messed up by attorneys who didn't understand their client's needs, didn't understand the tax code, unnecessarily complicated the crap out of an otherwise simple entity structure, so on and so forth.

Accountants and doctors are not immune. How many quack doctors are there? Plenty. Accountants? Just a bunch of nerdy, socially awkward types. Thanks to Ben Affleck, us accountants are also secret assassins. Thanks Ben, the secret is out. Way to go, wizard.

Some of the kidding aside, we have seen some attorneys do some ingenious things as well. The Watson CPA Group works with business law and corporate attorneys all the time. It is a great relationship since they know corporate governance and contract law, and we know taxation and businesses. Do not think you only need an attorney- you need both an attorney and sharp consultants.

The Watson CPA Group will do the following-

▲ Create Articles of Formation or Incorporation, and file with the Secretary of State,

▲ File an initial report if required,

▲ Check on local taxing jurisdictions for registrations (for example, San Francisco which has its own registration form and fee in addition to the State of California),

▲ Obtain your Employer Identification Number (EIN) from the IRS and

▲ Create an Operating Agreement (for single member LLCs only) or provide a MS-Word template set of By-Laws for corporations.

LLC, Professional Corporation or Corporation

Typically we will want to form an LLC and later elect S corporation status. However, certain states require certain professions such as accountants, attorneys and doctors to be professional corporations. These too can elect S Corp taxation.

Here is a side note- California allows corporate officers to opt-out of the State Disability Insurance (SDI) tax, which can easily exceed $900 annually. However, if you create an LLC and have it taxed as an S corporation, California says No since the underlying entity remains an LLC. If you create a corporation and elect S Corp taxation, then you can opt-out. Subtle difference.

Operating Agreements

Multi-member LLCs and Partnerships need agreements between the members and partners. As mentioned through this chapter, there are issues such as death, divorce, incapacitation, valuation techniques, etc. that need to be addressed. These agreements are legal in nature and represent rights, therefore the Watson CPA Group cannot assist in drafting these. However, we act in a consulting capacity with attorneys all the time to ensure a quality agreement is drafted that meets the client's needs and objectives. We have more details later in this chapter.

Accountable Plan

Unless there is a huge reason not to, we also draft Corporate Minutes for your Book of Record to adopt an Accountable Plan which is used for employee reimbursements (see Chapter 7, Accountable Plan). Lastly, and if necessary, we'll complete and submit the Form 2553 for S Corp election. This too requires Corporate Minutes. And Yes, there are reasons you might want to delay the S Corp election or not even elect at all. Keep reading.

Corporate Minutes and Books of Record

This is a bit old school. Back in the day, you needed an attorney and a $5,000 check to create a corporation since we didn't have the use of an LLC. The process was very formalized since only large businesses did it, and the states used the process to track the comings and goings of businesses operating in their jurisdiction. Plus these documents were public and used by shareholders.

Today, most closely held corporations and entities taxed as an S corporation do not bother themselves with this formality. And states have gotten increasingly lackadaisical on the enforcement of their rules and even the rules themselves. The Watson CPA Group still suggests maintaining your Book of Record for three reasons- helps to maintains the integrity of the corporate veil, some banks and other institutions might ask for it to allow you, the controlling shareholder, to act on behalf of the corporation (such as buying an automobile in the business' name), and the IRS from time to time will ask for it during an audit.

Business Banking

The three typical formation documents (Articles of Organization / Formation, EIN and Operating Agreement) are required by most banks for a business checking account. An Operating Agreement is not always required. The Patriot Act and Homeland Security want to clamp down on illegitimate business accounts and financial holdings. While it might throw off the Feds, Guido's Money Laundering LLC is out for your business checking account name unless you have an EIN, which defeats your purpose if you are Guido.

So, all banks will want either an EIN or a SSN to open a checking account regardless of it is a personal or business checking account. And an EIN is tied to your SSN. Follow the money, find the bad guys.

Note: You can also just get another personal checking account (typically for free from your current bank). However, if you plan on taking checks written in your business name, you'll need a business checking account. Then again, most people are utilizing direct deposit or some sort of ACH / EFT deposit which bypasses account names issues.

Remember, you can create a dba (doing business as) for your entity name. So, if your business is a franchise but you want a different LLC name on the checking account, you can be Big Bucks LLC dba Starbucks or Bad Coffee dba Starbucks. Remember, friends don't let friends drink Starbucks. Please, find a decent coffee for yourself.

S Corp Election

The S Corp election can wait. As mentioned throughout this book, $30,000 net income after expenses is the break-even point for an S-Corp. Not sure? Not to worry, we can elect S Corp as far back as three and a half (3 ½) years using special IRS Revenue Procedures (as opposed to the 75 days provided in the Form 2553 instructions). The Watson CPA Group files about 60-70 late S Corp elections each year, and we are batting 100% on getting them pushed through.

Therefore our advice is to wait until November or December to decide if the election makes sense, and then make it retroactive to the start of the LLC or January 1. So, get the LLC in place and wait on the S Corp trigger until it makes sense- and Yes, we provide this consultation for you.

More on the late election later but here is a spoiler-

▲ You could be in the middle of **March 2018**,

▲ Elect S Corp status back to **January 2017** and

▲ Run a late 2016 payroll event dated **12/31/17**. Boom! You just save 8-10% of your net income in taxes.

This is all legit, pain in the butt for us, but all legit and successful. The Watson CPA Group probably did this about 60 times last year, and we've been doing this for more than a decade without major hiccups. Not the ideal way in the eyes of the IRS- but then again, hate the game not the player. We are just working within the parameters of their rules.

Not sure if you want to have a full-blown S corporation? As stated earlier, the break-even point where an S Corp makes sense is about $30,000 in net business income after expenses. Why? Simple cost benefit analysis. The expense of running an S Corporation such as payroll and tax preparation equals the savings at $30,000.

Let's say you are teetering on that income figure, and not sure about running payroll and all that jazz. You could still run your business income and expenses through your tax return as a sole proprietor or another single-member LLC, and take the small self-employment tax hit. Then simply file a No Activity tax return for your S Corp. Legal. Legit. All good in the IRS hood.

If you expect to lose money the first two or three years, the S Corp election becomes a bit more complicated and more discussion is required- it is generally better to delay the S Corp election so you can avoid the costs and hassles of filing a corporate tax return. More importantly, a single-member LLC or sole proprietor can theoretically have unlimited losses where a partnership or S Corp cannot because of partner and shareholder basis rules. Briefly, as an S corporation you are both an investor and an employee. As an investor in any company, you cannot lose more than your investment (basis). Same thing here.

Here are some more gee-whiz stats

Industry	Tax Returns	Share
Professional, Scientific & Technical Services	702,282	16.7%
Wholesale & Retail	652,750	15.5%
Construction	544,711	12.9%
Real Estate	461,284	11.0%
Health Care & Social Assistance	354,625	8.4%
Accommodation & Food Service	234,534	5.6%
Waste Management & Remediation	209,690	5.0%
Finance & Insurance	162,832	3.9%
Manufacturing	157,884	3.8%
Transportation & Warehousing	152,086	3.6%
Other	575,000	13.7%
Total	4,207,678	100.0%

Your Spouse as a Partner (Happy Happy Joy Joy)

You might be one of three situations. First, you have a partner in your business already and there's no getting around it unless someone meets with an accident. Or, you work alone and don't see that ever changing. Or, you have options- either to add a partner now as you form your business or down the road. Let's assume you have the choice for now and you are considering your spouse.

Husband and Wife as Owners

Should you form an LLC with your spouse? No. Don't you see enough of each other at the house? All kidding aside, there are some definite Yes reasons to add your spouse-

▲ Expenses such as meals, business travel, mileage, cell phones, etc. have more deduction capability.

▲ Leverage the minority owned small business benefits (usually with government contracts).

▲ Increase 401k plan or SEP IRA contributions as a household.

▲ Reduce income base for operating spouse and subsequent reasonable salary testing (huh? Don't worry... we'll explore this more).

Two Options

If you and your partner are married, and you can actually tolerate each other's existence for the foreseeable future, you have two basic options-

▲ Elect to be treated as a qualified joint venture (as defined and allowed by the IRS), and file on Schedule C on your individual tax returns, or

▲ Form an entity, treat the entity as a partnership and file accordingly (either Form 1065 or 1120S).

How you arrive at these two options will vary depending on your state's property laws (community property versus common law property).

There are two types of states, community property and common law property. Here is some gee whiz information. Community property laws stem from Spanish law whereas common law property states originate from the English law system. Therefore it makes sense that most of the community property states are in the southwest portion of the United States plus the odd ducks up there in Wisconsin and Idaho.

Community property states dictates that the income is added into a "community" pot, and then divided equally between the joint taxpayers. And Federal laws will usually follow the state laws in terms of income joining and splitting. On a jointly filed tax return this is moot, but if you need to file a separate tax return this gets complicated. But regardless of the taxation issues, there are also some procedural issues with business ownership.

Community Property State

Two people, married, in a community property state are not a partnership unless they elect to be treated as such. If you are not electing S corporation status now or in the near future, we would advise **not** to elect to be a treated as a partnership. Keep it simple.

Electing to be treated as a partnership will complicate things from a tax preparation perspective, does not provide any added tax benefit, and forces you into one of two situations, which are both ultimately equal. You could prepare a partnership tax return and create separate K-1s for you and your spouse at 50% each, or prepare a partnership tax return and create a joint K-1.

What the heck is a joint K-1? Rare, Yes, but the K-1 would be issued to the primary taxpayer's SSN but read "Bob and Sue Smith, JTWROS". When your personal tax returns are prepared, this joint K-1 gets spread among both you and your spouse equally, and therefore the income might be taxed with additional, unnecessary Social Security taxes.

Or…

A husband and wife owning an LLC in a community property state can be considered one owner, or in the case of an LLC, one member and therefore become a disregarded entity as opposed to a partnership. The business activities are then reported on Schedule C of your Form 1040. However, if you properly prepare your individual tax returns, you would split the business activities equally between you and your spouse. Let's run through these three scenarios once more-

▲ Elect partnership with separate K-1s at 50% each, or

▲ Elect partnership with joint K-1, or

▲ Remain a disregarded entity and evenly split activities on two Schedule Cs (you and your spouse), and report them collectively on your individual tax returns (Form 1040).

All three of these scenarios are identical from a self-employment and income tax perspective. Remember, each person has to pay Social Security taxes which is the bulk of the self-employment tax equation up to $128,700 of income (for the 2018 tax year). So if you are forced to push income equally to you and your spouse, you could easily pay more self-employment taxes than necessary. You may avoid this by being a single-member LLC.

Remember grammar school, may is permissive and might refers to chance. You may go to the bathroom. It might rain today.

Two scenarios to drive home this point-

▲ Scenario A- The business earns $200,000 in net income. You pay Social Security taxes up to $128,700 for 2018, and Medicare taxes on the whole amount.

▲ Scenario B- The business earns $200,000 in net income. You and your spouse pay Social Security taxes up to $100,000 each if your spouse is also a member or partner in the business (Yes, an S corporation could alleviate some this, but you get the idea).

The only way to avoid this equalization in a community property state is to file separate tax returns and claim that you did not know about the community income (seems farfetched, Yes). You could always move to a common law property state such as Colorado which is lovely (we promise).

Or, prove to your family and friends that you are trainable by reading this book, and **not add** your spouse to the business entity. Most elegant and preferred choice when living in a community property state, and wanting to avoid the additional Social Security tax as illustrated above.

Or, eclipsing the threshold where an S corporation election makes sense, which we will explore in fascinating detail.

> **Note:** Making an S Corp election can prove problematic if your spouse is a non-resident alien or if your spouse does not consent to the election (even if he or she does not own the company with you). More on this later.

Common Law Property State
Similarly to community property states, a husband and wife (or same-sex couples) have two options- file a partnership tax return or elect to be a qualified joint venture.

Two major differences to note here right away- in common law property states, the presumption is that you and your spouse are a partnership. In community property states, the opposite is true- the presumption is that your business entity is essentially a qualified joint venture.

The other major difference is that in a common law property state, you can chop up the business activities based on a pro-rated basis of involvement / interest in the company. For example, your husband supports your consulting business by handling the books; perhaps his involvement is only 15%. This is converse to community property states which generally divided things equally (whoever thought a marriage was a 50-50 relationship was fooled long ago, but here we are).

Some other details allowing married business partners to be a qualified joint venture include the following-

▲ You and your spouse are the only members (owners) of the joint venture, and

▲ You file a joint tax return, and

▲ You both materially participate in the business operations (which has legal IRS definitions attached to it such as number of hours and activities), and

▲ You are not operating the business as a limited liability company (what?!).

The last one is the deal breaker for most people. According to IRS rules, if you and your spouse operate a multi-member LLC, whereby each of you are members of the LLC, then you must file as a partnership using Form 1065 in common law property states. Most people are confused on this including attorneys and other CPAs. Don't believe us? No worries, refer to these wonderful IRS resources-

www.wcgurl.com/5401

www.wcgurl.com/5401.pdf

Two reasons why a qualified joint venture for a husband and wife team might make sense over a partnership. First, a disregarded entity (single-member LLC) or a husband and wife team that elect to be a joint venture can theoretically have unlimited losses reported on Schedule C and your joint Form 1040. This is in contrast to a partnership where your losses cannot reduce a partner's basis below zero. In other words, if you invest $5,000 in a partnership you can only lose $5,000. Without going into crazy detail, this is different than a partner's capital account (for example, you inject property into the partnership that is worth $10,000 but you only paid $2,000 for it, your capital account will show $10,000 but your basis in only $2,000).

Sorry, there's only one reason. Oops.

Having said all this, the Watson CPA Group still prefers to file partnership tax returns even for married couples since it allows us to track your capital accounts and other basis information. If you sell the business or get divorced or bring on a new partner, then this history is readily available. Otherwise you have to rebuild this information.

The qualified joint venture election can be made on Form 8832. Here is a quick summary table for husband and wife teams-

Entity	Common Law Property	Community Property
Sole Proprietor	May be qualified joint venture (Schedule C for each, Form 1040).	May elect to be partnership (Form 1065). May elect to be disregarded entity (Schedule C, Form 1040)
Limited Liability Company	Must be a partnership (Form 1065). May be taxed as an S corporation (Form 1120S).	May elect to be partnership (Form 1065). May elect to be disregarded entity (Schedule C, Form 1040). May be taxed as an S corporation (Form 1120S).

You are saying to yourself, Yeah, but there have to be some good reasons to add my spouse to the ownership. You would be correct and here are some considerations

Disadvantaged Company
Women are a protected class, and therefore might receive favorable government contracts or grants as small business owners. Same sex couples might see increased favorable treatment as well. Don't forget about Veterans and other groups of people that might be leveraged. There are several acronyms out there-

DBE   Disadvantaged Business Enterprise (California uses this often)
MBE   Minority-Owned Business Enterprise
WBE   Women-Owned Business Enterprise
DVBE   Disabled Veterans Business Enterprise
WGBE   White Guy Business Enterprise

Yeah, okay, the last one was a joke. You should always explore these opportunities especially if you are engaging with governments. There are also companies who will certify your entity as one of the above since there has been a lot of fraud lately. Shocking.

Business Tax Deductions and Fringe Benefits
Refer to Chapter 8 for more information. However, dinners with your spouse could be booked as a business meeting making your meals and entertainment expense 50%

deductible. If dinner is considered de minimis then the meal is 100% deductible (see Chapter 8 about Tax Deductions and Fringe Benefits including de minimis rules). Typically routine meals with your business partner will fail the de minimis rules, and therefore will be deducted at 50% (which is still better than 0%).

Business travel to conferences or other business related trips can be 100% deductible when your spouse is also an owner-operator or employee. Business trips to Fiji? Probably not. There are rules on extravagance.

401k Plans, SEP IRAs and Social Security

401k plan contributions and other benefits could be extended to your spouse. However, if you are running payroll for any other reason (such as having a staff or electing S corporation status), you can simply add the spouse to the payroll without ownership to fund his or her 401k plan accordingly.

Each married co-owner can be contributing to his and her respective Social Security basis and obtain Medicare coverage independently. Some people especially in their 50s and perhaps 60s want to contribute to their Social Security basis. Sounds crazy, but each situation is unique and requires careful planning. So, perhaps this benefit is more of a qualified benefit.

Reduced Salary

If your spouse is an inactive owner of the company, then the operating spouse's salary might be reduced. For example, one of the criteria the IRS will use to determine if your salary is reasonable is the comparison to shareholder distributions. As we will discuss further in Chapter 6, one of the jumping off points is 1/3 of net business income after expenses and from there we massage the number to suit the operating spouse specifically. But if this 1/3 number is based on an ownership percentage less than 100% (such as 80% for the operating spouse and 20% for the inactive / investing spouse), then there might be some savings.

1/3 of 80% of $100,000 is $26,600
1/3 of 100% of $100,000 is $33,300

A $6,000 reduction in salary could save you over $900 in payroll taxes! Again, Chapter 6 has more information on this within the reasonable salary determination arguments.

Charging Orders

When you have a multi-member limited liability company, and there is a judgement against a member of the LLC, the creditor must obtain what is called a charging order from a court. Theoretically this forces the creditor to only obtain distributions from the LLC rather than the

LLC's assets. Adding a spouse creates a multi-member LLC situation, but there are some caveats. The end of Chapter 1 has more information on the concept of charging orders.

Husband and Wife Problems

Besides all the usual hurdles a married couple have to leap over, there are some additional concerns to keep in mind. To pay a salary to your spouse, work has to be done. This is similar to putting your children on payroll- a job description, tracking of hours or workloads, etc. should be done in case you questioned on the veracity of the spouse's employment.

If you are trying to classify your spouse as an inactive investor of the business, then you cannot pay a salary. This ultimately prevents your spouse from participating in a 401k plan, and expensing business travel becomes challenging since inactive shareholders don't normally attend conferences or meetings, hence the word inactive.

Another concern are certain professions- law, medical and accounting do not allow non-professionals to be owners in most states. For example, to be an owner of medical practice requires that you are also a medical doctor. There are some minor exceptions here and there, and each state is different. The overall theme is to double check with your local regulatory agencies first.

So you need to pick your poison, but you can always ask us for help.

Splitting the Salary Baby

For grins let's say you determine a reasonable salary to be $60,000 and now you want to hire your spouse. Since several duties will be shared and some duties will be entirely deferred to the new employee (your spouse), an argument can easily be made that the original $60,000 for one person is also the combined salary for two people. We refer to this as the Officer Compensation pie- if revenue hasn't changed, the pie remains the same size... just different slices.

For example, you could pay your spouse $25,000 while your salary is $35,000 (using our $60,000 salary example). This solves a lot of things. Now your spouse can contribute the maximum to his or her solo 401k plan. Child care expenses are now deductible since both parents are working. You can leverage more from the business in terms deducting additional meals, business travel, mileage, cell phone use, internet, etc.

Lastly, Line 7 on the S corporation tax return (Form 1120S) is Officer Compensation. This entry would be the $25,000 plus $35,000 or $60,000 total. So, your benefits expand but your payroll taxes remain the same (perhaps a bit more unemployment tax). Nice!

Net-Net Spouse Summary

On one hand you have the option of making your spouse an inactive shareholder which theoretically could defend a lower reasonable salary. For mid-range salaries ($30,000 to $50,000), your savings could be $900 to $1,500. Okay, that's one side of the coin.

The other side is adding the spouse as a shareholder and employee (or just employee), and sharing more expenses and adding to solo 401k plans. What does that get you in terms of money? At a 25% marginal tax rate, if you were to reduce taxable income by $10,000 because of additional business deductions, you save $2,500.

We consider solo 401k contributions and retirement planning as more qualitative than quantitative. Remember, retirement contributions are only tax deferrals- IOU's to the IRS that they patiently wait to collect when you retire. Therefore, when you withdraw retirement money you have to pay taxes. So the six million dollar question is marginal tax rates today versus marginal tax rates in retirement. Don't forget the benefit of deferring state taxes that you might not ever pay back if you relocate for retirement (Pennsylvania has caught on to this trick, and does not give you a tax deferral for 401k plans... no wonder the Eagles stink).

So the ultimate answer is weighing the payroll tax reduction (inactive shareholder) versus the income tax reduction (spouse as employee). Remember that the income tax deduction is not generated by solely giving your spouse a wage (assuming you file a joint individual tax return). The income deduction is generated by justifying increased business spending and solo 401k plan deferrals.

The best trick is to find a legal way to take the money you already spend and turn it into a small business tax deduction. Employing your spouse might help.

More Husband and Wife Stuff

If you are concerned about ownership transfer in case of death, we suggest taking care of this issue within your estate planning. Transfer of assets between spouses during death is generally seamless in most states. Contact an estate planning attorney for more comprehensive analysis and advice. Yes, the Watson CPA Group has an estate planning attorney in our office who can assist you with your Will and Trust, regardless of where you live. One stop shopping. For more information on The One Call Team, visit-

www.watsoncpagroup.com/toc

If you are concerned about separation of property during divorce, our experience and observation show that a single owner will still be required to obtain a business valuation from an expert and the business becomes a marital asset. Most courts use a method such as excess earnings to determine the value to the operating spouse, not necessarily the fair market value.

For example, a one-person consultant with a single client might not be able to sell the business because no one else could do the work. However, the business remains valuable to the operating spouse. This is the same as the POS you drove in college- you could sell it for $50, but to you the car was worth a zillion dollars. It ran well, the heater worked, etc.

Business valuations for divorces sounds like fun, doesn't it? A real hoot. The Watson CPA Group is heavily involved in forensic accounting and business valuations, so if you need help let us know. Remember, the goal of any divorce is to ensure both parties are equally upset. No one should be high-fiving as they leave the courtroom.

Spouse As Independent Contractor

You might also consider paying your spouse as an independent contractor. Why the heck would you want to do that? Well, there could be a situation where you don't want your spouse to be an owner or that person cannot be (in the case of a law firm, for example), yet you want your spouse to be able to contribute to his or her 401k. Furthermore, by putting your spouse on the payroll of your company, you might jeopardize other fringe benefits such as Health Reimbursement Arrangements (HRAs).

You might also want to pay your children as contractors so they can have a 401k without making your company implement a full-blown company-sponsored 401k plan. This stuff can get tricky, but please understand that you have some options.

Family Partners

As mentioned in other areas of this book, your family might benefit from adding children and / or parents to your entity. For example, you could have your children be 10% owners each. They in turn pay very little tax compared to you, and they can either gift the money back to you (good luck) or you can surrender and use this ownership method as a conduit to give them your money which is going to happen anyway.

For example, they are 25 years old making $50,000 on their own. Your business had net profits of $250,000. Because of exemptions and deductions, your child is in the 10% marginal tax rate whereas you are in the 28% marginal tax rate. Not a huge swing, but you get the idea.

Other examples include minor children. Yes, a minor can own shares in an S corporation. However, given the current kiddie tax limit of $2,100 for 2016, any distributions above that will be taxed at the parents' income tax rate. Unless... the minor child materially participates in the corporation. Huh?

There are seven tests for material participation, and the easiest one is 500 hours per year (or about 10 hours a week). The activity must also be regular, continuous and substantial (this is straight out of the ATG – Audit Techniques Guide from the IRS). So, if you nail down the material participation with your minor children, they can earn above the $2,100 kiddie tax limit (for 2016) and be taxed at their own tax rate as opposed to your tax rate. Yes, they can gift the money back to you or make a contribution to their retirement accounts. We prefer the former.

Wait! There's more. You can still claim them as a dependent if you provide over half of their support. How expense are kids? Really expensive!

Mom and Dad can qualify for this as well. And if you are an S Corp, you don't have to pay a salary to shareholders who do not materially participate in the business activities (inactive shareholders).

Other Formation Considerations

There might be some situations where layering entities or creating a brother-sister or parent-child type of overall structures makes sense.

Holding Company and Operating Company

This is one of the most common situations where you own two entities that do business between themselves. For example, you are a typical poor accounting firm with the usual high maintenance clients, and you feel that everything would be better if you also owned your own office building. You would create an LLC as the holding company which owns the building, and another LLC (and probably taxed as an S Corp) for the operating company.

This allows for some excellent ownership separation. For example, if you and your father-in-law own the building, he doesn't have a stake in your accounting firm, and vise-versa. You might also want to make one of your key employees a business partner in your operations, but he or she should not have a stake in the building. Chinese Wall.

This arrangement can also reduce self-employment taxes or payroll taxes since this conduit changes the color of money. Huh? Your accounting firm's income is earned income, taxed both at the self-employment tax level (or payroll tax level) and the income tax level. However, you reduce this earned income by the amount of rental expense and that subsequent rental income on the other end is considered passive, and only taxed at the income tax level. Beauty. You must have a lease and the rent must be market rates.

Parent-Child Arrangement (Income Flows Up)

You might have two business entities, and you want to combine them but they are also very different. For example, you are a realtor and your spouse is an IT consultant. We could create a holding LLC called Smith Ventures which owns the realtor LLC and the IT consultant LLC. In other words, the realtor LLC and IT consultant LLC have a single member, and that single member is the holding LLC.

The holding LLC would then make the S Corp election, and all the LLC income would flow into the S corporation as wholly owned subsidiaries. Remember, single-member LLCs are disregarded entities and are reported on the sole member's tax return. In this case the sole member is the S corporation.

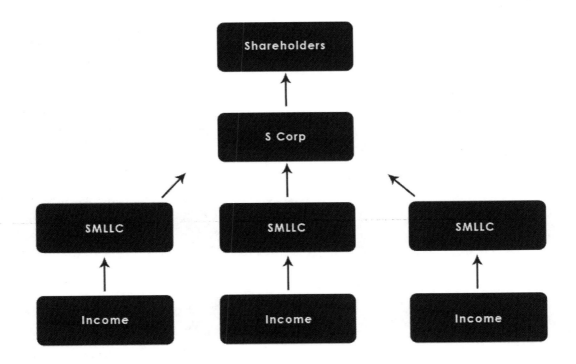

This entity structure solves some big problems yet creates some minor inconveniences. Instead of running multiple S corporations each with payroll processing and tax returns, all the payroll for the shareholders is handled out of a single S Corp. Each single-member LLC (SMLLC) is a disregarded entity and therefore on a singular tax return is required at the S corporation level.

Another benefit is that one of these business units, subsidiaries or whatever you want to call them can be carved away and later sold off. You could also expand ownership in one without expanding ownership in the whole structure (see below).

On to the minor inconveniences. Each entity should have its own checking account and set of books. Common expenses such as an umbrella policy or tax preparation fees would be paid at the S corporation level, while subsidiary-specific expenses such as website hosting would be paid at the LLC level.

Also, if you want to take a distribution out of one of the subsidiaries, truly the S corporation would receive the distribution first, and then make another distribution to you, the shareholder. A double hop. In other words, transfer money from the SMLLC's checking accounting to the S corporation's checking account to your checking account.

Another inconvenience is that each entity might be slapped with high annual fees from the state in the form of filing fees, or franchise taxes (like California) or both. The benefits might still outweigh the costs, but be careful.

This is a common strategy between husband and wife teams where the business entities are completely different, yet the household wants to enjoy the benefits of an S corporation. Plus, one of the spouses can expand ownership in his or her respective entity without upsetting the whole apple cart.

Bonus- one spouse could also have a 401k plan in one entity without affecting the other 401k plan in the other entity. For example, one entity has employees and the 401k plan has elected safe harbor to not fail HCE testing. No problem. The other 401k plan at the S corporation level maxes out each shareholder's contributions. There are certain rules about control groups, but this example gets around it (more information in Chapter 9 – Retirement Planning).

Parent-Child Arrangement (Income Flows Down)

Another thought along these lines involves a multi-member LLC where you and another non-spouse partner are the members. Later in Chapter 3 you'll learn that one of the limitations of an S corporation is that distributions must be made in the same percentage as ownership. So, if you are 50-50 with another shareholder, distributions must also be 50-50.

Backup for a moment. If this multi-member LLC was not taxed as an S corporation, the Operating Agreement could dictate a different schedule of distributions. For example, you and another insurance agent team up. But you want an Eat What You Kill revenue model. In this case, you could be 50-50 partners, but have the distributions be tied to the production of each insurance agent. No problem.

You S Corp this thing, and now it blows up. Regardless of production or revenue splitting detailed in your Operating Agreement, or whatever, distributions must be 50-50 since that is the ownership percentage among the two shareholders. But you still want to save on self-employment taxes. What can be done?

We create three entities. A holding company that is a multi-member LLC (MMLLC), with each member being an S corporation. Each S corporation is owned 100% by each principal involved. Stay with us on this one. The following example shows three S corporations as members of the MMLLC, but just ignore one side if you are two-person show.

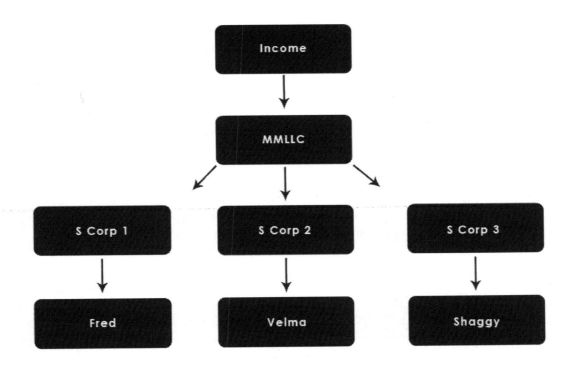

The MMLLC is really a funnel. All revenue goes in, all common expenses are paid out such as internet, copier lease, admin functions, etc., and an Operating Agreement dictates how the distributions are to be handled. K-1s are issued to the members which happen to be S corporations. And then those S corporations pay a reasonable salary to its respective sole shareholder and distribute the remainder.

There are some excellent benefits with this arrangement beyond the revenue splitting and saving of self-employment taxes. Each S corporation is independent. In using the previous schematic, Fred could buy whatever company car he wanted. Velma could work from home and reimburse herself for a home office. Shaggy could rent an office since his place is... well... a dog house of sorts. Each S corporation can run expenses through as it sees fit without upsetting the other business partners.

We see this arrangement commonly in medical groups (surgery groups, physicians, doctors, anesthesiologists, nurse anesthetists, etc.), insurance agents and financial advisors. It is very common in entities where the revenue is not shared equally, but rather on production.

401k plans in this situation is tough since it is a controlled group (technically what ERISA and the IRS call an Affiliated Service Group). More information can be found in Chapter 10 on controlled groups, and how retirement planning within this scheme works.

Multi-Member LLC That Issues Invoices

A simpler way to accomplish the same thing as above is to create three entities again, but the multi-member LLC is owned by you and the other guy, not the S corporations. The S Corps then issue consultation invoices to the multi-member LLC in the amount of the revenue split driving the multi-member LLC income down to zero. The K-1 to each member would show zero for member income, and the invoices would be ran through the S corporations as business income. So this still accomplishes the Eat What You Kill revenue splitting and changes the color of money through distributions from the S Corp.

This would be beneficial if you didn't have an Operating Agreement or if you are afraid that an Operating Agreement could be too restrictive from year to year.

We **do not** suggest issuing 1099s in this scenario. First, a 1099 is only required to be sent to non-corporations. Even though you might have created an LLC and then later elected S Corp status, you are now considered a corporation and your vendors are not required to send you a 1099 (although many do).

Second, a 1099 has EINs and possibly SSNs. Since these dots can be connected by the IRS, the issuance of a 1099 might invite unnecessary scrutiny. The IRS agent's question becomes "Why did you issue a 1099 to a partner rather than let the income flow through a K-1?" "To avoid taxes, headaches" is probably not going to go well.

A multi-member LLC with a zero for taxable income (or close to it) is a no harm no foul tax return. In other words, it flies well below the radar. Having said that, this is not the most elegant option- we still prefer the previous diagram as a long-term solution.

Expanding Ownership

Expanding ownership will be discussed in more detail in Chapter 3, but we quickly wanted to add some more reasons for the compartmentalization of your multiple business units into LLCs. Let's say you have a home inspection business and a home remodel business. Similarly to the holding company / operating company arrangement, you might want to expand ownership in the remodeling business unit and not the inspection business unit.

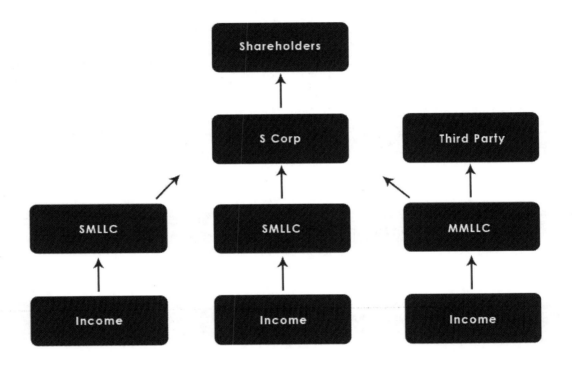

By having separate LLCs, both initially owned by an S corporation, you can accomplish various ownership expansions, such as adding a third party as a co-owner of one of your subsidiaries (MMLLC in the diagram above). In other words, the MMLLC would have two members; your S corporation and the other guy. The other guy could be an S corporation as well. In this scheme you would need two business tax returns; a Form 1120S for the S Corp and a Form 1065 for the MMLLC (Partnership Tax Return). Your S Corp would receive a K-1.

Joint Ventures

Using the same example above, the two insurance agents could simplify by entering into a joint venture agreement that allowed for revenue and expense sharing, without the formality of the business entity structure above.

Be careful here. The IRS could impute that this is a partnership and demand a partnership tax return. Not much more will be said here since the Watson CPA Group is not a huge fan of joint ventures in this fashion, and most attorneys say it is very expensive to draft this agreement. Automobile manufacturers have the budget to enter into joint ventures.

Using a Trust in Your Formation Considerations

While discussion with a qualified estate planning attorney is essential when using a Trust, here are some basics about Trusts to better understand how they incorporate with your world.

Trusts do two things really well. First, they usually help bypass probate. If you own property in three different states, then probate must be opened and closed in all states. It is long. It is expensive. It is public.

Second, they help you, the dead guy, dictate policy from the grave. If you want to ruin a 30 year old's life, give Junior a million dollars. A Trust can dole out money according to a schedule. Special needs kid? Drug addict? Nut-job son-in-law? A Trust can protect your interests long after your cold.

Trusts might also protect your children. Here's an example. You die. Your wife wears a skirt and heels to the funeral, and waits the obligatory 4-6 weeks before dating again. She gets married because your dying words were, "I want you to be happy." She lives another decade and then dies suddenly. Now this dude has all the money and doesn't care about your kids. Wonderful.

The only difference for women is that men would only wait 2-3 weeks to start dating, the rest remains unchanged.

Revocable Trusts are also called living Trusts. This is where the grantor and the trustee can be the same person. If a revocable trust owns real estate, the grantor can burn the place down, paint it purple or sell it. Since the grantor has ultimate authority over the trust asset, there is no creditor or asset protection afforded. Zippo. None. Don't believe the hype the asset protection hype. If you want protection, you have to give up control.

Irrevocable Trusts are the roach motel- you can check in assets, but they can't check out. The grantor does not have any authority over the trust; only the trustee does. The trustee cannot be you, the grantor. The trustee could be your best friend, but cannot be influenced by you. The trustee has to make decisions with the Trust's interests in mind as a fiduciary.

Some people try to install poison pills in an irrevocable Trust where if certain events happen, the assets revert back to the grantor. Be careful on this. The IRS recently ruled in Private Letter Ruling 201426014 that the "provision in trust that provides that, in the event that both the children are no longer serving as members of the Distribution Committee or if there are fewer than two serving members, the trust property will be distributed to the grantor, and the trust shall terminate, constitutes a reversionary interest under Code Sec. 673." This is one example of a poison pill that backfired. This was a revocable / living Trust disguised as irrevocable.

Those items that have built in beneficiaries such as life insurance and investment accounts might be placed in a Trust, but they do not have to be since these assets bypass probate automagically. However, if you want these proceeds metered out according to a schedule, then the Trust needs to be the beneficiary. Get some planning!

Litigious assets are usually encapsulated in an LLC prior to being placed in a Trust. Automobiles is an example of litigious assets, but they are usually directly owned by an individual. Real property such as rental real estate is another great example. But what if you wanted to have your rentals pass through your estate and skip probate?

[fancy graph showing you how to complicate your life is coming up]

Many business and corporate law attorneys will suggest only using an LLC with an Operating Agreement. In our experience, the control of a Trust with the guidance of a trustee makes a Trust more attractive and better equipped to handle the transfer than an Operating Agreement. Therefore, several estate planning attorneys (and the Watson CPA Group) recommend the following arrangement-

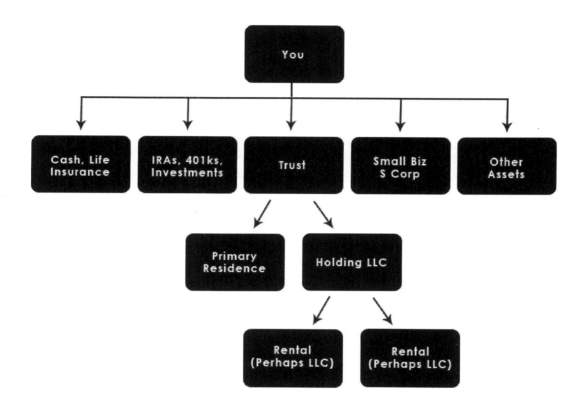

Operating Agreements

If you are a single-member LLC or if your business partner is your spouse, this information might not apply. But if you are in business with another person, even a brother or sister-in-law, then a beefy Operating Agreement is a must have, at least eventually.

Operating Agreements are like By Laws for an LLC, and they protect the rights of the members and define the parameters in which the members can operate. In general, attorneys do an adequate job drafting this critical document, but there are some holes that the Watson CPA Group feels compelled to mention.

Death, Divorce, Incapacitation

Death and divorce are easy, and attorneys have this in their templates all the time however incapacitation is often left out, or only briefly mentioned. Look at the recent idiot Donald Sterling who was found mentally unsound and could not run his company. If your business partner is Donald Sterling who is not dead nor divorced much to LA's chagrin, you might want a contractually obligated and legally enforceable plan to get rid of his member interest.

Do you need one doctor? Two doctors? What is the triggering threshold? Traumatic brain injuries are no laughing matter of course, but you need to protect yourself if they occur. It is not just incapacity from a mental perspective either; your business might suffer if a member cannot physically perform the role either.

Accounting, Corporate Waste

Most attorneys draft language that state any member can request a formal accounting of the expenditures and financial records. However, they often neglect to build thresholds where all members must sign off on an expense. For example, let's say you are a minority shareholder at 25%, and the other three members are also 25% each. Interestingly, the other three members are also a voting block since they are all family members as well. What's to prevent them from buying a company car for someone other than you?

In Colorado we are seeing a flood of marijuana investors. This is a cash business of course and all these minority investors are pouring their savings into a new pot farms. It is not a bad investment; first to market, stake your claim, build mega farms, control the pricing, etc. However, and this is a big however, it is still a cash business. Don't you want a little assurance that the majority owner is not skimming the till?

Do you know how the IRS can determine your sales volume as a bar? They look at your purchases which is why most bars have to buy from a distributor. Determine the cost of goods purchased slap on a regional markup, and boom, you have sales regardless of what the cash deposits say.

Distributions

Oftentimes the business will have income, but no cash since it is re-investing back into the business. However, as a shareholder of an S corporation or a member of a garden variety LLC, you will pay taxes on business income and not distributions. Theoretically you could have a big tax bill based on income but never see the cash.

Another common example is when you are the minority shareholder or member. The majority elects to not pay distributions, basically starving you out. My partner would never do that? Really. Ok. But everyone else not living in fantasy land, an Operating Agreement can protect from this situation.

Dispute Resolution

Templated Operating Agreements usually have language about dispute resolution, and specifically mediation. Mediation is fine, and some courts have a standing order that parties will attend mediation prior to trial. However, mediation is not binding and parties don't necessarily have to enter into mediation with good faith. Trials take a long time- anywhere from 12 to 24 months, just to get to opening statements.

Arbitration is like mini-court and the rules of discovery and evidence are usually more relaxed. They can be expensive since you are paying for your attorney plus the arbiter who is usually a retired judge or attorney. However, they can also be efficient.

Regardless of mediation, arbitration or trial, make sure your Operating Agreement has expeditious dispute resolution provisions, and incentives for all parties to be efficient and bargain in good faith.

Business Valuation

So a member wants out, no problem, but what is the value of the business? Should you use a formula to determine the value? Something based on revenue? A full-blown business valuation (our retainer is $5,000 for a conclusion of value business valuation engagement)? What if you and your business partners cannot agree on the selection of the business valuation expert? Make sure there are provisions in your Operating Agreement.

As a side note, if the value cannot easily be derived from a formula, then the out-member and the remaining members each pick a business valuation expert. Then those two experts pick a third as a neutral.

As we've said in the past, just because you are working with an attorney or an accountant doesn't mean you are working with a smart person. The Watson CPA Group can act as a consultant with your attorney when drafting these documents.

Exit Plans, Business Succession

Nothing lasts forever, even the Cubs will eventually win a pennant. If your business partner is not your spouse, understand that you could suddenly find yourself in business with his/her spouse or children. Image you and your partner. Happy as a clam. Successful. Cement truck. Dead. She left everything she owned to her whacked out children including her portion of the business. Now you and her kids are partners. Wonderful. Do scenes from Horrible Bosses come to mind?

But valuation and funding are the biggest hurdles. For example, the company might be worth a zillion dollars, but has no cash. Or the value is all tied up in assets, such as houses, buildings or machinery. Exit plans or Buy-Sell Agreements really make sense only when the business has value.

In many cases, the remaining partner or partners can simply start up a new company in a different name, and carry on as usual. Huh? Example time. Let's say you and your partner are accountants. Living the high life, declining Matt Lauer interviews, driving fancy cars, etc. One day you decide to call it quits. In this situation, both partners could simply split the office equipment and break away with his or her portion of the business and move on as individuals.

See Chapter 10 for more information on Buy-Sell Agreements.

Liability Protection Fallacy of an LLC

Can you be sued personally if you operate an LLC? Yes. And you can easily lose on both a business and personal level. There are several myths out there regarding the use of an LLC as a shelter from potential lawsuits and litigation. Some of the hype has been created by attorneys who used to charge upwards of $1,000 to form an LLC. Need to pay for condos in Maui, presumably. We accountants tease attorneys that LLC really means Lawyer's Likely Choice.

Remember, attorneys are not necessarily smart because they went to law school. People are smart, and smart attorneys are people who were already smart and then chose law as a profession.

While consultation with an experienced attorney is strongly recommended for your unique situation, as business owners ourselves we feel the excitement of the LLC has overshadowed the reality of our litigious society. In other words, if your acts, errors or omissions injure someone even though it was under the auspice of your LLC, good chances you will be personally named in the lawsuit and held liable as the owner of the LLC.

The word liability in the LLC truly refers to **financial liability**. Please read on.

For the matter of this liability discussion, LLCs, S Corps, C Corps and limited partnerships are considered the same. No liability protection is asserted for sole proprietorships, general partnerships and general partners in limited liability partnerships. Sure, this is a huge generality, and exceptions always exist depending on agreements and state law.

Types of Liability

There are three areas where you can be held personally responsible- criminal, contractual and torts. Torts is probably most people's concern, and torts can either be-

▲ negligence where you have a general duty to act in a reasonable way and you didn't (like drive your car safely), and

▲ intentional torts where there was a purposeful act to harm.

There are other tort buzzwords like gross negligence, careless disregard, defamation, etc. Remember, negligence is the opposite of diligence.

Piercing the Corporate Veil

Officers and directors of corporations are routinely held liable for the actions of the corporation. This is called piercing the corporate veil. Can you say Enron?

Piercing the corporate veil typically is most effective with smaller privately held business entities (close corporations) in which the corporation has-

▲ a small number of shareholders

▲ limited assets, and

▲ separating the corporation from its shareholders would promote fraud or an inequitable result

While this is referring to a corporation, the same philosophy is apply to a limited liability company. Does that sound like your LLC? Yes. And could it happen to you? Yes. Is there a small chance of this happening? Who knows? We say risk it, put it all on red and let it ride. Just kidding. No one bets on red.

Even a two-member LLC would easily be considered a closely held entity. If those members were grossly negligent in the way they managed the business, separating the corporation from its shareholders (or LLC from its members) would certainly promote unfairness from a liability perspective. This is our opinion of course, but we want to share with you some of the behind-the-scenes perspectives from the courts and law that might not be readily considered when forming an LLC.

Another perspective- if you owned shares of Ford Motor Company, you were not personally responsible for the damage caused by the Ford Pinto even if you were a shareholder.

However, if you were a corporate officer who ignored (gross negligence) the potential for harm, you could be held responsible, even criminally. In other words, fix that loose railing before your tenant hurts himself (using an LLC owning a rental as an example).

The general rule across the country is that individuals acting on behalf of a company are personally liable for their tortious conduct even if they did so on behalf of the company. So, to protect your personal assets you need to fund the LLC with enough resources to pay for a lawsuit. This defeats the purpose of not having to pay personally.

There might be situations where an investor has a lot to lose personally as compared to his or her smaller co-investors- so perhaps funding the LLC on an equal basis to hedge against potential lawsuits or to have similar language in an Operating Agreement or Partnership Agreement can mitigate some exposures.

Furthermore, if you own multiple investments and LLCs, and you think you can protect the other assets in the event of a lawsuit on one, think again. In our non-legal opinion and observation of events, if you face a credible lawsuit arising out of your acts or omissions there is a chance everything you have is going to be pursued by the injured party's attorney including your personal residence, cars, college funds, LLCs' assets, Snuggie collection, etc. Yes, even the leopard one.

Other Things to Think About
You are a reasonable person. Does it seem reasonable for someone to hide behind the auspice of an LLC or a corporation when they do bad things? Of course not. Public policy shouldn't allow for this. So it follows that if you maintain an unsafe rental property or if you are reckless while driving the company car, you should be sued, and you should lose.

Some attorneys will argue that if you mix personal and business funds together, even accidentally, you might erode the separate of you, an individual, and the business. For example, a business owner will pay for car insurance through the business. The car is owned personally by the business owner, and the owner is getting reimbursed for mileage. Therefore the car insurance is not a deductible business expense, and is coded as an owner draw or distribution. In this scenario, a court might determine that the "veil" between you and the business is getting thin, and might be determined to be too thin.

Same with Corporate Minutes. Some argue that if you do not keep up with the housekeeping and governance of your corporation, you can chip away at the corporate protection.

Protecting Yourself

After all the gloom and doom, there is one element of protection. If your employee's conduct creates a liability for himself and one for the LLC, the owner of the LLC may be absolved. This can get tricky depending on the conduct, and any instructions the LLC provided to the employee. This is attorney type stuff.

So, what do you do? In addition to your general business liability insurance, you should secure a decent umbrella policy both at the personal and commercial level. This is our strong recommendation for liability arising from your acts, errors and omissions. General umbrella policies are $400 to $700 per year. Something to note is that your liability limits on the underlying assets such as buildings and cars might have to increase to reach the floor (starting point) of the umbrella policy. This prevents gaps in insurance.

Errors and omissions insurance varies depending your profession (realtor versus financial advisor versus insurance sales).

It appears that many credible lawsuits will sue to the limit of coverage to avoid lengthy and expensive trial litigation. Again, please consult your attorney and insurance agent for your unique situation. Yes, the Watson CPA Group in connection with The One Call Team can offer assistance. For more information, visit-

www.watsoncpagroup.com/toc

The LLC Protection (An Example)

LLCs and corporations protect the owners from being personally responsible for the company's debts and obligations unless the owners or officers personally sign for the loan (called a recourse loan). However, in today's lending climate it will be very difficult to get a business loan in the name of the LLC without having to sign a personal guarantee on the note. Business debt without a personal guarantee is called a non-recourse loan since the bank or lender does not have a recourse against the individual. Tough to get, expensive at times and requires significant equity (60% loan-to-value is the general rule of thumb).

How this works is straightforward. Let's say you own three businesses, one is an LLC operating a pizza joint, another LLC owns a rental with a ton of equity, and another LLC is used to trade stocks, bonds and options. The rental was purchased with a non-recourse loan. The rental house has extensive mold, is un-insured for mold, and eventually is foreclosed leaving some creditors holding the bag. Picture the poor guy in Monopoly. Those creditors **cannot attach or seize** your pizza joint or your portfolio since they are held in other LLCs. This is an overly simplified example, and there are probably some rare and narrow instances where you could still be in trouble, but generally this strategy works.

A common arrangement is the self-rental which is discussed in more detail later, but here's a glimmer. You operate an LLC as a business and you also buy the office building with another LLC, of course with a non-recourse loan (the only collateral is the building itself and **not** your personal promise to pay). The business also has a line of credit. Depending how all the debt is structured, each of these assets (the business and the building) has a Chinese Wall between them.

Another strategy that is older than dirt is equity stripping. It is a process of encumbering your assets to the point where there is no value for lack of equity. In the simplest of forms, you pull cash out against your assets, and separate your cash from the assets. Be very careful. There are "bogus friendly liens" triggers where a person will use a Nevada corporation to file a lien against the asset, however the asset and corporation are owned by the same person (or some related party). This lien is subsequently pierced or tossed. Equity stripping can be a good asset protection strategy, but it requires careful planning.

Again, banks are smart. You are not the first Tom, Dick or Harry to come around. We should probably update the names to reflect the current smattering- how about you're not the first Parker, Logan or Dakota to come around. Most lenders require personal guarantees on every loan.

But, there is some wiggle room on financial shielding using a limited liability company. If you sign a contract for internet service, or for a copier lease, or some other commitment, you might be able to get away with executing the agreement under the LLC. So, if your business fails the LLC might be liable for the remaining contract obligation and not you.

This only works if you maintain the separation between you, the person, and the LLC. Co-mingling of funds and other "veil piercing" activities can blow this up. Be careful, and seek sound legal advice.

Liability State Nexus

We'll chat about nexus from an income tax perspective in the next few pages- this little tidbit is about nexus from a liability perspective. Several corporations are created in what some people perceive as corporate friendly states, such as Delaware or Nevada. But when it comes to liability especially tort liability, you will be generally sued in a jurisdiction where you have an economic and / or physical presence.

Yes, an attorney will show up and attempt to fight jurisdiction. But he or she might lose. Now you have to hire an out of state attorney to fight your out of state lawsuit. Sounds like a grand plan.

So if you file Articles of Formation, Organization or Incorporation in another state such as Delaware, maintain a presence in Kansas and cause damages in Kansas, you will probably be sued in Kansas. Yes, you can write contracts that clearly dictate the forum of law, but now you are asking a Kansas court to possibly understand and enforce Delaware law. According to several attorneys that we work with, if you march into court pinning your hopes on Delaware law being enforced by a Kansas court, you have already lost.

Also most parties will want the jurisdiction to be in their backyard. You trip and fall in a Wal-Mart and sue Wal-Mart, you are not having to fly to Bentonville, Arkansas to file the lawsuit. Although Table Rock Lake to the north of Bentonville is amazing, you want to sue in your local town, using local courts and jurors. After your big fat judgement, fly to Table Rock Lake in your private jet. Good stuff!

If you have a presence in all 50 states, using Wal-Mart as an example again, you have to pick a state to call home regardless, and then file as a foreign entity in all the other states. Then perhaps picking a more friendly corporate state makes sense. Attorneys call this forum shopping, and it makes sense when you clearly have a choice.

For 99% of the small business owners out there, keep it simple- organize in your home state. You truly have only two major concerns. Where contract disputes will be argued, and that can dictated within the contract. The other concern is tort liability, and that is usually mitigated with insurance.

Yet another example. A lot of real estate investors will incorporate in Nevada (for example) because of the seemingly friendly business laws, and then buy rental properties in Colorado. This requires a foreign entity registration in Colorado. It is a near guarantee that if you are grossly negligent in the maintenance of your rental, you will be sued in Colorado. So why the heck are we forming in Nevada? Or Wyoming? Or Delaware? The theory is that a Colorado court would then interpret and enforce the other state's law in your lawsuit. Good luck with that.

Please don't believe the hype. Do your homework! Do you know of anyone in all your walks of life and circles that fought a lawsuit based on some other state's law? Perhaps, but sleeping at night solely based on this layer of protection might not be that comforting.

There are some situations such as several remote principals collaborating on a business where the "home state" becomes murky. For example, the Watson CPA Group has a client where three brothers own a hotel in a Caribbean country. We formed a Florida LLC since two brothers were residing in the foreign country and the third was residing in New York.

We have another client where the three principals lived in Oregon, Texas and New Jersey. We formed the entity in Wyoming, and filed for foreign entity in each state.

Charging Orders

If you are financially in trouble, and a creditor wants to take your assets, your multi-member LLC and its assets might be safe. Instead of taking the LLC directly, a court can issue a charging order which allows the creditor to receive any distributions from the LLC. The theory is quite simple- if you are in business with another person, and that person has financial trouble, why should it be your problem? Your only problem should be where to send the profit distribution check for that person's distributive share.

A charging order puts the creditor in line for any financial rights that the debtor has, but does not convey any management rights. Therefor the creditor cannot order the LLC to make a distribution. However, many states have allowed the creditor holding the charging order to foreclose on the membership interest of the debtor. Yuck. This is done under the auspice that the debtor will not be able to re-pay his obligation. So now the creditor is the permanent owner of the financial rights of the debtor's portion of the LLC, but the creditor still does not own any member interest in the LLC. This results in the debtor owning a portion of an LLC that he will never receive any money from since his financial rights are gone.

It doesn't stop there. Some states and certain courts can also assign the full interest (ownership and financial) to the creditor. This create a big mess for the other members of the LLC who suddenly need to scrape up enough money to pay off the creditor so as to not be tethered to them as a co-owner.

What does all this mean? Some attorneys want to automatically add a spouse to the LLC so it suddenly becomes a multi-member LLC with the financial protection of a charging order. Sure, why not? There is some protection there with very little effort.

As a side note, here is Delaware's verbiage about charging orders under Title 6, Section 18-703-

> (d). The entry of a charging order is the exclusive remedy by which a judgment creditor of a member or a member's assignee may satisfy a judgment out of the judgment debtor's limited liability company interest and attachment, garnishment, foreclosure or other legal or equitable remedies are not available to the judgment creditor, whether the limited liability company has 1 member or more than 1 member.

Makes you want to run out and form your LLC in Delaware. Again, if you are marching into court with a boatload of financial woes, and hanging your hat on charging orders for your financial protection, you might have bigger problems. Creditors are wise to this, and they usually make you sign for and guarantee liability as an individual.

Also, if you form an LLC in Delaware and operate in Colorado, you will need to file as a foreign entity in Colorado. If you receive process of service in Colorado for a lawsuit, you are now asking a Colorado court to interpret and enforce Delaware law in your matter. Courts and judges are not fond of this ask.

Nevada Fallacy of an LLC (or Delaware, or Wyoming, or where ever!)

We just listed out the three most debtor-friendly states, but that's where it ends. You might have heard that you can avoid taxes by forming an LLC in Wyoming or Nevada- is that true? Sure if tax fraud comes easy to you. Sorry Charlie, your profits will technically be allocated to the states in which you operate. Here is a sample allocation which **some states** use to calculate your tax liability-

▲ Payroll- One third of your profits are allocated based on payroll. So if you have payroll expenses only in Colorado and California, but are incorporated in Nevada, one third of your LLC's profits are split between Colorado and California. Nothing is allocated to Nevada.

▲ Property- The second third of your profits are allocated based on property ownership and where it is located, such as real estate, inventory, etc.

▲ Sales- The last third of your profits are allocated based on sales and sales nexus, but this can get extremely sticky since the definition of where a sale occurs is grey- is it point of sale (seller's location), point of purchase (buyer's location), title transfer, fulfillment centers, etc.? Where a sale actually occurs is an argument which states and taxpayers can go around and around with- you can only imagine how it will end fighting a state with virtually unlimited resources and time coupled with their presumption of being right.

So, yes, under nexus rules perhaps a small portion of your profit can be attributed to Nevada- yet, this is not because you were incorporated in Nevada, it's because you had a presence in a state that does not impose an income tax. Same would be true for all your sales in Wyoming, Washington, Texas, South Dakota, etc. where strict corporate income taxes do not exist. In addition, several states impose a gross sales receipts tax and other forms of alternative minimum tax although their corporate income tax rate is zero.

Note: This is a sample. Some states gives sales a larger weight. Others ignore payroll and property. Talk to your allocation buddies at the Watson CPA Group.

State Nexus

This allocation boils down to nexus. And states are getting much more aggressive with claiming nexus so the income generated in that state is taxable. This might make people unhappy, but the reasoning behind it is fair in our opinion. You target a certain group of customers who live in a certain jurisdiction, and you sell computers. Why would Best Buy in the same tax jurisdiction have to pay income taxes in that jurisdiction while you do not? Please don't use the "it's just little ol' me versus the big box store" excuse. Seems a bit unfair if you are Best Buy, or Wal-Mart, or Apple.

Those customers in that jurisdiction perhaps enjoy a smaller tax rate and are able to have more purchasing power. That smaller tax rate might be offset by higher tax rates for the businesses. Business A (Best Buy in this example) has to subsidize the customers in the taxing jurisdiction while Business B (you) does not. Best Buy would be a bit upset in this example.

Avoiding taxes is the American way. We get it. But something about the 14th Amendment and equality and pursuit of happiness comes to mind. Then there's that darn 16th Amendment.

States define economic presence differently. Some states, such as California, use a sales dollar threshold (sometimes referred to bright-line) to determine nexus. The Watson CPA Group is getting close to having enough California business to necessitate filing as a foreign entity there just based on sales. Yuck, since the income tax rate is twice as much as Colorado's. California also has a presence test where if you have an agent working for you in California, then you have income tax nexus.

Remember, this is only income sourced to that taxing jurisdiction. About half the states have nexus rules and thresholds. Can't get enough? Here is a Journal of Accountancy article from 2010-

www.wcgurl.com/1515

Don't forget the basics such as bank accounts, licenses and permits. If you must be licensed in another state to legally conduct business such as an agent for an insurance company, this in itself might create nexus.

This book dives deep into the issue of nexus in the Chapter 4 – State Nexus Problems. Topics such as sales tax, FBA (Fulfillment By Amazon), throwback rules, and interstate commerce rules.

Foreign Qualification

This has nothing to do with international business. When your business has either a physical or economic presence in another state, you must register as a foreign entity. This is usually a formality, but some states might require your company to be in good standing with the home state. So keep up with your annual filings.

Conversely, you might simply want to create another LLC in the satellite state. This allows you to separate financial liability- for example, you might get sued in one state with unfavorable tax laws yet protect your interests in the other state (separate LLC). Bankruptcy laws change by state as well. Something to consider.

Nevada Fallacy Recap

So, don't believe the Nevada hype. You can probably get away with not paying state income taxes on your own, but as tax and accounting professionals we are bound by such inconveniences like ethics and law. Sorry.

Another example to chew on- you have a home office in Maryland. You commute to DC to work for your only client. You incorporate in Maryland since that is where your home office is and you pay yourself a wage subject to Maryland income taxes. Wait there's more. You also have a presence in Washington DC requiring a DC corporate tax return as a foreign entity in addition to your Maryland corporate tax return.

The bottom line is that Nevada tax laws benefit business owners with a presence in Nevada. As Zig Ziglar would say, You might get a free lunch on consignment, but eventually you'll have to pay. We encourage you to not game the system, and if you want to, the Watson CPA Group cannot be a part of it- we have too many clients relying on us to do the right thing. Pay your fair share of taxes, just not a dollar more.

Having said that, there are a zillion reasons why forming a corporation in a tax friendly state does make sense. But those are case-by-case scenarios. Nothing is a slam-dunk or carte blanche either way. The right questions must be asked and answered to reach the best decision.

Using a Self-Directed IRA or 401k to Buy a Rental, Start a Business

Since this chapter is about starting a business, there's no better place to talk about self-directed IRAs. What the heck is a self-directed IRA? Just because you make investment choices within your retirement accounts, does not mean they are self-directed. Sure, in a practical sense they are. But a self-directed IRA in the context of this section is about a very specific investment vehicle.

Why would you consider this option? Let's assume that you want to invest into rental properties (which is a great augmenting retirement strategy by the way.. we are huge fans), but all your money is tied up in an IRA. You are 50 years old, and can't touch it without penalty. The bank won't let you borrow against it. You might be hosed.

However, if you set up a self-directed IRA and roll your existing IRA into it, you can have the IRA invest into the rental property. But there is another reason why this might make sense. The S&P 500 index for the past 20 years has returned 9.22%. Not bad. Yet in some situations, rental properties might beat or in some cases, crush, the returns of the stock market. And it creates some diversification within your financial planning.

The other option with a self-directed IRA is to start or purchase a new business. A new business might need cash to invest into equipment, franchise fee, marketing, operational cash, etc.

If you want to expand your horizons into real estate notes, equipment leasing, livestock, private debt and equity placements, and oil and gas you can also use a self-directed IRA. Be careful here. Suitability might be your biggest hurdle. Talk to your financial team (such as The One Call Team) before squandering your life savings on ocean front property in Arizona.

And a 401k may be used as well. A 401k differs slightly from an IRA since it tied to your business. So you get the high contribution limits and no income phase outs of a 401k, and the ability to act as fund manager and purchase assets directly for the benefit of the 401k.

The first step is research companies who handle self-directed IRAs and ask very pointed questions. Second step is to move your money into the self-directed IRA. Certain companies provide for this transfer. Then direct your IRA to make an investment into a business. What's the catch? There's always a catch. Here are the things to look out for.

▲ No S-Corps or Partnerships. The way these entities are structured, business profits are returned to the shareholders. Profits cannot fall into the hands of the IRA account owner. Tainting of retirement dollars is the big thing here. So, your best recourse is a C-Corporation or a single member LLC.

▲ <u>Prohibited Transactions</u>. The business cannot invest directly in collectibles, art, rugs, antiques, metals other than gold, silver and palladium bullion, gems, stamps, coins (except certain U.S.-minted coins), alcoholic beverages, and a few other tangible items related to personal property. Ok- there goes half your list for sure. Yup, cross palladium of your list.

In addition, friends, business associates and siblings may invest in the business via a self-directed IRA, but your parents, children or spouse may not. The strict arms-length perspective of the business dealings must be maintained.

▲ <u>Key Employee / Investor</u>. You cannot be the key employee and key investor in the business. Nor can you own a controlling interest of the business. Basically, someone else has to have the right to hire or fire you such as a Board of Directors. The "someone else" is the grey area in all of this, and warrants more discussion.

The net-net of this is that the IRS does not allow you personally to receive money that was slated for retirement (at least without penalty until you are 59.5 years old). There are some other devils in the details, but this is certainly a great option. And Yes, we can help you through the sticky and tightly governed process.

To reiterate, a self-directed IRA o 401k is very cool. It allows you to move money you normally could not use into an account that can now be used to get yourself into a rental or a hot franchise. All without having to find cash elsewhere.

[Rest of page intentionally left blank]

Chapter 2
S Corporation Benefits
(updated December 23, 2017)

Avoiding or Reducing Self-Employment (SE) Taxes

A common complaint from those who own their own business is self-employment tax. Can you avoid, reduce, eliminate or lower your self-employment taxes or SE taxes? Yes, to a large extent actually but it takes some effort.

If you own a business as a sole proprietor or as a garden variety single-member LLC (one owner or shareholder) your business income will be reported on your personal tax return under Schedule C and is subject to self-employment tax (currently 15.3%) **and** ordinary income tax. So, you could easily pay an average of 40% (15.3% in SE taxes + 25% in income taxes) on all your net business income in Federal taxes. Wow, that sucks! Similar taxation for partnerships / multi-member LLCs too.

Drive this concept into your head, pretty please. On business income as an LLC or partnership, you are being taxed twice. Once at the self-employment tax level and again at the ordinary income tax level. Income taxes are a concern, but they are not the crux of the S Corp election and subsequent tax savings. In other words, the primary benefit of an S corporation is the reduction in self-employment taxes, not income taxes. Deductions available to an S Corp are available to a sole proprietor (health insurance, HSA, 401k, business expenses, etc.).

We are all humans, and we generally spend what we make. If you are not prepared for 30% to 40% in taxes for your business income, it could be a shocker on April 15.

The recent tax reform and specifically the pass-thru taxation changes in Section 199A do not alter the theory of self-employment tax savings. The additional pass-thru deduction afforded to small business owners complements the benefits of an S corporation. Please bear with us as we go through the mechanics of saving self-employment taxes with an S Corp. In Chapter 6 we will show you several examples of how the Section 199A works with and without an S Corp election.

How SE Tax Is Computed

A bit of disclosure is in order. Self-employment taxes are 15.3% which is derived from the "employer" portion at 7.65% and the "employee" portion of 7.65%. However, a small business gets to deduct its portion of payroll taxes from income before determining the taxable income. Huh?

Think of your last job where you received a W-2. The employer might have paid you $100,000 and withheld your portion of Social Security and Medicare taxes on your behalf. The company also had to pay its portion of Social Security and Medicare taxes, so its total expense was the $100,000 salary plus $7,650. Similar concept with sole proprietorships and LLCs.

Here is an illustrative table-

Net Business Income	100,000
less SE Tax Adjustment at 7.65%	7,650
Taxable Business Income	92,350
SE Tax at 15.3%	14,130
Tax Deductible Portion	7,065

Do you see the $14,130 or 14.13% of $100,000? That is essentially your effective rate of tax on self-employed business income because of the deductible portion of 7.65%. Probably doesn't make you feel any better but there you go.

Quick Analysis of S Corp Savings

If you own a business and have elected to be treated as an S Corp (Subchapter S) for taxation, the business now files a corporate tax return on Form 1120S. What's the big deal? Before we get into that, let's look at some quick numbers. These are based on using a salary of 40% of net business income for incomes up to $500,000 and then decreased incrementally to 30% for the millionaire at $2,500,000 below (real case actually). The 40% / 30% is for illustration (we will discuss reasonable shareholder salary is silly detail).

Here is our summary table-

Income	Total SE Tax	Salary	Total Payroll Tax	Savings $$	Delta %
30,000	4,239	12,000	1,836	2,403	8.0%
50,000	7,065	20,000	3,060	4,005	8.0%
75,000	10,597	30,000	4,590	6,007	8.0%
100,000	14,130	40,000	6,120	8,010	8.0%
150,000	18,711	60,000	9,180	9,531	6.4%
200,000	20,050	80,000	12,240	7,810	3.9%
300,000	22,972	120,000	18,174	4,798	1.6%
500,000	29,991	200,000	20,494	9,497	1.9%
1,000,000	47,537	350,000	24,844	22,693	2.3%
2,000,000	82,630	600,000	32,094	50,536	2.5%
2,500,000	100,177	750,000	36,444	63,733	2.5%

Chart Notes
Let's review some interesting things about the data on the previous page.

The bulk of payroll taxes are Social Security and Medicare taxes, which are combined to be called FICA taxes. You might have other payroll taxes such as unemployment (Yes, some states require it even for one-person corporations) and state disability insurance (SDI).

As mentioned, salaries started at 40% thru $500,000 and then reduced to 30% at $2M and $2.5M. This is a jumping off point. The IRS standard is "reasonable shareholder salary" which includes all sorts of non-qualitative things such as your expertise, Bureau of Labor Statistics, comparison of salary to distributions, zodiac sign, favorite color, etc.

Medicare taxes of 2.9% continues into perpetuity for LLCs and partnerships who do not elect S corporation status. Not only does this go on into perpetuity, it also goes on forever. This is one of the major component of savings in the upper incomes since Medicare taxes are capped at the amount of salary with S Corps. In other words, if you earn $1M you will pay Medicare taxes on the net income, but if you elect S Corp status and pay yourself a $400,000 salary you only pay Medicare taxes on the $400,000.

The Medicare surtax starts for those earning $200,000 and filing single, and $250,000 for those filing jointly. This too continues into perpetuity for LLCs and partnerships. In the data, we assumed a joint tax return. For example, at $500,000 net business income there is a $1,906 Medicare surtax. But if this business elects S corporation taxation and pays $200,000 salary, there is not a Medicare surtax. There is not a net investment income (NII) tax on the S corporation ordinary income either (more on that loophole later).

Savings as a percentage of income starts to drop off at $128,700 which makes sense given the Social Security cap for 2018. And those savings bottom out around $300,000 net business income and then begin a decent climb rate. Without getting into excruciating details and mental gymnastics, there is an interesting dynamic at $300,000 between Medicare taxes including the surtax on the LLC / partnership income, the salary being paid within an S Corp election, and Medicare taxes associated with that salary.

The Source of the Savings

The S Corp election of your Partnership, LLC or C corporation changes how the business reports income to the IRS. An S Corp prepares and files a Form 1120S which is a corporate tax return. That in turn generates a K-1 for each shareholder. Remember, shareholder, investor and owner are synonymous terms for our discussions.

As stated earlier, a K-1 is a statement that each shareholder receives, and it is similar to a W-2 since it reports the income that each shareholder is responsible for from a taxation perspective. As we discussed earlier, there are three types of tax returns that generate a K-1.

▲ Partnership / MMLLC (Form 1065)

▲ S Corporation (Form 1120S), and

▲ Estate or Trust (Form 1041)

There are two types of K-1s for the purposes of our self-employment tax conversation- one is generated from a partnership tax return and the other is generated from an S corporation tax return. These K-1s look nearly identical and both are reported on page 2 of Schedule E and your Form 1040. Schedule E is the tax form used for rental properties, royalties and **other investment income** including business income from a partnership or an S Corp.

However, a K-1 generated from a partnership tax return which has ordinary business income in box 1 and / or guaranteed payments in box 4 **will** typically be subjected to self-employment taxes for an active partner or member. Conversely, ordinary business income in box 1 on a K-1 from an S corporation will **not** be taxed with self-employment taxes. The S corporation election changes the color of money (we love this saying).

> **Note:** S Corps do not have guaranteed payments like partnerships might- S Corps would call these payments wages or salary. A partnership (and an LLC for that

matter) cannot pay its partners or owners a wage or salary. IRS frowns on this. Any periodic payment that is recurring in a partnership to one of the partners is called a guaranteed payment and is reported separately from partnership income. Both might be subjected to self-employment taxes.

You might hear terms such as pass-through entity or disregarded entity- a disregarded entity is a single-member LLC. As the terms suggests, it is disregarded, and therefore does not have to file its own tax return since the taxable consequence is reported on the owner(s) personal tax returns as a sole proprietorship.

A pass-through entity passes its Federal tax obligation onto the partner of a partnership, the shareholder of an S corporation or the beneficiary of an estate or trust. States might impose a business tax or a franchise tax on the partnership or S Corp directly (they legally cannot impose an income tax... more in Chapter 3 about interstate commerce rules).

For purposes of Section 199A pass-through deduction, disregarded entities are treated the same. Recall the definition from Chapter which treated sole proprietors, real estate investors, limited liability companies (and the variants) and S corporations to all be treated the same when determining the qualified business income deduction under Section 199A.

Quick Recap, The S Corp Money Trail

So, when your partnership, LLC or corporation is taxed as an S Corp you are considered both an employee and a shareholder (think investor). As an employee, your income is subjected to all the usual taxes that you would see on a paystub- federal taxes, state taxes, Social Security taxes, Medicare taxes, unemployment and disability.

However, as a shareholder or investor, you are simply getting a return on your investment. That income, as the Romneys, Gates and Buffets of the world enjoy, is a form of investment income and therefore is not subjected to self-employment taxes (tiny exception for income over $200,000 (single) or $250,000 (married) where Medicare surtax is charged).

When we say self-employment taxes, we are really talking about Social Security and Medicare taxes. From a sole proprietor perspective, they are self-employment taxes. From an employee perspective, they are Social Security and Medicare taxes. Same thing.

Let's look at another visual in terms of how the money travels-

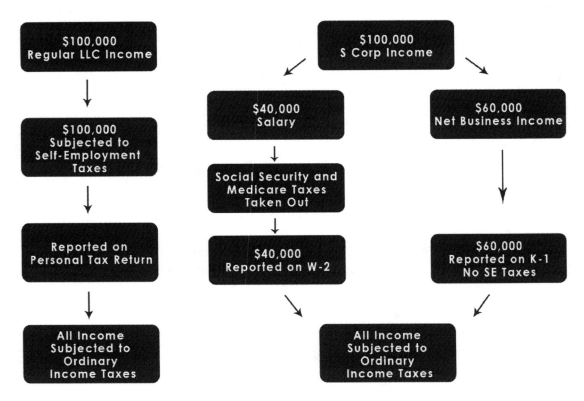

The four boxes on the left is the money trail of your sole proprietorship, LLC or partnership. The series of boxes on the right is the money trail of your entity being taxed as an S corporation. Note the $60,000 chunk of income on the far right hand side that is not being taxed at the self-employment tax level. This is the source of your savings.

Also note that all your $100,000 is being subjected to income taxes. This is a common misconception- a lot of business owners believe there is a magical income tax reduction with an S Corp election. Not true. The only reduction is in self-employment taxes. All other tax deductions such as operating expenses, home office expense, mileage, meals and entertainment, etc. are equally deductible with or without an S corporation.

Still not sure or not convinced? No problem... please check out Line 57 on your Form 1040 tax return. This number reflects the self-employment taxes paid on your business income. We want to reduce this by 60 to 65%.

Other S Corp Benefits with Salary Considerations

The previous data showed significant savings using a 40% salary without self-employed health insurance (SEHI). Again, we are only focused on the self-employment tax and payroll tax savings at this point. Section 199A from the Tax Cuts & Jobs Act of 2017 will be wormed into overall tax savings in Chapter 6. While reducing overall taxes and leveraging the pass-thru tax deduction cannot be ignored, we are isolating payroll taxes to drive home a critical point.

What happens when the company pays for your health insurance?

Tax Savings with Health Insurance

When your S corporation pays for your self-employed health insurance (SEHI), including coverage for your family, that amount is added to Box 1 Wages on your W-2. So, your income is artificially increased by the annual amount of premiums. However, there are two huge concepts you need to embrace.

First, Box 3 Social Security Wages and Box 5 Medicare Wages **do not** get increased by the amount of premiums paid. Here is a silly looking, but illustrative W-2.

Box 1 Wages	50,000	Box 2 Federal Tax Withholdings	21,735
Box 3 Social Security Wages	**40,000**	Box 4 SS Withholdings	2,480
Box 5 Medicare Wages	**40,000**	Box 6 Medicare Withholdings	580
State Wages	50,000	State Tax Withholdings	4,347

Don't get tweaked on the Federal and State tax withholdings. We'll explain that in Chapter 6 (spoiler alert- we increase income tax withholdings to help budget for the K-1 income that is combined with your W-2 income on your individual tax return).

Your focus should be on Box 3 and Box 5- these are the boxes that we want to reduce to the best of our abilities and with reasonableness.

Subsequently Box 4 and Box 6 is the calculation of the Social Security and Medicare taxes based on the amounts in Box 3 and Box 5. As you can see, your compensation is $50,000 but only $40,000 is being used to compute Social Security and Medicare taxes. Why is this? Some taxable fringe benefits, such as health care benefits (self-employed health insurance premiums and HSA contributions), is only added to Box 1 Wages, and not Box 3 or Box 5. Boom!

How does this translate to the corporate tax return? Line 7 of Form 1120S is "Compensation of officers" and the $50,000 in Box 1 above would be entered there (we'll chat about the effects of solo 401k plan deferrals in a bit). Line 21 of Form 1120S is "Ordinary business income." Line 7 as compared to Line 21 is one of the ways the IRS will consider a challenge of your S corporation with respect to reasonable shareholder salary (the IRS also looks at your K-1 as compared to your W-2, both connected by your Social Security number).

Got it? Good. Next concept.

The second concept is that self-employed health insurance (SEHI) premiums are effectively deducted on Line 7 of Form 1120S as Officer Compensation. Therefore the salary paid to the shareholders plus health insurance directly reduces Line 21 on Form 1120S which is your taxable ordinary income generated by the S corporation.

However, your W-2 shows $50,000 in taxable wages and this will appear on Line 7 of your Form 1040. Hmmm… how does that work? We know what you are thinking- you are paying income taxes on the full $50,000 since the W-2 shows $50,000 but you were paid $40,000… where is the tax savings? This concern would be true except that you are considered self-employed as a greater than 2% shareholder, and therefore the health insurance premiums are deducted on Line 29 of your Form 1040 as an adjustment to income. This is a $1 for $1 reduction in your gross income to arrive at your adjusted gross income (AGI) on Lines 37 and 38.

Just to reiterate- the deduction and subsequent tax benefit of self-employed health insurance is done on the corporate tax return. The deduction appears on your individual tax return, but it is a net zero as we've illustrated above (we accountants call this an in and out). If this doesn't resonate quite yet, don't worry. However, we have seen this screwed up several times when clients run their own payroll and / or prepare their own individual tax returns. Be aware and know that you should have a Line 29 entry on Form 1040 if you are paying self-employed health insurance premiums. Period.

So, we have an artificial increase in salary by the amount of SEHI and our reasonable shareholder salary testing is improved, but Social Security and Medicare taxes are computed on a lessor amount. Winner winner chicken dinner.

There are more examples of this stuff in Chapter 6. Also, the handling of self-employed health insurance in this manner is encouraged by the IRS as outlined in Fact Sheet 2008-25.

Here is the blurb if you can't get enough-

The health and accident insurance premiums paid on behalf of the greater than 2 percent S corporation shareholder-employee are deductible by the S corporation as fringe benefits and are reportable as wages for income tax withholding purposes on the shareholder-employee's Form W-2. They are not subject to Social Security or Medicare (FICA) or Unemployment (FUTA) taxes. Therefore, this additional compensation is included in Box 1 (Wages) of the Form W-2, Wage and Tax Statement, issued to the shareholder, but would not be included in Boxes 3 or 5 of Form W-2.

A 2-percent shareholder-employee is eligible for an AGI deduction for amounts paid during the year for medical care premiums if the medical care coverage is established by the S corporation. Previously, "established by the S corporation" meant that the medical care coverage had to be in the name of the S corporation.

In Notice 2008-1, the IRS stated that if the medical coverage plan is in the name of the 2percent shareholder and not in the name of the S corporation, a medical care plan can be considered to be established by the S corporation if: the S corporation either paid or reimbursed the 2percent shareholder for the premiums and reported the premium payment or reimbursement as wages on the 2percent shareholder's Form W-2.

Payments of the health and accident insurance premiums on behalf of the shareholder may be further identified in Box 14 (Other) of the Form W-2. Schedule K-1 (Form 1120S) and Form 1099 should not be used as an alternative to the Form W-2 to report this additional compensation.

That was IRS Fact Sheet 2008-25 which can be downloaded here-

www.wcgurl.com/8247

Moving on… Here is a summary of the savings assuming a 40% salary **and** a $10,000 annual health insurance premium.

40% Reasonable Salary, With Health Insurance

The following table highlights the significant savings when factoring self-employed health insurance into the reasonable salary calculations.

Income	Total SE Tax	Salary	Total Payroll Tax	Delta	Delta%
30,000	4,239	2,000	306	3,933	13.1%
50,000	7,065	10,000	1,530	5,535	11.1%
75,000	10,597	20,000	3,060	7,537	10.0%
100,000	14,130	30,000	4,590	9,540	9.5%
150,000	18,711	50,000	7,650	11,061	7.4%
200,000	20,050	70,000	10,710	9,340	4.7%
300,000	22,972	110,000	16,830	6,142	2.0%
500,000	29,991	190,000	20,204	9,787	2.0%

35% Reasonable Salary, Without Health Insurance

As mentioned, the previous illustrations are based on a reasonable salary that was 40% of the business income after expenses. If your reasonable S Corp salary is less than this, your savings increase. For grins, the table below shows the results and subsequent savings using a 35% reasonable salary figure. Check out the $150,000 figure! $10k in savings.

Income	Total SE Tax	Salary	Total Payroll Tax	Delta	Delta%
30,000	4,239	10,500	1,607	2,632	8.8%
50,000	7,065	17,500	2,678	4,387	8.8%
75,000	10,597	26,250	4,016	6,581	8.8%
100,000	14,130	35,000	5,355	8,775	8.8%
150,000	18,711	52,500	8,033	10,679	7.1%
200,000	20,050	70,000	10,710	9,340	4.7%
300,000	22,972	105,000	16,065	6,907	2.3%
500,000	29,991	175,000	19,769	10,222	2.0%

The salary calculation part of running an S Corp is one of the biggest challenges, but it also allows for most wiggle room for argument if necessary. Chapter 6 will touch on the various tools we use to determine a reasonable shareholder salary including-

▲ IRS Revenue Ruling 74-44

▲ IRS Fact Sheet 2008-25

▲ Tax Court Cases

▲ Bureau of Labor Statistics / Risk Management Association Data

▲ Rules of Thumb (Biz Valuation, 1/3 1/3 1/3)

Here is some initial food for thought from a 2013 tax court case-

Sean McAlary Ltd. Inc. v. Commissioner, TC Summary Opinion 2013-62- the IRS hired a valuation expert to determine that a real estate agent should have been paid $100,755 salary out of his S-Corp's net income of $231,454. Not bad. He still took home over $130,000 in K-1 income, and avoided some self-employment taxes. The valuation expert had used Bureau of Labor Statistics data to determine the average salary for real estate agents in the taxpayer's zip code.

Here is the entire tax court summary opinion-

www.wcgurl.com/8244

Please don't be that guy who extrapolates the previous tax court case into something else. BLS data is only one aspect of determining a reasonable salary. As mentioned, there is more on the salary stuff in Chapter 6 and pinning your entire argument on BLS data might leave money on the table.

Until then, consider the following summary which outlines the savings at various income levels and salaries (including one with self-employment health insurance)-

Income	40% Salary No Health Ins.	40% Salary $10k Health Ins.	35% Salary No Health Ins.
30,000	2,403	3,933	2,632
50,000	4,005	5,535	4,387
75,000	6,007	7,537	6,581
100,000	8,010	9,540	8,775
150,000	9,531	11,061	10,679
200,000	7,810	9,340	9,340
300,000	4,798	6,142	6,907
500,000	9,497	9,787	10,222

Good stuff!

Why are we belaboring the heck out of this? In other words, does payroll really need to be dialed in this tightly? Consider that paying a salary which is $10,000 too high will cost you $1,410 in unnecessary payroll taxes. Read that again. If you paid yourself $100,000 when a reasonable salary could have been $80,000, you paid $2,820 too much in payroll taxes. What would you rather spend $2,820 on?

So, payroll calculations need to be just a bit tighter than bar napkin quality and just a hair below NASA precision.

Officer Compensation with Solo 401k Plan Deferral

Previously we showed you a mock-up of a W-2 with self-employed health insurance premiums added to Box 1 as Wages. When you have a solo 401k plan and make employee deferrals, that reduces Box 1 of your W-2. However, Line 7 of the corporate tax return will still show the gross salary paid plus self-employed health insurance premiums as officer compensation. In other words, contributing to a 401k plan does not reduce your officer compensation below a level where the IRS might challenge your reasonable salary determination. If you worked for Google making $100,000, and Google collects $18,000 and sends it off to the 401k people on your behalf, Google's wage expense remains at $100,000. Same thing here. We will give you more examples including a table showing how this shakes out in Chapter 6.

Tracking Fringe Benefits

Again, more information on this in Chapters 5 and 6, but before we go too far down the road, your business needs to track the amounts paid for fringe benefits so they may be included as Officer Compensation. Specifically-

▲ Self-employed health insurance premiums,

▲ Health Savings Account (HSA) contributions,

▲ Health Reimbursement Arrangement (HRA) reimbursements, and

▲ Personal use of company assets such as vehicles and airplanes.

There are others, but these are the biggies. If you are using accounting software or even Excel, each of these should be a separate category. If you wanted to get fancy, you could have an account labeled "Officer Compensation" with sub-accounts being Wages, SEHI, HSA, HRA and Other. At tax time, your profit and loss statement would then be framed and hung on our smart client wall. Yes, we have a not-so-smart client wall too which is thankfully much smaller since it is temporary until we give you the "see… how it works is…" tutoring during a Periodic Business Review.

[Rest of page intentionally left blank for shameless self-promotion]

S-Corp Hard Money Facts, Net Savings

Sales pitch alert! The Watson CPA Group specializes in S corporations which have a small number of shareholders, and often just a one-person show. Did you know that 95% of all S Corps have only one shareholder, and 99% of all S Corps have three or fewer shareholders? Small business owners is all we do!

Because it is a core competency for us, we have created an S Corp package that includes the following-

	Aspen	Vail	Breck	Keystone
S Corp Reasonable Salary Calculation	Yes	Yes	Yes	Yes
Section 199A Pass-Thru Optimization	Yes	Yes	Yes	Yes
S Corp Payroll Filings and Deposits	Yes	Yes		
Annual Processing (W2s, up to five 1099's)	Yes	Yes		
S Corporation Tax Prep (Form 1120S)	Yes	Yes	Yes	Yes
Individual Tax Prep (Form 1040), One Owner	Yes		Yes	
Estimated Tax Payments	Yes	Yes	Yes	Yes
2018 Tax Planning, Mock Tax Returns	Yes	Yes	Yes	Yes
Unlimited Consultation, PBRs	Yes	Yes	Yes	Yes
First Research Industry Reports	Yes	Yes	Yes	Yes
Small Business Tax Deductions Optimization	Yes	Yes	Yes	Yes
Solo 401k Plan	Yes	Yes	Yes	Yes
IRS Audit Defense	Yes		Yes	
Annual Fee	**$2,940**	**$2,640**	**$2,460**	**$2,160**
Monthly Fee	**$245**	**$220**	**$205**	**$180**

Couple of things to keep in mind- we make very little profits on payroll processing… we offer it as a convenience to our clients. One throat to choke with a single call can be reassuring but if you want to run your payroll, go for it! And… the benefit of the Watson CPA Group preparing both tax returns is that we slide things around depending on income limitations, phaseouts, alternative minimum tax (AMT), etc. Having our arms around both can yield some good tax savings!

Some more things to consider- Since only a partial year remains, our usual annual fee is pro-rated to not charge you for services you didn't use (like payroll and consultation). However, a large chunk of our annual fee is tax preparation which is typically a fixed amount of $1,300 (both corporate and personal). Whether we onboard you in January, July or December, we have to prepare a full year tax return. This increases the monthly fee for the remaining months of 2018 but the monthly fee will later decrease in January of 2019 to reflect the amounts above.

Break-even analysis is based on our annual fee of $2,940. If an S corporation saves you 8% to 10% (on average) in taxes over the garden variety LLC, then $2,940 divided by 8.5% equals $35,000 of net business income after expenses.

You can always find someone to do it for less- we know that. At the same time, we have a vested interest in your success and provide sound tax and business consultation as a part of our service. Here is a link to our Periodic Business Review agenda that we cover throughout the year so our consultation to you is comprehensive-

www.watsoncpagroup.com/PBR

We also have written a webpage on end of year tax planning-

www.watsoncpagroup.com/EOY

Common S Corp candidates and current clients for the Watson CPA Group are consultants, financial advisors, physicians, chiropractors, doctors, surgeons, anesthesiologists, nurse anesthetists, insurance agents, photographers (the profitable ones), online retailers, FBA retailers, among several others. We also have several medical groups and financial advisor teams.

W-2 Converted to 1099

One of the biggest pushes into the S Corp world is when your employer decides to convert you from W-2 to 1099. To refresh your memory, when you are paid a W-2 salary your employer pays for half of the Social Security and Medicare taxes associated with your income. Conversely when you are paid as a 1099 contractor, you pay both halves of the Social Security and Medicare tax.

Another nice feature of being paid a W-2 salary is the built-in budgeting since your taxes are taken out before the direct deposit into your checking account. On the other hand, 1099 income is raw- just a big ol' fat check ready to spend.

Companies like to have contractors versus employees since it cuts down on cost and offers more flexibility. Some companies can easily exceed a factor of 1.6 for a fully burdened labor rate. For example, if you are being paid a $100,000 salary, the cost to the employer could be

$150,000 after you factor in payroll taxes, 401k contributions, pension funding, health insurance, vacations and sick pay, office resources, etc. This would be a factor of 1.5.

Another benefit is when a company needs to shrink, it simply ends the contract or reduces it dramatically without much hoopla. If Northrop Grumman laid off 10,000 workers there would be congressional hearings. If they ended 10,000 contracts with sub-contractors, no one pays any attention to it.

Some employers, such as Verizon, have recently gotten in trouble by converting too many W-2 employees into 1099 contractors. The IRS and several states see it as an end-around.

Regardless, when entertaining being converted from W-2 to 1099, consider the fully burdened labor rate of your employer. If you were making $100,000, you really need to make at least $130,000 or more to come out ahead. You win, they win. Don't forget that as a 1099 contractor you now can rifle a bunch of expenses through your business that were otherwise limited or not allowed… but don't leak that out during negotiations.

Lastly, create an LLC and tax it as an S corporation.

Net Investment Income, Medicare Surtax and S Corps

To help fund the Affordable Care Act (Obamacare), an additional Medicare surtax is tacked on to your net investment income. Recall that as an S corporation owner, you are both employee and investor. When you trigger the high income threshold for the Medicare surtax, then you could pay 3.8% (2.9% Medicare plus 0.9% surtax) on some portions of your income.

The tax is calculated by multiplying the 3.8% tax rate by the **lower** of the following two amounts:

▲ net investment income for the year; or

▲ modified adjusted gross income over a certain threshold amount ($200,000 for single filers and $250,000 for married filing jointly).

Again, whichever is lower (how nice of Congress?).

The IRS defines net investment income for the purposes of calculating the unearned income Medicare contribution tax includes interest, dividends, capital gains, annuities, royalties, rents, and pass-through income from an passive business such as **S Corps** and partnerships. Yuck. Why did they have to pointedly name S corporations?

But! And this is a big but! Like a Nel Carter butt. If you materially participate in your S Corp this income is **not** included in the net investment income calculation. 99% of the small business owners out there who elect to be treated as an S Corp will also qualify as materially participating. As an aside, 95% of all S corporations have one shareholder, and 99% have three or fewer shareholders.

Here is the laundry list the IRS uses for testing material participation-

To materially participate in a business for a particular year, the shareholder must meet one of the following seven tests discussed in Temporary Regulations Section 1.469-5T(a)-

▲ The shareholder participated in the activity for more than 500 hours during the year;

▲ The shareholder's participation in the activity constituted substantially all the participation of all individuals in the activity;

▲ The shareholder participated for more than 100 hours in the activity, and the shareholder's hours were not less than those of any other participant in the activity;

▲ The activity is a significant participation activity for the year, and the shareholder's aggregate participation in all significant participation activities exceeded 500 hours;

▲ The shareholder materially participated in the activity for any five of the past 10 years;

▲ The activity is a personal services activity where the shareholder materially participated in the activity for any three years preceding the tax year; **or**

▲ Based on all the facts and circumstances, the shareholder participated in the activity on a regular, continuous, and substantial basis.

This list is an "or" list, therefore you only need to fit into one of the buckets to trigger the material participation designation. Interestingly, these regulations are titled Temporary Regulations but they have been around for a very long time. Like forever. Maybe even forever and ever.

Material participation is a common theme with the IRS, and in some respects it changes the color of money similar to an S Corp election. A silent investor in an S corporation will have passive income and might be subject to Medicare surtax on that income. That same investor now materially participates, and the same income is now considered non-passive (or quasi-earned but without self-employment taxes) and is sheltered from the Medicare surtax.

Three Types of Income

Let's back up a bit. Our book loves to spill the beans so-to-speak with the net-net fun facts, and then dig a hole under the house for the foundation. Wow. All kinds of metaphors. There are three types of income- earned, portfolio and passive. There is also a small subset of passive income called non-passive income.

Earned Income

Earned income is income that is a direct result of your labor. This income is usually in the form of W-2 wages or as small business income reported on Schedule C of your personal tax return, both subjected to Social Security and Medicare taxes (self-employment taxes).

Portfolio Income

Portfolio income is income generated from selling an asset, and if you sell that asset for a higher price than what you paid for it originally, you will have a gain. Depending on the holding period of the asset, and other factors, that gain might be taxed at ordinary income tax rates or capital gains tax rates. Interest and dividends are other examples of portfolio income.

Capital gains is not a form of income per se. Capital gains simply defines how your portfolio income will be taxed. Subtle difference.

Portfolio income is not subjected to self-employment taxes, but as illustrated earlier it might be subjected to net investment income (NII) Medicare surtax.

Passive Income

Passive income bluntly is income that would continue to generate if you died. Morbid. How about this? Passive income is income that would continue to generate if you decided to do nothing and sunbathe on some beach. That sounds better. Passive income includes rental income, royalties and income from businesses or investment partnerships / multi-member LLCs where you do not materially participate.

Passive income is also not subjected to self-employment taxes. But similar to portfolio income, it might be subject to the Net Investment Income tax. So, if you own a rental house, the income generated from the rental house is considered passive income. As a side note, taxpayers used to label themselves as Real Estate Professionals under IRS definition to allow passive losses to be deducted; now we are seeing the same label to avoid Net Investment Income tax on rental income.

Additionally, if you wrote a book and receive royalty checks, that income is also passive and not subjected to self-employment taxes. But, if you write several books and consider yourself a writer, then you are materially participating in your activity and your income is earned income. And Yes, you would pay self-employment taxes on that income.

Non-Passive Income

But there is another funny thing. K-1 income generated from an S Corp where you materially participate is considered non-passive income. It is not necessarily earned income and it is not passive income. It is something in between, but definitely without the Social Security and Medicare tax element.

As an aside, expatriates, or expats for short, can exclude up to $102,100 for 2017 of earned income while working overseas. Many establish S corporations stateside for their contract gig- both the W-2 and K-1 income up to $100,800 are excluded from income tax.

Therefore as a shareholder in an S corporation you will receive a K-1. How this income is labeled can change depending on your involvement. Material participation makes your K-1 income non-passive income, otherwise it is passive income. As mentioned earlier, this changes the color of money.

Where is this all leading to? Good question.

More Net Investment Tax, Self-Rentals and S Corps

The net investment income tax was a topic that was briefly broached earlier. Generally speaking, passive income such as rental income will be considered net investment income and subject to the Medicare surtax. Why do you care?

It is common for a business owner who relies on machinery or equipment to have two business entities. One entity is an LLC that owns the assets. The other entity is an S corporation which leases the assets from the LLC to use in the business. This directly reduces the S Corp's income, and might possibly reduce the amount of salary required to be paid by the business to the shareholders. Good news.

Here is an example.

	S Corp Owns Building	LLC Owns Building S Corp Rents from LLC
Gross Income	100,000	100,000
Rental Expense	0	30,000
Net Income	100,000	70,000
Reasonable Salary (assumed at 40%)	40,000	28,000
Payroll Taxes	5,640	3,948
Savings		**1,692**

This is an overly simplified example and leaves out depreciation, etc., but you get the idea. In addition, we used a 40% salary calculation which might be different in your situation. Regardless, the apples to apples comparison shows a nice little savings of $1,692. As mentioned in Chapter 1, the arrangement also allows you to have different partners in each entity allowing you to expand ownership in the operating entity while retaining full ownership in the leased asset (building).

More good news. The LLC's activities are considered self-rental activities meaning that you are creating a transaction with yourself. Provided that this arrangement is at market rates, the IRS accepts this relationship. Moreover, the self-rental income is **not** considered passive and therefore **not** subjected to the net investment income tax calculations.

We know what you are thinking... wait for it... Yes, this changes the color of money (how many times have we said this?).

Here is the code. Regulations Section 1.469-2 boringly read-

> (f)(6) Property rented to a non-passive activity. An amount of the taxpayer's gross rental activity income for the taxable year from an item of property equal to the net rental activity income for the year from that item of property is **treated as not from a passive activity** if the property-

> (i) Is rented for use in a trade or business activity (within the meaning of paragraph (e)(2) of this section) in which the taxpayer materially participates (within the meaning of Section 1.469-5T) for the taxable year; and

> (ii) Is not described in Section 1.469-2T(f)(5).

Read that first paragraph again. Only attorneys and legislators could have taken a simple concept and made it unnecessarily complicated. Let's summarize. If you have a self-rental situation with a business where you materially participate, that income is not considered passive income.

Self-rental situations are not just limited to buildings. You could lease your car to your S corporation. No, this isn't the same as leasing a car from a dealership. This is where you own a piece of equipment, let's say an automobile, and you lease it back to your company for your company's use. Sounds exotic, but it is quite simple. More about this in Chapter 7 – Fringe Benefits.

This is about the equipment used in your trade or craft. Field engineers and landscapers are just a few that come to mind who benefit from a self-rental situation.

Wait! There's more. There's always more.

Interest income generated from loans to the S corporation are also excluded from the net investment income tax calculations to the extent of your allocable share of non-passive deduction. Huh? Example time.

Jim Smith and Sharon Jones own JS Toys as 60-40 partners. Jim received $1,000 in interest income from the business because he lent the company money. Jim owns 60% of the business. Therefore, Jim can exclude $600 from his net investment income since that is his allocable share of non-passive income. The remaining $400 would be subjected to the net investment income tax calculation. Yes, we accountants love a stupidly convoluted tax code- keeps you confused or bored, and keeps us employed.

Make sure this stuff is handled correctly. You might be paying a Medicare surtax gratuitously.

Income Types Recap

We talked about a lot of things regarding the type of income and how it is treated. Here is a brief recap-

▲ Earned income is subjected to self-employment taxes for self-employed, or payroll taxes in the form of Social Security and Medicare taxes for the W-2 employee. Easy.

▲ Portfolio income is generated by selling assets and is taxed at the capital gains rate or ordinary income tax rate depending on how long you owned the asset. Interest and dividends are also considered portfolio income. Also easy.

▲ Rental income is considered passive income which is taxed at the ordinary income tax rate only (as opposed to being taxed twice, once with self-employment taxes and again with ordinary income taxes). Rental losses are considered passive losses.

▲ Passive losses can only be deducted from passive income, generally. But there are exceptions of course.

▲ Passive losses may be deducted against other forms of income such as earned income, portfolio income and non-passive income up to a $25,000 limit. This requires your participation to be considered active, which is a much easier threshold than material participation. Usually a 100 hours will do it.

▲ The deduction of passive losses with active participation becomes limited when modified adjusted gross incomes exceed $100,000 and are reduced to zero at $150,000. Those disallowed losses are carried forward into the future to be used when incomes or dispositions of assets allow.

▲ Non-passive income cannot be offset or reduced by passive losses except the magical $25,000 figure. So, if you have $100,000 in passive losses from your rental properties and $100,000 in income generated from your self-rental to your business, your non-passive income can only be reduced to $75,000.

▲ There are PIGs (Passive Income Generators) which have been under IRS scrutiny as abusive tax shelters since their sole purpose is to generate passive income in the beginning to offset other passive losses.

Tilt. This can be confusing. Please contact the Watson CPA Group for more assistance and hopefully clarification.

Chapter 3
The 185 Reasons to Not
Have an S Corp or LLC
(updated December 23, 2017)

Introduction

Not everything that glitters is gold so there are a handful of downsides, some manageable, to the S Corp election or having an LLC. A lot of these examples stand alone, and some of these depend on the net income of the business and other external factors. The Watson CPA Group can help guide you through the decision-making process.

And No, there are not 185 reasons- it was just a self-proclaimed catchy number. Most of these reasons in the beginning of this chapter focus on S corporations. However, there are some general pains with having any type of formalized entity, and those are near the end.

Specifically, in this chapter we will review these disadvantages to having an S corporation-

▲ Increased cost (tax preparation, payroll taxes)

▲ SEP IRA limitations

▲ Trapped assets

▲ Disparate distributions

▲ Other W-2 income

▲ State taxes

▲ Among other smaller issues

Specific to S corporations, we ask these general questions of each business owner before diving into the nitty-gritty-

▲ Does your business earn over $35,000 net income after expenses? Say Yes.

▲ Are you located in New York City or Tennessee where S corporation tax rates are egregious and suck up all the federal tax savings? Say No.

▲ Do you have other W-2 income that exceeds or comes close to exceeding the Social Security limits of $128,700 (2018)? Say No. If you say Yes, we need business income to exceed $200,000 in #1 above.

▲ Is this a going concern? In other words, is the business going to continue to earn the same income or more each year? Say Yes.

▲ Do you have an LLC or some other entity in place that can be elected to taxed as an S Corp? Say Yes. If you say No, we have options just not elegant ones.

Are you still here? Excellent news... then read on!

Additional Accounting Costs

Paying shareholders through payroll and filing a corporate tax return costs money- but with a potential 8% to 10% savings of net income, the benefits will exceed the costs especially if the net business income after expenses exceeds $35,000. This is **net income after expenses**- not gross. So many business owners think in terms of gross income- we don't care about gross income and the IRS doesn't care about gross income when it comes to taxable income, and the sensibility of an S Corp election.

Since the cost of payroll services and corporate tax return preparation is relatively fixed, the more profit you earn the more you'll save. Something to discuss and consider.

> **Quick Numbers**: Let's say $100,000 in net income saves you $8,500. The Watson CPA Group charges $2,940 ($245 per month) for corporate and personal tax returns, payroll and estimated taxes, income tax modeling and planning, and unlimited business consultation. Therefor a $100,000 S corporation saves you close to $5,500 after our fee, and we do all the work.

If you already have a partnership, and you file a partnership tax return your break-even point is about half, or $20,000. If you also run payroll within your partnership because you have a staff, then the annual cost of having an S Corp should be zero. So now your $100,000 actually puts $8,500 in your pocket.

In other words, a large chunk of the $2,940 is business tax return preparation and payroll. Therefore, if you already pay for these services within your business then they are considered sunk costs when contemplating the S Corp election. Consideration of sunk costs should be removed from decision making.

We are not considering the huge benefits from pass-thru qualified business income tax deductions as outlined in Section 199A of the Tax Cuts & Jobs Act of 2017. At this point, in this chapter, one of our primary focuses is the delta between a non-S Corp and an S Corp. Real numbers and real examples are coming up in Chapter 6. Be patient...

Additional Payroll Taxes

The IRS will expect unemployment taxes (FUTA) on all W-2 wages paid, including corporate officers. Currently in 2017, the first $7,000 will be taxed at 6% with a credit of up to 5.4% for unemployment taxes paid to your state (SUTA). Some states such as Alaska, Kansas, Minnesota, Nebraska, Oregon, Washington state and Washington D.C. will allow you to opt out of state unemployment.

Before you opt out of your state unemployment taxes, consider two things. First, you get a credit for the state unemployment taxes paid when you file your Federal unemployment taxes on Form 940. This is a big deal. Here is how it works-

Minnesota (for example) has a wage base of $31,200 (2016). Let's say the average SUTA rate is 2.6% and your salary is $40,000. You would pay $811 to Minnesota for unemployment. Then, because you paid into a Minnesota's unemployment system, the IRS only charges you 0.6% of the first $7,000 or $42. So... $811 + $42 = $853. If you opted out, you would only pay 6% of the first $7,000 or $420. Opting out in Minnesota at this wage base makes sense.

In Colorado, where you cannot opt-out but provides a good illustration, the wage base is $12,200. If your SUTA rate was 2.1% then you would pay $257 to Colorado and $42 to the IRS for a total of $298. If you could opt out and did opt out, the IRS would charge you 6% of the first $7,000 or $420. A tiny savings, but a savings nonetheless.

Some states, such as California, are in arrears with the federal government on unemployment debt payments and as such the credit the IRS provides is reduced. For example, the FUTA rate is 0.6% if you pay SUTA, but for California businesses the FUTA rate is 2.7% in addition to the SUTA rate. California is projected to be all caught up on its federal unemployment debt in 2018 thanks to the backs of resident taxpayers, and the FUTA rate will revert to 0.6%.

Note the subtle difference- full FUTA rate is 6% and the reduced rate is 0.6%. The simple decimal move is sneaky.

Second... and this one you might laugh at... second, if you shut down your S corporation you might be eligible for unemployment benefits. Remember, unemployment benefits are administered by the state and if you opt out because of your corporate officer exemption, you could be limiting yourself unintentionally. Yeah, this is crazy but beware just the same.

Some states, such as California and New Jersey, also impose a state disability insurance (SDI) payroll tax when you run payroll on the shareholders. Specifically, California charges 1.0% with a maximum of $1,149 for 2018. Yuck. You can opt-out from California if your underlying entity is a corporation.

To summarize some of these various terms that you might hear-

▲ FUTA and SUTA- unemployment tax. Unavoidable. You might be able to opt out, and as the Minnesota example above illustrates, there is a tax savings.

▲ SDI- state disability insurance. Might be able to opt out for single-owner corporate officers in California.

▲ Workers Compensation Insurance- has nothing to do with unemployment or state disability insurance, and is not interchangeable with those terms. This is purely insurance coverage for on the job injuries and is provided by private insurance such as State Farm, All State, Farmers, etc. Ask your local insurance agent if you can opt out. Typically you can since you don't plan no suing yourself for a paper cut or a rogue paperclip stabbing.

Be aware that additional payroll taxes can nibble at the S Corp savings, but frankly it is small. The worst case scenario might yield a $1,200 reduction in savings such as California if you cannot opt out of state disability insurance (SDI). Average case scenario is probably around the $500 mark.

SEP IRA Limitations

If you earned $200,000 in your garden-variety LLC your SEP IRA contribution is 20% of $200,000 or $40,000. But if you elect S corporation taxation, your SEP IRA is now 25% of your W-2. Let's say you paid yourself $70,000 in wages, your SEP IRA contribution would be $17,500 versus $40,000.

However, if you leveraged a solo 401k plan instead, your total contribution is now $18,500 plus 25% of your W-2 or $36,000. Another way to look at the SEP IRA versus 401k calculation is 401k = SEP IRA + $18,500 + $6,000 (if 50 or older).

The reduction in what you can save in your SEP IRA or solo 401k cannot be viewed in isolation. In the $200,000 example above, your S Corp savings might exceed $12,000. Also recall that tax deferrals are merely little IOU's to the IRS. As such, the small reduction in contribution limits and the small tax deferrals and even smaller ultimate tax savings (provided your retirement marginal tax rate is less than your current tax rate) are shadowed by the savings of an S corporation.

Trapped Assets

As the only shareholder of an S Corp, you might think that everything the business owns you also personally own. Not true. The relationship you have with your S Corp is not a marriage where mine is mine and yours is mine too.

Part 1

If you want to move assets out of an S corporation or convert them to personal use, you will trigger a taxable event. A potentially big one. When assets are distributed to the S Corp shareholders, they are distributed at fair market value. Cash is easy. An automobile is generally not a big deal. But real estate can kick your butt.

We recently had a consult with an S Corp owner whose business owned a hotel building. On the advice of an inexperienced CPA he revoked his S corporation election. This triggered a distribution of corporate assets at fair market value. The basis in the hotel building was $400,000 and the fair market value was $2,000,000. This sparked a $320,000 capital gain tax event reported on his K-1. Capital gains is a success tax, right? But when you don't actually get the cash from the transaction, this tax could be impossible to pay. Keep appreciating assets out of an S corporation people!

Sole proprietors and garden-variety LLCs enjoy a bit more flexibility under certain circumstances.

Part 2

Assets within your S Corp can also be problematic upon death. If you own an asset at the time of death, the asset is re-valued and your heirs get a step-up in basis (cost). So when they sell the asset their gain is lower. For example, you buy a painting for $5,000 and when you die, the painting is valued at $20,000. If your heirs sell the painting for $22,000, they will only realize a $2,000 taxable gain.

If the asset is sitting in the S Corp upon your death, the S corporation's stock value might get a step-up in basis through an appraisal. However it might prove harder to demonstrate than the increased value of one particular asset. Look at it another way. S Corps don't die, and therefore assets within the business don't get a step up in basis upon a shareholder's death.

We'll acquiesce. This trapped asset problem is super rare yet so many owners love to have personal stuff owned by the S Corp.

Distributing Profits, Multiple Owners

S Corp shareholders are distributed profits as a percentage of ownership whereas multi-member LLC's use an operating agreement. Electing S Corp status in certain situations can create headaches for silent partner or angel investor situations and other non-traditional ownership structures.

Fluctuating Revenue Splitting

An S Corp election can be problematic for partnerships who have an **Eat What You Kill** arrangement. For example, the Watson CPA Group has a client where the entity was comprised of two insurance sales agents. They created a multi-member limited liability company to share in some of the costs and to gain some economies of scale by working together. After common expenses were paid, the operating agreement distributed remaining profits as a percentage of revenue generated by each of the partners. So, one year could be 60-40 and the next year could be 45-55. This worked fine with no problems.

However, if this multi-member LLC elected to be taxed as an S corporation the arrangement blows up since shareholder distributions must be made on a pro-rata basis of ownership. In using the above example, an insurance agent might be a 50% shareholder but should only receive 40% of the distributions according to the revenue split. No bueno. Here is why this is a problem-

Net Business Income	100,000	

	Batman	Robin
Beginning Basis	5,000	5,000
Apportioned Income	50,000	50,000
Ending Basis	55,000	55,000
Shareholder Distributions	60,000	40,000
Ending Basis	-5,000	15,000

In this example, Batman is receiving 60% of the distributions as a 50% shareholder. The negative ending basis cannot happen without ugly consequences in S Corps. You could solve this by changing salaries- however this usually creates unnecessary additional payroll tax burdens in the attempt to equalize the income.

A more elegant way to solve this problem, as mentioned in Chapter 1, is to simply create two more S corporations who are 50-50 members in the LLC. The operating agreement will still dictate the pro-rata share of distributions on a fluctuating basis yet the income is sheltered by the taxation of an S Corp. We did this in the insurance agency example, and each insurance sales agent was 100% owner of his respective S Corp.

Minority Shareholders

Similar problems occur with minority shareholders or silent investors. The author, Jason Watson, served on a jury trial about a decade ago. An S corporation was formed with three people. One owner was a 10% shareholder, while the other two were split evenly as a husband and wife team. Not looking good from the start.

The minority shareholder, the 10% guy, was constructively ousted from the daily operations of the company. He was not paid a salary. He did not receive any money from the company. Distributions were not made to any shareholder, but the husband and wife team paid themselves a salary and used expense reimbursements as a way to funnel money out.

The company began earning money, lots of money, and the minority shareholder was getting K-1s showing taxable income of several thousands of dollars. Good right? No. Not good. He had to report taxable income, but never saw any money in the form of a shareholder distribution. The husband and wife team were upset too since they could not take distributions without having to pay the minority shareholder. No one was willing to budge.

Had this entity had a strong operating agreement which forced distributions, minority problems can be avoided. One of the provisions we advocate for when working with attorneys is to establish a cash reserve for operations and then distribute 40% of the remaining amount once a year. This forces the entity to at least cover the shareholders' typical tax obligation associated with the K-1 income.

Other W-2 Income

You might not reap all the benefits of an S Corp election and subsequent self-employment tax savings if you have other W-2 income. Let's say you are an IT consultant for ABC Company, and you also do some outside consulting. If ABC Company pays you $130,000 in wages, you are already max'ing out your Social Security contributions, and therefore any supplementary income regardless of your entity will automatically avoid additional Social Security taxes. You still obtain a small savings in Medicare taxes, which can be material.

We find this to very common among medical professions. Many times a surgeon or anesthesiologist will be full-time for a hospital or medical group, but also moonlight on the side for smaller towns with smaller hospitals with even smaller budgets.

The problem with piling extra W-2 salary from your S corporation onto W-2 salary from your main job is the S-Corp's portion of payroll taxes. While both salaries might exceed your individual Social Security cap ($128,700 in 2018), any salary in excess will unnecessarily increase the tax burden of your S Corp by 6.2% (the employer portion of Social Security taxes). Huh?

In other words, your main job will stop collecting and paying Social Security taxes once you reach the annual limit. However, since Social Security taxes are paid by both the employee (you) and the company, when you run payroll with your S corporation, the company will collect and pay Social Security taxes just like your main job. On your individual tax return you will get your excess refunded to you on Line 71 of Form 1040. That's the good news. The bad news is that the S Corp's portion will not be refunded. This is lost forever.

[a table that hopefully makes sense is on the next page]

Here is yet another table to explain this further-

Salary from Old Job	150,000
Income from Business	200,000
Medicare w/o S Corp	**7,600**
Salary	65,000
Payroll Tax w/ S Corp	
ER Social Security	4,030
ER Medicare	943
EE Medicare w/ Surtax	1,463
Total	**6,435**
Initial Savings	1,165
Accounting Fees (low)	1,300
Net Savings (loss)	-135

Ok... here we go. Let's say you had a job that earned $150,000 and they converted you to a contractor where you plan to make $200,000 net income after expenses. You eclipsed your Social Security maximum with your old salary, so the $200,000 is only subjected to Medicare taxes plus the surtax, or **$7,600** ($200,000 x 3.8%).

Now we elect S Corp for your business and pay a salary of $65,000. The total taxes paid not considering your portion of Social Security which will be refunded is **$6,435**. ER is short-hand for "employer" and EE refers to "employee." The initial savings is $1,165. However, now you have to run payroll and file a corporate tax return. Therefore, the savings are gobbled up by normal professional fees.

So, in this situation perhaps a garden variety LLC is more prudent from a cost-benefit and headache analysis. Having other W-2 income, however, could actually work in your favor- more on that later in this book (see Tricks of the Trade).

As a side note, having multiple sources of income can mess up your withholdings. Each source of income on its own withheld correctly, but when combined, the total income was in a higher tax bracket and unfortunately under-withheld. Again, payroll tables don't know about other jobs or sources of income, and can only make assumptions. Some tax planning is a must. More about tax planning within your S corporation payroll in Chapter 6.

State Business Taxes (Not Just Income Taxes)

State tax laws might not treat S Corp income and subsequent K-1 income in the same benevolent manner as the IRS. Recall that S corporations do not pay a federal income tax directly. Rather the income is passed onto the shareholders who are then taxed at their individual tax rates. However, some states impose an additional tax. For example, California imposes a 1.5% franchise tax on S Corp net income with a minimum of $800. Yuck. So your 8% savings turns into 6.5%.

Other income tax free states, such as Texas, have similar taxations and various exemptions too. Franchise tax is another buzzword you might come across. Why do they call it a franchise tax, or a business and operating tax as they do in Washington State? They can't call it income tax because of the Interstate Income Act of 1959. Yup. Way back when, and it is battled every year in court, in various representations.

Before we get into that, there are two issues at play here and we'll pick on California to illustrate some points. One, if you are an S corporation headquartered in California you will be subjected to the franchise tax. Period. End of story.

But the other side of the coin is state nexus (which was broached earlier) where you are not physically headquartered in California, but have a nexus either physically or economically in California. This too would subject your income sourced from California to the franchise tax.

In some cases you might have nexus in California but not any California sourced income, and you will unfortunately be subjected to the minimum franchise tax of $800 (as of 2017). Nutty. You have nexus, but no taxable income, and you still pay the minimum franchise tax? Yes. This happens when you create an LLC but all your income sources are outside California and they exceed certain thresholds. There are other situations where this can happen.

Conversely, if you are a sole proprietor in California (and not an LLC or corporation), you do not pay a franchise tax. Yes, you will be subjected to Federal self-employment taxes which is why you want to consider an S Corp election. So therein lies the rub. Franchise tax versus self-employment tax.

About half of the states have some sort of franchise, business or excise tax. Back to the Interstate Income Act of 1959- it is against Federal Public Law 86-272 for states to charge an income tax on foreign businesses in certain circumstances. Remember, foreign does not mean domestic and international. Foreign is a business registered in Nevada doing business in California, as an example. Here is a snippet of Federal Public Law 86-272-

No state, or political subdivision thereof, shall have power to impose .. a net income tax on the income derived within such state by any person from interstate commerce if the only business activities with in such state by or on behalf of such a person during the taxable year are either, or both, of the following-

1. The solicitation of orders by such person, or his representative, in such State for sales of tangible personal property, which orders are sent outside the State for approval or rejection, and, if approved, are filled by shipment or delivery from a point outside of the state; and

2. The solicitation of orders by such a person, or his representative, in such State in the name of or for the benefit of a prospective customer of such a person, if orders by such customer to such person to enable such customer to fill orders resulting from such solicitation are orders described in paragraph (1).

States are therefore prevented under Public Law 86-272

▲ from taxing out-of-state businesses on income derived from activities within the state

▲ if the activities are limited to mere solicitations of **tangible personal property**, and

▲ the orders are processed from outside the state.

Note how this centers on tangible property and not services. Huge distinction! Is internet hosting a service or tangible personal property? How about an eBook? This is discussed more in a later chapter, and the current news is not great. The future isn't good either.

So the wizards at various states came up with a tax that is **not** based on income or as least not called an income tax. Some states tax your gross receipts, no matter what your expenses are! Amazing. It is also noteworthy that Public Law 86-272 does not protect businesses located in and doing business in the respective state (only interstate activities, not intrastate activities). But it appears that states keep things consistent, and impose a franchise tax, a business tax or an excise tax on local businesses just the same. Genius.

Here are some sample state links-

www.wcgurl.com/1304	California
www.wcgurl.com/1302	Oregon
www.wcgurl.com/1307	New York City
www.wcgurl.com/1311	Tennessee
www.wcgurl.com/1314	Texas

Major New York tax reform was passed in April 2015 which aligned taxation between New York City and New York State. NYC was like Rome, and was off in the weeds as compared to New York State. Regardless, New York S Corp tax rate is 8.85%. Tennessee is 6.5%. Texas is about 1% with exclusions and exceptions, which is similar to Washington. Washington DC has a tax it imposes on S corporations, but tax is exempt if over 80% of the revenue is from personal service.

Do you want more wrinkles? Here you go- California (we just love to pick on them) has a unique rule to their franchise tax. As a garden-variety LLC, you are taxed on gross receipts in addition to the $800 franchise tax. For example, you could have $1,000,000 in gross receipts and $1,000,000 in expenses. Your franchise tax would be $800 + $6,000 although you do not have any net income. Yuck.

However, if this LLC is taxed as an S corporation then it would pay 1.5% of the net income or $800 whichever is higher. Using the example above California's franchise tax would be $800 versus $6,800. Therefore the lesson is that you might be forced into electing S corporation status in California just to avoid its silly gross receipts tax.

In summary at some point as income increases close to $200,000 or more, a non-S corporation entity (sole proprietor, LLC or partnership) could actually pay fewer taxes without the S Corp election depending on the state and your unique circumstances. But nothing is simple and the rules are like spaghetti.

To complicate things even more, you have to apply nexus rules to all this. You might not be subjected to another state's franchise or business tax if you don't have an economic or physical presence in that state.

The issue of state business taxes and nexus is discussed in nauseating detail later in this chapter. More buzzwords such as economic presence, throwback rules, tangible personal property, commerce and due process clauses, etc. Bottom line- talk to your nexus experts at the Watson CPA Group to nail this down.

Deducting Losses

With an S corporation or partnership you need sufficient shareholder / partnership basis in your business to deduct losses. For example, if you invested $10,000 into your business but the business lost $30,000, as an S Corp shareholder you can only deduct losses up to the amount of your shareholder basis (in this example, $10,000).

Think of Google. You invested $10,000 into Google stock and they go out of business, you only loose $10,000. Remember that with an S corporation you wear two hats- one as an employee, and one as an investor (shareholder).

Depreciation Losses

How does a loss in an S corporation happen? Most one-person S corporations are cash based and don't have a lot of equipment. However, for the sake of argument we will assume you bought a piece of equipment for $100,000 and borrowed $100,000 to pay for it. The equipment also qualified for Section 179 depreciation deduction allowing you to deduct (or attempt to deduct) the full amount against business income. Great! The benevolent IRS king is alive.

Let's assume that the business income prior to depreciation was $60,000 (and depreciation was $100,000). The S corporation tax return would still show a $60,000 net business income amount, but your K-1 would show a $70,000 amount for Section 179 deduction. Why $70,000? You had $10,000 in basis (using the example above) plus the $60,000 net business income. 10k + 60k = 70k, even in Canada.

You would be able to deduct $70,000 as a loss. The $30,000 remainder of the Section 179 deduction that was not taken or used would be carried forward to future years. Yuck! Sorry, the once-benevolent IRS king is now an imposter.

[Rest of page intentionally left blank for a table]

Here is a table to demonstrate the depreciation conundrum more clearly. We love tables.

Taxable Income Prior to Depreciation	60,000
Depreciation	100,000
Shareholder Basis	10,000
Business Income on K-1	60,000
Section 179 Depreciation on K-1	70,000
Loss Taken on Personal Tax Return	**-70,000**
Section 179 Depreciation Carryforward	30,000

Business Debt

Another example that can really blow up your world is a loan. Let's say the S corporation borrows $100,000 regardless if you personally sign and guarantee it. If you withdraw this $100,000 as a shareholder distribution to buy a lightly used Porsche 911 for your teenage daughter, the amount in excess of your shareholder basis would be taxed as capital gains to you. This gets complicated right quick, but can also be a big problem. If you are flirting with this scenario please tread lightly.

Partners in partnerships who are responsible for partnership debt might be able to add the loan amount to their partnership basis, and the above distributions would not be problematic.

As a single-member LLC without the S Corp election, business losses have no theoretical limit on your personal tax return since the entity is disregarded. Technically this assumes that all your money into the business is "at-risk" but that is usually the case.

The net-net is that corporate debt needs to be considered depending on the entity type.

Shareholder Loans and Tax Planning

Any additional money injected into your S Corp should be treated as additional paid-in-capital which adds to your shareholder basis, rather than calling the money a shareholder loan. If your S Corp fails, you may deduct the additional investment as a capital loss. However, any loan you made to the S corporation becomes a miscellaneous deduction subject to thresholds, limitations and alternative minimum tax (AMT) on Schedule A. Yuck.

Everyone wants to label a cash injection into a business as a loan to the S corporation. This is absolutely silly. If you materially participate in your S Corp there is **no tax benefit** or advantage. This is a bad debt versus capital injection scenario- money goes from you to the business, but is treated differently depending on what you call it. Oftentimes we'll convert shareholder loans from prior tax returns into paid in capital to better position the client.

Let's not forget that the IRS hates shareholder loans. Is there a promissory note? Payment schedule? Appropriate interest? If not, you could be technically in some trouble. We recently had a revenue agent say that the IRS uses Schedule L on the S corporation tax return (Form 1120S) to flag this. Who knows? Blowing smoke? Perhaps.

Again, don't do shareholder loans! Having demanded that, many accountants face the reality of balance sheet issues from ghosts of lousy accounting past and must book imbalances to shareholder loans. This is not elegant, but at the same time a balance sheet must... well... balance, as the name implies. Regardless, promissory notes and payment schedules need to be drafted if this occurs.

As an aside, if you lend money to your garden variety LLC that has not elected S Corp status, the interest paid to you is taxable at the income tax level of course but the overall LLC income is reduced by the interest expense and therefore you save self-employment taxes if you can justifiably reduce your salary. You are essentially pulling money out of the LLC without paying self-employment taxes. There might be a Medicare surtax trigger, but generally this is a great tax saving technique if your LLC is not earning above the magical $35,000 net income threshold.

[Rest of page intentionally left blank for a table]

Here is another table.

	No Owner Loan	With Owner Loan
Income	25,000	25,000
Interest Expense on Owner Loan	0	5,000
Taxable Business Income	25,000	20,000
Taxable Interest Income	0	5,000
Income Taxes @ 25%	6,250	6,250
SE Taxes @ 15.3%	3,825	3,060
Total Tax	10,075	9,310
Savings		**765**

Not a huge amount, but you get the idea.

Stock Classes

One of the rules of an S Corp is to only have one class of voting stock, and this can be a problem at times if you are trying to bring in a new partner or create a vesting schedule for future owners. You can actually have two classes of stock as long as the only difference is the voting rights between the stocks. See IRC Section 1361(c)(4). Quite the page turner.

So if you want to provide distributions to a person but not give them control, assign him or her nonvoting stock (such as a retired parent who needs some money and enjoys a lower tax bracket than you).

Truly stock classes don't trip up many S corporations. What can prove to be tricky and expensive to solve is expanding the ownership of the S Corp through key employees or other graduated buy-in situations. Keep reading.

Vesting and Expanding Ownership

You, or someone you know, might have had a job where the company match to your 401k was vested over time or the company had a restricted stock grant that only triggered after so many years of service. For most of our readers this concern is moot since the idea of expanding ownership is not on the radar. However, life is funny and you never know how your path might change directions with left turns at right angles.

If the transfer of stock and subsequent ownership is not handled correctly within your S corporation, this could be considered a second class of voting stock which nullifies the S Corp election. So, if you are contemplating bringing in other owners or partners please read on. If you are not considering it, please read anyway so you have some basic knowledge of the problems.

Basis Problems

If you have a successful S Corp and you sell 10% of your stock to a key employee, you suddenly create a zillion headaches. First, what is the valuation of the stock? A valuation too low might be considered compensatory triggering an income tax obligation for the employee buyer.

What is the cost basis of the shares? This is arguably easier since we would just look at your shareholder basis to determine the capital gain (if any). However, many business owners freak out when they are faced with a capital gain when selling a minority interest in the business.

For example, the Watson CPA Group has a client who established a value of his business based on a long calculus. His basic argument was that he injected intellectual property into the business and therefore his shareholder basis was $250,000. No doubt, this guy was smart and his business was probably worth $250,000 from the beginning. However, he neglected some accounting basics and IRS law.

In its simplest form, you cannot create basis in a company without paying income taxes on the money used to establish the basis. Huh? Let's say you have $1,000 in your pocket. You paid income taxes on that $1,000. You buy stock for $1,000 and sell it for $1,500. Your basis is $1,000 and your gain is $500. Piece of cake.

Same with a business. You wrote a check for $250,000 and you paid income taxes on that money. When you sell your business for $400,000 you will have a $150,000 gain because the $250,000 was already taxed.

Therefore, you cannot create basis out of thin air. In the case of intellectual property, the owner would have had to pick up $250,000 worth of income on his individual tax return somewhere in the past in order to have $250,000 of basis in his company. Same with a loan. If the bank gives you a loan, either through the business or through you personally, the principal payments are **not** tax deductible. Therefore if the personal loan is your injection to create basis in your business, it too is done with after-tax dollars.

Another way to look at this is your personal home. You borrow $300,000 to buy a $300,000 house. Over the course of 30 years you paid over $500,000 in total payments but when you sell the house, your basis remains at $300,000.

Does this make sense? No? Crud. Perhaps have a nice Dale's Pale Ale and give us a call. We can try walking through it another way. We might need a Dale's too! Yum.

Back to the headaches of selling 10% of your company to someone else. This 10% owner now gets a K-1 with 10% of the S Corp's net business income as taxable income. All shareholder distributions must be allocated among all shareholders. So, you want to pull out $9,000 to pay for your family vacation, you also need to write a $1,000 check to your new 10% shareholder buddy. Cancel the flights. You might have to drive to vacation.

Death, divorce and incapacitation. Does your operating agreement deal with death, divorce or incapacitation? You need to. What is incapacitation? Do you need two doctors to sign off? If the remaining shareholders have first right of refusal on the re-purchase of the crazy man's stock, how is that valued? It will be hard to negotiate in good faith with someone who is incapacitated.

Speaking of value, 10% of the shares issued to the new shareholder have very little value. Since the S corporation is closely held, there is not a market to establish the value of the shares. A bank would probably not use the shares as collateral. The majority shareholder (you, in this string of examples) could run the company into the ground or simply shut the business down. The 10% shareholder has very little recourse outside of dissenting shareholder lawsuits (unless there is some contractual obligation governing these possibilities).

Lastly, the 10% shareholder might want to be involved with daily decisions or long-term decisions. Sure, the majority doesn't technically have to listen or even care, but that isn't the most professional way to foster the new relationship. Office politics suddenly becomes a reality in a business in which you never had to consider it.

So, what can you do? You have several options to bring in new owners without creating immediate problems, and you can get creative.

Employee Stock Ownership Plan (ESOP)

ESOPs are a great way to reward and incentivize employees. They also create a market for the shares of a departing owner or an owner who wants to expand ownership to the employees. Remember, if you have a growing company and you want to start working on an exit strategy or transition plan, using your own staff as future suitors might be the best idea. They have been vetted over time and know the business very well.

Here are the basics of an ESOP. A company creates a trust where shares or cash to buy shares are contributed to the trust account. Each share is allocated to individual employee accounts. You can discriminate based on years of service, full-time versus part-time and age. There are rules on this of course. The default is 1,000 hours of service in a plan year and 21 years old.

You can also create vesting schedules. For cliff vesting where the employee has either 0% or 100%, the maximum vesting schedule is three years. And for graded vesting schedules, the maximum is six years. This is because an ESOP is a qualified defined contribution plan and must follow the rules.

3-Year Cliff Schedule		6-Year Graded Schedule	
Year	Vested %	Year	Vested %
1	0%	1	0%
2	0%	2	20%
3	100%	3	40%
		4	60%
		5	80%
		6	100%

You can find vesting rules in IRC Section 411(a)(2)(B).

Here are some other takeaways on ESOPs. The percentage of ownership held by the ESOP of an S corporation is tax-deferred. For example, the S Corp earns $500,000 and the ESOP owns 40%. $200,000 of the taxable income should be added to the ESOP and allocated to each employee participant. This is a tax deferral not a tax deduction. When the employee sells or withdraws the shares (such as retirement) there will be a taxable event based on the individual's tax rate.

This makes sense since an S corporation is a pass-thru entity. So if an ESOP trust owns a portion of the stock, the beneficiaries of the trust (employees) will have a deferred tax obligation.

As an aside, a common theme in income taxation is one person's deduction is another person's taxable income (mortgage interest is a great example). A great exception is charitable donations- your deduction is not a taxable gain to the charity. Back to the ESOP- if a company may deduct the cash or stock contribution into an ESOP, the taxable income is later picked up by the ESOP participants when the money is taken out.

Here are some more takeaways. The law currently does not allow ESOPs for partnerships or professional corporations. Departing employees' shares must be re-purchased. Costs of these plans can be substantial (as much as $40,000 depending on complexity, according to the National Center of Employee Ownership).

If you are seriously considering this please review Section 401(a) of the Internal Revenue Code in between P90X reps at the gym, contact the NCEO (**www.nceo.org**) or contact the Watson CPA Group.

Hybrid Purchase Schemes

If the ESOP doesn't suit your needs and if you are afraid of introducing additional ownership through a simple stock sale, the sky is the limit on creating your own scheme. Time to put your thinking cap on.

The Watson CPA Group recently consulted on a buy-in scheme involving several millions of dollars. A trust was created and funded with profit incentives. In approximately ten years, if profit goals were achieved, the trust would be fully funded and a partnership would come to life. The funds would be directed by the trust and trustee to purchase a large chunk of the business for the benefit of the new LLC.

Initially the attorneys involved had an arrangement set up where three key employees would eventually be the members of the LLC (in other words, partners in a partnership). However, it was suggested by the Watson CPA Group that even key employees might come and go. Instead, each employee invited to participate would be granted units from a pool depending on years of service. Units could also be re-deposited back into the pool upon departure of a key employee.

This allowed seniority and longevity to become valuable, but the owner could also assign additional units as he saw fit depending on an employee's individual contribution. The owner was also able to grant some units to his children to ensure their long-term legacy and wealth transfer.

In addition, the funding was augmented by cash value whole life insurance to protect the current owner's interests and to help fund the transfer of ownership.

Recap of Expanding Ownership Issues

Creating ESOPs, buy-in schemes, Buy-Sell Agreements, and the like, for an S corporation requires a talented business law attorney in concert with business consultants who can draft the corporate governance documents correctly. This stuff is state-specific but also must follow national guidelines within the IRS, ERISA, DOL, etc. Let us know if you need help in selecting a proper attorney, and adding some creativity and protection to your scheme.

Bad Loans to the S-Corp

If your loan is not in writing or does not have a firm schedule for repayment, it might be labeled as a second class of stock which will nullify your S Corporation. We know it's a pain but go through the hassles of creating a proper instrument when lending money to your company. See IRC Section 1361(c)(5)(B). More amazing information! Or is it spellbinding?

As with most things in the IRS world, there are exceptions and many exceptions are called Safe Harbor provisions. In this situation, there is a straight debt safe harbor which allows for a loan by a person who is eligible to hold stock in an S Corp or is a business engaged in lending. The loan must not be convertible into stock, and there are some other rules. Let's not muddy the waters quite yet since this is rare.

As mentioned earlier in this chapter, shareholder loans are generally a bad idea and might not be as elegant as basic cash injection.

Social Security Basis

If you believe Social Security will remain funded by the time you retire, you might be short-changing yourself since your salary will be used to gauge future retirement benefits. Remember, K-1 income from your S Corp is not subjected to self-employment taxes and therefore will not count towards your Social Security benefits basis.

Conversely the tax money you save today can make excellent retirement investments which can counteract the loss in Social Security benefits. In other words, the savings in Social Security taxes today might exceed the loss in future Social Security benefits if those savings are invested correctly. The Watson CPA Group has several in-house financial planners to model this scenario.

Consider this- if your salary is around $64,000 you will be eligible for about two-thirds of the maximum Social Security benefit (for 2017). This Primary Insurance Amount calculations are computed annually by the Social Security Administration. The PIA formula computes two bend points which dictates a reducing sliding scale of benefits. Your Social Security bang goes down at each bend point of salary buck. Economists call this diminishing marginal benefit.

Payroll Taxes on Children

Children do not pay any Social Security or Medicare taxes until they reach 18 years of age if he or she-

▲ works for a parent who owns a sole proprietorship or partnership (recall that a multi-member LLC is taxed as a partnership),

▲ works in domestic service (babysitting, chauffeurs, etc.), or

▲ delivers newspapers (the law really lists newspapers.. who does this anymore?)

However, with an S Corp election this blows up because the child is now working for a corporation, and not the parent. In other words, when you run your business as a sole proprietor, you and the business are one in the same. Same thing with a single member LLC and a partnership. But an LLC with an S corporation election now becomes a corporation for taxation purposes, and your child loses this exception.

For example, your sole proprietorship or LLC could pay your child $20,000. He or she would not pay payroll taxes (Social Security and Medicare), and neither would you as the employer. Your child could then gift the take-home money back to you and your spouse. It is presumed that his or her tax rate would be lower than yours, and therefore you created some tax arbitrage. There is not a kiddie-tax issue since this is earned income. Furthermore, depending on how fruitful you are or your religion, you might have a hefty amount of salaries being paid to your gaggle of children bypassing payroll taxes.

Yes, he or she would have to file a tax return. But you would still claim the exemption as a dependent. No, having babies is not good tax advice. Kids are expensive. Really expensive.

There are gamers out there who will set up a single-member LLC which is solely owned by the Mom or Dad. Then, this LLC charges a consulting fee to the S Corp and then pays out the proceeds as salary to the children. In theory this bypasses payroll taxes (Social Security and Medicare) since it is an LLC that is paying the salary rather than the S corporation. We do not know how this would play out in tax court. Oftentimes we see theory making sense on paper just to have it be viewed as an end-around by the court.

Having said this, there might be several situations where paying your children a salary from your S corporation continues to make a lot of sense. More in this and other fringe benefits in Chapter 8.

C Corp to S Corp Problems

There are several potential problems when electing a C corporation to be taxed as an S corporation. First is called the built-in gains tax, or BIG tax for short. If the C corporation has net unrealized gains on appreciated assets, you must track these assets for a certain period of time. This also means your assets need to be appraised as of the conversion date.

For example, if an S Corp that was recently converted from a C Corp sells some real estate that increased in value when owned by the C Corp, the S Corp will probably pay taxes on the appreciation even though the corporation is now an S Corp. The BIG tax is for any asset sold within 5 years of S Corp election (it was a 10 years look back period, then whittled down to 7 due to the American Recovery and Reinvestment Act of 2009 and then 5 thanks to the Small Business Jobs Act of 2010). Here is an example-

> MyCorp was a C corporation for several years until it recently made an S Corp election following some good advice. The only asset had a value of $100,000 at the time of election and its basis was $20,000. Two years later the asset was sold for $140,000 without consulting with MyCorp's accountant.
>
> Because there was a net built-in gain at the time of the S Corp, it will be subject to corporate income tax on $80,000 of its gain. The remaining $40,000 of its gain is not subject to corporate tax.
>
> However, the entire $120,000 gain ($140,000 less the basis of $20,000) is taxed to the shareholders of the S corporation (but it is reduced by the amount of tax that MyCorp had to pay on the gain).

See Sections 1366(f)(2) and 1374 of the Internal Revenue Code (IRC) if you find yourself in the unique position of not having enough information on the BIG tax.

More bad news- Normally, Net Operating Losses (NOLs) can be carried forward and used in future years for C Corps. On the other hand, unused NOLs will be lost forever with an S corporation election unless the C Corp can use it for previous years through amended tax returns. Otherwise the NOL cannot be used by the S Corp nor its shareholders.

Other issues arise from accounts receivable, inventory, and rents, royalties and investment income. More discussion is always required when dreaming of converting your C Corp to an S Corp. And don't worry, we won't judge you on the reasons you were a C corporation from the beginning (there aren't many legitimate reasons).

Going Concern

Is your S Corp going to be needed next year, or the year after that? While an S Corp might make sense in the immediate future, the costs and hassles of startup and shutdown need to be amortized or spread out over a handful of years at the minimum. In other words, if your consulting gig might turn into a W-2 job next year, perhaps wait or defer the creation of an S Corp.

Marriage in itself is not a reason to elect S corporation status. But an S Corp is like a marriage- easy to get into, hard to get out. The S Corp election needs to be revoked, the business needs to reclassify itself as an LLC, a final tax return needs to be filed, payroll accounts need to be closed, etc. At times it is easier to shut down the entity and re-light another one.

We are not trying to alarm you or dissuade you, but at the same time many people forget about the back-end issues. Yes, the Watson CPA Group can take care of all this.

Recap of S Corp Downsides

There are several issues where an S Corporation election does **not** make sense. Be wary of all the accountants and other business owners who automatically check the Yes box when asked about making the election. Attorneys screw this up was too often as well. As you can see, it is not for everyone or every situation.

As always, the Watson CPA Group charges $150 for 40 minutes of consultation where we will ask questions to ensure the fit is correct and that it makes sense. If you decide to engage us for future services, we credit back the $150. Three options exist from the consult-

▲ A solid Yes, or

▲ A solid No, or

▲ Another appointment to dig deeper into the facts and your objectives to ensure the fit is right.

This is our core competency. We suggest taking advantage of it (Yes, more shameless self-promotion but in our heart of hearts we just want to help you avoid a mistake or a series of mistakes).

Growing Company, Debt Service

Another problem a business entity might face, regardless of S Corp status, is debt service.

In a perfect world, if you had a $10,000 K-1, hopefully you received close to $10,000 in cash. But growing companies might be re-investing all their cash back into the business and if a company has high debt service, taxable income might be present without cash. For example, your company made a $65,000 loan payment. Perhaps $60,000 of this was principal payment since the loan is near the end of its term, and the remainder was interest.

If the company has $100,000 in earnings before accounting for debt service it will only have $35,000 in cash but have $95,000 in taxable income. This in itself is not bad, but the company might not be throwing off enough discretionary cash flow for the owners. Huh? Example time.

Net Business Income	100,000
Principal Payments	60,000
Interest Expense	5,000
Cash Available	35,000
Taxable Business Income	95,000
Effective Tax Rate	30%
Tax Due	28,500
Cash Surplus / Deficit	**6,500**

The tax rate above is made up to illustrate the point. In this example you have $35,000 in cash available for a shareholder distribution, and $28,500 will be eaten up on your individual tax return for taxes leaving $6,500 for happy meals and taco Tuesdays.

Another concept to point out is that depreciation of an asset is supposed to alleviate some of this problem. Let's say you purchased some equipment for $100,000. Similar to the example above, you had a high portion of your debt payment being applied to the principal amount of the loan. This reduces your cash yet taxable income is left unchanged.

However, depreciation is a non-cash reduction in taxable income and helps alleviate the principal loan payment problem. Here is an example using the same table above.

	Without Depreciation	With Depreciation
Net Business Income	100,000	100,000
Principal Payments	60,000	60,000
Interest Expense	5,000	5,000
Depreciation Expense	0	25,000
Cash Available	35,000	35,000
Taxable Business Income	95,000	70,000
Effective Tax Rate	30%	28%
Tax Due	28,500	19,600
Cash Surplus / Deficit	**6,500**	**15,400**

The depreciation amounts and effective tax rates were made up numbers to illustrate this point. As you can see, depreciation can alleviate some of the cash crunch. Then again, if you elected to depreciate it instantly with a Section 179 deduction, then you are back to square one. This is one of the examples where the bird in the hand is not worth two in the bush- the pleasure of an instant tax deduction via Section 179 which lacks the stamina to help you in future years (which presumably are at a higher income).

> **Note:** This really isn't a reason not to elect S corporation status- it is a problem for any business entity.

Cash is king. Plan ahead before paring down debt.

Chapter 10 on Business Valuations, Sale has some more examples, including how depreciation might be your friend in the cash, debt service and tax issue.

Chapter 4
State Nexus Problems
(updated November 15, 2016)

This in itself is not a reason to avoid the S corporation election, but there is not a better place for this material. State nexus stuff is getting very complicated so we decided to make this a separate chapter since it will continue to grow over time.

Every year all 50 states plus the District of Columbia and New York City participate in a survey conducted by Bloomberg. Here is the link for the latest results, but a warning is in order first. The 2015 report is 429 pages (yet the table of contents is rich with detail to find your particular area of interest).

www.wcgurl.com/1744

There are several concepts here and a ton of material. Here is the mini table of contents-

▲ Nexus Theory

▲ Constitutional and Legislative Standards
Commerce and Due Process Clause
Public Law 86-272

▲ Sales Tax, Income Tax

▲ Physical and Economic Presence, Nexus Attached

▲ Services and Tangible Personal Property (TPP)

▲ Costs of Performance, Market-Based Approach

▲ Allocation and Throwback

▲ FBA, Drop Shipments, Trailing Nexus Revisited

We will explore each of these in turn, and then attempt to bring it all together with a recap. The operative word is attempt since this stuff is changing all the time and will continue to evolve through court decisions, state legislation and the impending congressional moves.

And this section is not designed to address all your nexus concerns or be a solution. We are merely shining a light on all the angles to this massive problem. Our darn forefathers couldn't imagine internets (yes plural), and other things like trains, planes and automobiles.

Nexus Theory

Nexus is a Latin word meaning to bind, join or tie. Simply stated, tax nexus is the minimum amount of contact between a taxpayer and a state, which allows the state to tax a business on its activities. Every state defines nexus differently using terms such as physical presence or economic presence, and those concepts will be discussed in a bit.

There is also a concept called trailing nexus where an entity that once had nexus in a state ceases activities that created nexus in the first place. This is a point of contention between taxpayers and states, and is commonly created by Fulfillment By Amazon (FBA) and other online retailers.

The theory behind the trailing nexus concept can be better illustrated with an example. If your company sent a sales rep to Washington for several months to solicit orders, it is safe to say that after the sales rep leaves a residual effect would remain. This in turn would generate sales (business activity). As an aside, Washington is one of the few states that defines trailing nexus explicitly. Pot + Coffee = Progressive Law.

Constitutional and Legislative Standards

Time to go back to school. The Due Process Clause of the United States Constitution requires the seller to have some "minimum contacts" with the taxing state. The seller must reach out and purposefully avail itself of the benefits of that state. Courts have held that a physical presence is required to meet the Due Process Clause, but that is eroding and being redefined every day.

Once this is satisfied, which is no easy task for a state, a four-part test of the Commerce Clause must be met.

Article 1, Section 8, Clause 3, of the Constitution empowers Congress to prohibit a state from unduly burdening interstate commerce and business activities. The law authors were very concerned with states colluding or combining forces near major trade hubs and routes, and thus created the Commerce Clause. A vision of gangs holding up covered wagons in California.

The United States Supreme Court in *Complete Auto Transit v. Brady (1977)* stated that a seller must meet the following four-part test to be forced to collect a tax:

▲ The seller must have substantial nexus (physical presence) in state;

▲ The tax cannot discriminate against interstate commerce;

▲ The tax must be fairly apportioned; and

▲ The tax must be fairly related to services provided by state.

The common theme after physical presence is fairness. The only time a tax is fair is when you pay the minimum amount.

Moving onto legislative standards. Public Law 86-272 was quoted earlier in this chapter and basically prevents state from imposing income tax on businesses whose only activity in the state is the solicitation of orders provided the orders are accepted and delivered from a point outside the state (interstate commerce). And this only refers to tangible personal property (TPP) and not services. At the time of this law, services were inherently personal and required a close, physical presence to perform (proximity). That has changed with telecommuting and the pure definition of a service (more on that in a bit).

So we have three standards yet states vary across the board based on the definition and triggering of nexus.

Sales and Use Tax, Income Tax

There are two issues at play, and they are not necessarily connected. First is sales and use tax which frankly receives the most attention because of online retailers. Some theory. When you purchase a computer at your local Best Buy, the seller is collecting sales tax in a fiduciary role. In other words, it is collecting **your** sales tax obligation for you on your behalf, and remitting it to the authorities. Nice of them, right?

If you buy this same computer from an Amazon retailer, the seller might or might not collect sales tax on your behalf. If the retailer does not collect sales tax, it is still your responsibility to pay this sales tax along with your state income tax return. No one does this of course. The Watson CPA Group has asked 25,000 times in the past decade, and we have never heard a Yes from a client. But understand that you are **required to pay sales tax** if not collected by the online seller.

States are getting sick of the under-reported sales tax obligations. Therefore several are going after businesses with strong internet presence. Here is a summary about New York's "Amazon Law" from Cbiz-

> *In practice, such an online selling scheme may work as follows. A retailer selling neckties has a shop in Florida, and it wants to increase sales by selling over the internet. The retailer sets up a website, and decides that to generate traffic on its website, it will partner with other online websites. In this example, the retailer places an ad on the website of the New York Times. When a customer reaches the retailer's website by clicking on the link at newyorktimes.com, the "click-thru" is logged. If the retailer makes a subsequent sale as a result of the click-thru, the New York Times is paid a commission. As a result of the Amazon law, New York assumes that the relationship has created nexus for the online retailer.*

The other issue is income tax. Just because a retailer has an obligation to collect sales tax does not necessarily mean they have an instant income tax obligation. Some states have a fruit of the poisonous tree mentality where sales tax nexus creates an income tax nexus and vice versa. And don't forget that states cannot impose an income tax per se, but they can impose a business tax or a franchise tax or a whatever tax that smells, walks and talks like an income tax but isn't call an income tax.

Remember too that Public Law 86-272 protects TPP only from a strict income tax. However states are the using the same "non-income tax" tax as a work around for everything from tangible personal property to services.

Physical and Economic Presence, Nexus Attached

In a 1992 U.S. Supreme Court case docketed as *Quill Corporation v. North Dakota*, the court established a physical presence test for sales tax nexus. The court did not address income tax, and since this decision states have varied quite a bit on attaching nexus to taxes other than sales and use tax.

Several appellate courts have limited the Quill case to sales and use tax nexus, and have deferred income tax nexus to economic presence rather than physical presence. According to Bloomberg's survey at the beginning of this topic, only 7 states applied the physical presence test in determine an income tax nexus leaving 43 states to apply an economic presence test for income tax nexus. It is safe to say that the 7 will decrease over time.

Let's consider California's economic presence rules. A company is considered doing business in California if it meets any of the following conditions-

▲ They have property in California, with a value of $50,000 or 25% of total property, whichever is less.

▲ They have payroll in California, in the amount of $50,000 or 25% of total payroll, whichever is less.

▲ They have sales in California, in the amount of $500,000 or 25% of total sales, whichever is less.

California's numbers above are a bit out dated since they are annually adjusted for inflation. In 2015, the sales trigger is roughly $525,000.

These hard numbers is called bright-line nexus. You simply meet a numeric threshold, and you magically have nexus in that state. Several states have a preponderance of the evidence set of rules using phrases such as "businesses earning significant income." Really!? Sounds like fun trying to defend that.

And to make matters worse, your business might be protected by Public Law 86-272 if you are simply soliciting orders for tangible personal property in California. But if you are selling services in California, even with independent contractors, there is no protection and the income will be taxed if you meet one of the three criteria above.

More bad news. Your company might not have income associated with California but be deemed as doing business in California. Seriously! And, in this case you would be subjected to the $800 minimum franchise tax regardless. Yuck.

Here is the direct language from California's Franchise Tax Board website-

> *An out-of-state taxpayer that has less than the threshold amounts of property, payroll, and sales in California may still be considered doing business in California if the taxpayer actively engages in any transaction for the purpose of financial or pecuniary gain or profit in California.*
>
> *Partnership A, an out-of-state partnership, has employees who work out of their homes in California. The employees sell and provide warranty work to California customers. Partnership A's property, payroll, and sales in California fall below the threshold amounts. Is Partnership A considered to be doing business in California?*
>
> ***Yes. Partnership A is considered doing business in California even if the property, payroll, and sales in California fall below the threshold amounts. Partnership A is considered doing business in California through its employees because those employees are actively engaging in transactions for profit on behalf of Partnership A.***
>
> *Corporation B, an out-of-state corporation, has $100,000 in total property, $200,000 in total payroll, $1,000,000 in total sales, of which $400,000 was sales to California customers. Corporation B has no property or payroll in California. Is Corporation B doing business in California?*
>
> ***Yes. Although Corporation B's California sales is less than the $500,000 threshold, Corporation B's California sales is 40 percent of its total sales which exceeds 25 percent of the corporation's total sales ($400,000 ÷ 1,000,000 = 40%.)***

California is a fun state to research since they are usually on the forefront of legislative changes and updates, and there is so much economic activity. The following link is California's FTB1050 where they outline in plain language a list of protected activities and unprotected activities as they relate to Public Law 86-272 (tangible personal property).

www.wcgurl.com/1751

There are 51 other examples aside from California (including Washington DC and New York City). Please do the homework!

Some more fodder for your consideration. In two U.S. Supreme Court cases, *Scripto v. Carson (1960)* and *Tyler Pipe v. Washington Department of Revenue (1987)*, the court affirmed that a third party can create nexus. The court specifically stated what matters

> *"is whether the activities performed in the state on behalf of the taxpayer are significantly associated with the taxpayer's ability to establish and maintain a market in this state for the sales."*

This third party connection is detrimental to Amazon and eBay retailers (and the like) and discussed in more detail later.

Services and Tangible Personal Property (TPP)

Public Law 86-272 protects TPP as we previously mentioned. But services are fair game for states to tax. Generally speaking states do not impose a sales tax on services but they can impose a franchise, business or privilege tax.

To make things more interesting, the definition of a service is expanding in light of ecommerce and cloud computing. For example, most states characterize cloud computing as a sale of intangibles or services, but Utah considers cloud computing as the sale, lease or license of TPP. Subtle difference, yet important.

Let's say what you do is a service. What is the standard for determining nexus for your business? Read on please.

Costs of Performance, Market-Based Approach

Prior to Al Gore inventing all the internets, most states used the costs of performance as the method to determine nexus. If your butt was in Colorado and you provided a service to people in California, the costs of performing the service would be in Colorado and therefore you would not have nexus to California. You would only be subjected to Colorado income taxes.

Given the latest Bloomberg survey, there is a growing minority of states that are using the market-based approach. This can be loosely defined as the assignment of revenue based on the location of either

▲ the service provider's customers, or

▲ where the customers received benefit from the service provided.

Consider a web server. 38 states plus the District of Columbia and New York City would consider a web server physically located in their taxing jurisdiction as enough of a presence to find income tax nexus. And most would find sales tax nexus as well. Wow. 38 is a high number.

Allocation and Throwback

Allocation of the sales and subsequent income is at the top of this heap of nexus mess. States don't want to unnecessarily complicate things, but they do want money.

Throwback is a common concept but not every state uses it. Again, we'll pick on California. Under the old rules, when a California company ships TPP to another state, and that company does not have nexus in that state, the sales are "thrown back" to California since it is considered a California sale.

Interestingly enough, there are cases where a sale would not have a tax home at all. Let's say you sold a service to a customer outside of California. Using the market-based approach and under California's new rules of bright line nexus (turn back a few pages to review), sales exceeding $500,000 in another state are not thrown back to California. So, if you had sales in another state that did not trigger a filing in that state, these sales could arguably be allocated outside of California but disappear into a black hole. Sounds crazy, but true.

Allocation issues such as these can create tax arbitrage. And there are other examples of the same dollar being taxed twice by different states. It truly is a mess. States recognize this growing problem and are working together to eliminate the loopholes. In about three perhaps four hundred years we'll be good to go.

FBA, Drop Shipments, Trailing Nexus Revisited

Fulfillment By Amazon (FBA) and other fulfillment services add a new dimension to the nexus conversation. States are scrambling to figure it out so tax revenue can keep up with population growth and resource use.

Avalara is a consultation company who specializes in sales tax issues, and they wrote a wonderful article on FBA and what it means to you. We will attempt to paraphrase some of the concepts here, but if you want the full details use the following link-

www.wcgurl.com/5858

The first concept is nexus, which we've beaten to death. But here is a different spin for those selling products online. There are four common nexus creating activities-

▲ Your Location

▲ Inventory

▲ Warehouse Use, and

▲ Fulfillment Services

The common theme to these four activities is Where is your stuff? More importantly, is your stuff in a state that ships within the state, and if so, does that state have a sales tax obligation? In other words, if a competitor located in the same state that you are selling your tangible personal property (TPP) through an online channel is collecting sales tax, then you probably have a similar obligation. Location. Location. Location.

There is guilt by association as well. If the distributor, warehouse, fulfillment center, storage facility, or whatever else you want to call it has nexus within the state you are selling to, then you also have nexus by the fact they are storing and handling your stuff. The essence of the facility argument for a state is that the facility is helping you create a marketplace for your goods.

There are some fine lines with who holds title and when does title transfer. For most online retailers and sellers, title arguments probably won't do much good unless there is a lot at stake and you have a war chest to spend on attorney fees.

The next concern is materiality. If you've determined that you have nexus and are required to collect sales tax, is the obligation material? If you sold $200 worth of stuff to a Colorado Springs consumer, is the $16 in tax worth the headaches? Remember, if you do not collect sales tax from a consumer, he or she is still obligated to pay sales tax on his or her individual state income tax return. Unless, of course, your nexus and materiality tips the scale, and you have the responsibility to collect sales tax on behalf of the consumer.

States can spend some time on going after the head of snake, such a medium-sized online retailers or states can spend a lot of time going after the consumer. Drug user versus drug dealer.

There are voluntary disclosure initiatives to allow online sellers to come clean with their dirty sales tax deeds. Several states will waive the penalties and limit the lookback to only three years. You must weigh the chance of the hammer versus the certainty of a light tap.

The issue of trailing nexus must be considered as well. For those familiar with Amazon and FBA services, you understand that your inventory is continuously being shifted to different states. Just because your inventory no longer exists in a state does not mean your nexus is instantly cutoff. This concept was broached in the beginning of this section, and is reiterated here to stress the importance of keeping up with the Kardashians and the location of your stuff, and who you owe an obligation to. Good luck.

Recap of State Tax Issues

We attempted to provide several angles and concepts to the state taxation issue. There are very few hard and fast solutions. There are tax attorneys and consulting firms who do nothing but argue and litigate state nexus issues.

If there is nexus, is there allocation? If there is allocation, who gets what? If there is a sales tax obligation is there an income tax (or franchise tax or business tax) obligation? Can you have one and not the other? Are your services considered tangible personal property by some states?

Be careful. States are taking on the giants like Best Buy, WalMart, Amazon, etc. And they now appear to be shifting their focus to those companies who do not have deep pockets to fight or pay fines. If what you are doing smells wrong or keeps you up at night, it probably is worth looking into.

Chapter 5
S Corporation Election
(updated July 13, 2017 watching Wimbledon, Federer was betterer)

Formation (Election) of an S-Corp

There is a misconception floating around out there that an S-Corp is a standalone entity. Not true. There are several entity types, but the three most common are

▲ Limited Liability Companies (LLCs), either as a single member or multi-member

▲ Partnerships, including all the variants (LP, LLP, LLLP, etc.), and

▲ Corporations (C-Corps), including Professional Corporations (PCs).

Each can elect to be treated as an S-Corp for taxation purposes under subchapter S of the revenue code.

So while we might talk about your "S-Corp", we are truly talking about your LLC, partnership or C-Corp being treated as an S-Corp for taxation. While there are partnerships and C-Corps out there who elect to be treated as an S-Corp, this book generally focuses on the "S-Corp LLC" where the underlying entity is an LLC being taxed as an S corporation. However, the information is valid for each entity type.

Also, the words member and shareholder are synonymous as well from a conversational perspective- the state considers owners to be members but the IRS considers the owners to be shareholders when issues like distributions, basis, etc. Same is true for equity accounts on the balance sheet.

Electing S-Corp Filing Status, Retroactive for 2017

Yes, you are able to engage in revisionist history and retro activate your S Corporation election to January 1 and have your income avoid a large chunk of self-employment taxes. Which year? Good question, and Yes, of course, it depends. First things first. You must be eligible to become an S-Corp for taxation purposes-

▲ you must have an LLC, partnership or C-Corp already in place,

▲ your entity must be domestic,

▲   have 100 or fewer shareholders,

▲   have shareholders who are individuals, estates or exempt organizations, and not have any non-resident alien shareholders, and

▲   have only one class of stock (you are allowed to have voting and non-voting as one class)

There some other devils in the details, but 99% of the LLCs, partnerships and C-Corps out there qualify.

If you do not have an entity already in place, there are organizations that sell shelf companies. Note the word shelf- not shell. These shelf companies have EINs, file tax returns and all their history sits on a shelf hence the name shelf company. How this works is beyond our book and usually required a conversation.

Late S Corp Election, Oops

Form 2553 (the S-Corp election form) must be filed with the IRS. It is typically due within 75 days of forming your business entity or March 15 of the following year. However in typical IRS fashion there are 185 exceptions to the rule and the late S corporation election is another example. The IRS provides relief for the late filing of Form 2553. Historically, IRS Revenue Procedures 2003-43 and 2004-48 used to be the governing rules but the IRS has simplified it (imagine that!).

IRS Revenue Procedure 2013-30, effective September 3 2013, allows an entity to get relief and elect S-Corp status within 3 years and 75 days from the date the election was originally intended to be effective. Holy cow. Three years!

The IRS is basically saying that if you walk and smell like an S-Corp, then you are an S-Corp.

So, if it is November 2017, and you want to go back to January 1 2017, no problem. If it is March 2018 (tax season) and you are freakin' out because you forgot to make the election earlier, you can still go back to January 1 2017. No that is not a typo... we are talking about going back to the previous year's January 1!

There are hiccups. Isn't hiccups such a friendly word? Sort of like bumps in the road. Bruises is another word that is about as hollow as hiccups and bumps. No one says pitfalls or disasters anymore, just hiccups. Bottom line is we can engage in some revisionist history on March 1 2018 and create an officer compensation event for December 31 2017. No worries.

If your current CPA or tax professional says No, we suggest you find a new accountant. The Watson CPA Group has been doing this for over a decade (there was relief provisions prior to the 2013 IRS Rev Proc as well) without major problems. You might incur some late filing penalties which usually can be abated under the First Time Abatement statutory relief program. We will review on a case by case basis.

Once the facts and circumstances are reviewed and everyone thinks the S Corp election is the way to go, there are three things that happen simultaneously-

▲ Fax Late S Corp Election Form 2553 to the IRS

Fee: **$375**

▲ Open Payroll Accounts for 2018

Fee: **$300 to $450** (depending on state, OH and PA are the worst, super yuck)

▲ Issue a 1099-MISC as Officer Compensation (in lieu of a late payroll)

Fee: **$350** (this includes tax planning and estimated tax calculations)

▲ Prepare S Corporation Tax Return on Form 1120S

Fee: **$800 to $1,100**

So about $2,000 give or take a few bucks however you will be saving anywhere from 8% to 10% of your net business income depending in your situation. Also remember that the late S Corp election and payroll account setup is a sunk cost. In other words, you would need these things done regardless of late S Corp election for the previous year or waiting until next year. Bite the bullet now. Get it done.

In the past, to obtain relief with a late S-Corp election during the tax season, we would prepare and file Form 1120S (corporate tax return) and attach Form 2553 (S-Corp election) to it. Today, there are two paths. If we can file the S Corp tax return (Form 1120S) by March 15, then we send off the Form 2553, wait for the IRS to approve and then eFile the tax return. New school.

Conversely, if we cannot file the tax returns in a timely manner, we usually have to paper-file the tax returns along with Form 2553. This is the old school way and there are times it is the only way.

Everyone once in a while the IRS loses its mind and rejects the late S Corp election. We always get it pushed through. Always. Unfortunately the rejection or some other nasty gram of a notice arrives on your doorstep at 5:01PM on a Friday. Briefly freak out, send the documents to us, and then have a Coke and a smile- it'll be OK.

At the very worst we have to obtain a Power of Attorney from you, call the IRS and give them a "see... how it works is..." spiel. The Watson CPA Group has 100% in getting these three events pushed through. Your mileage might vary, but we are also very successful with getting late payment penalties abated with the IRS. Each state is different, and some are unsympathetic. Again, the savings will outweigh the costs (or we wouldn't let you do it).

Another Option, Dormant S Corp

Not sure if you want to have a full-blown S Corporation? The break-even point where an S Corp makes sense is about $35,000 in net income after expenses (remember, our all-in S corporation package is $2,940 and the savings is 8-9%- $2,940 divided by 8.5% is $35,000). Let's say you are teetering on that income figure, and not sure about running payroll and all that jazz. You could still run your business income and expenses through your tax return as a sole proprietor or another single member LLC, and take the small self-employment tax hit. Then simply file a No Activity tax return for your S Corp.

Missing Payroll, Now What?

There is a near certainty that we can make the S Corp election retroactive to January 1 of 2017. As mentioned earlier, one of the pillars of S Corps is to pay a salary to the shareholders. If you are reading this after Thanksgiving dinner and yet another Cowboys loss, it is time to step on the gas and get payroll setup so a payroll event can be ran before the end of the year.

But if it's 2018, and 2017 is all over, there are three options (in descending order of elegance)-

▲ **Issue a 1099 to Yourself**- Really?! For real? Hang in there on this one. What we can do is issue a 1099-MISC for a portion of the company net income to yourself which will be reported on Schedule C of your personal tax return. In turn, this income will be subjected to self-employment taxes. Remember self-employment taxes and Social Security and Medicare taxes are the same thing.

The amount of the 1099-MISC is entered into Line 7 of Form 1120S as Officer Compensation. Therefore from an Officer Compensation to net business / K-1 income comparison, this technique still satisfies the reasonable salary sniff.

While the IRS might frown upon this option, at the end of the day they are typically satisfied since employment taxes are essentially being paid. Again, this is not as elegant as the W-2 option, but it certainly works for the first year.

Additionally, if you were to lose an IRS challenge on reasonable salary determination the IRS would impute income on Schedule C. We are simply following what they would eventually do anyway. Again, this is a first-year mulligan. A one and done. Payroll must be set up for the following year, and normal W-2 and other filings must be done.

▲ **Reclassify Distributions as Wages**- We used to do late payrolls since we processed payroll manually, in-house. We have now partnered with ADP to handle all our payroll processing (we still consult with you on a reasonable shareholder wage and make the payroll entries into ADP). ADP is wonderful, but they are rigid. As a result, no late payrolls.

We list this option is case you or someone else wants to run a late payroll event after December 31, but we advise against it. If you want to see a flurry of IRS and state notices, and waste time wading through it all, then go for it.

▲ **Roll the Dice**- As paid tax professionals, the Watson CPA Group cannot advise this course of action. Having said that, we have observed several taxpayers labeling the first year as a mulligan, not creating a W-2 or a 1099, and taking his or her chances. Audit rates are about 0.4% for S-Corps, and currently the Treasury Inspector General of Tax Administration (TIGTA) is charging the IRS with the task of auditing S-Corps that do not pay a salary and who report losses for three or more years. As a result, profitable S Corps appear to be flying under the radar especially if you only miss one year of paying a salary (your first year).

What could happen? The IRS could simply impute wages, create payroll liabilities and send you a bill. We've seen S Corporations get these types of notices. This is not ideal since the state is not getting its share of things such as unemployment and disability, and the IRS is sharing data with states.

Again, rolling the dice is not our professional advice, even if it rhymes. We do not want some stray bullet hitting us from the IRS trying to hit you- we will decline the engagement if you want to roll the dice. We don't want your problems to become our problems.

Conversely, let us do it right. You sleep well at night. More rhymes. Everyone wins.

Of course the Watson CPA Group can take care of all this paperwork for you!

> **Huge Emphasis:** We cannot stress enough that having an LLC in place is cheap insurance even if you don't ever elect to be an S Corp. While IRS guidance is hazy, it our recommendation plus the recommendations of tax attorneys and other consultants that the effective date of the S Corp election should not occur before the earliest date that the LLC has members, acquires assets or begins conducting business.

Mid-Year Payroll

It's July and your golf game is just as crummy as it was in May so you start focusing on your business. You talk to us, and we decide that the S corporation election is the way to go. We don't go back to Q1 and Q2, and run late payroll. That is an unnecessary can of worms. We simply open payroll accounts for Q3, determine your reasonable salary, compute your tax obligation and chop it up between Q3 and Q4.

No, the IRS does not get alarmed when you start payroll in the middle of the year. No, they are not concerned about the lopsidedness of your payroll. Yes, there might be some underpayment penalties if you haven't made any estimated tax payments.

Nuts and Bolts of the Election

Behind the scenes there are some technical things going when electing to be an S-Corp. The LLC essentially transfers all of its assets and liabilities to the corporation in exchange for the corporation's stock and then distributes stock to its shareholders to complete the liquidation. Sounds cool. Read IRS Regulations Section 301.7701-3(g)(1) if you can't get enough.

The transfer is tax free of course unless the LLC's liabilities exceed its assets. If this applies to you, please consult with us. Also, Form 8832 Entity Classification Election is generally not required since the Form 2553 S-Corp Election supersedes it.

If you have an existing Operating Agreement it will need to be updated so it aligns with your entity being taxed as an S corporation. We can help guide you on this.

S Corp Equity Section

Massaging of the equity section of your balance sheet is required when being taxed as an S corporation. Here is some nauseating accountant jargon. On January 1st, the effective date of the S corporation election, the equity section would have five accounts-

▲ Capital Stock

▲ Additional Paid-In Capital (for each shareholder)

▲ Shareholder Distributions (for each shareholder)

▲ Retained Earnings, and

▲ Net Income

Unlike a C corporation, an entity being taxed as an S corporation can only have one class of stock, so preferred stock is not allowed, yet common stock within an S corporation structure can still have voting and non-voting rights. This section of our book is regarding an LLC but if a C corporation elected to be taxed as an S corporation (for example), Dividends Paid would still be tracked within the equity section purely for legacy purposes. However, S corporations do not pay dividends. Rather shareholders receive distributions.

The challenge becomes how to "fund" the Capital Stock and Additional Paid-In Capital accounts. Typically an LLC will be initially funded with the owner injecting cash and perhaps some equipment to start the business. This would have been a debit to Cash and Equipment separately, and a Credit to the owner's Capital account. Upon S corporation election, the Capital account would be closed out to Capital Stock using a pre-determined par value such as $10 per stock and a nominal number of shares such as 100, or $1,000 in Capital Stock.

We recommend keeping the Capital Stock account as small as possible because it provides the most flexibility in taking future Shareholder Distributions without affecting Capital Stock. The remainder would be a credit to the Additional Paid-In Capital account(s).

Since it is common for small businesses to operate as LLC's for several years and to have incomplete records (shocking), the "funding" of the equity accounts might have to wait until the end of the first year of S corporation election to maintain sanity. For example, on December 31st Capital Stock and Additional Paid-In Capital are zero, including Retained Earnings.

The following three journal entries would be made-

▲ Net Income would be closed out with a credit to Retained Earnings, and

▲ Shareholder Distributions throughout the year would be closed out with a debit to Retained Earnings, and

▲ A correcting entry would be made with credits to both Capital Stock and Additional Paid-In Capital using the same guidelines of keeping Capital Stock a nominal value such as $1,000, and a debit to Retained Earnings.

You really don't care about this, do you? No worries, we provide these journal entries during tax preparation.

Another technique where historical records are incomplete would be using the amount of cash in the business checking account on January 1 of the first year of S corporation election as the initial capital injection. The entry would be a debit to Cash, and credit to Capital Stock and Additional Paid-In Capital. While these techniques are not as elegant as tracing the capital structure from the beginning, it does create efficiencies and simplicity within a small business.

Terminating S-Corp Election

S Corps have relished being the class favorite for all kinds of reasons as stated in this book. However, the original C-Corp could be making a comeback. Based on projected trends corporate tax rates may be on the decline. At the same time, individual tax rates recently hit epic proportions especially considering the 3.8% surtax on net investment incomes for high earners. Your individual rate could easily hit 43.4%. Yikes!

Yes, you can change back and the present-day solution is accomplished by either liquidating, or terminating the S Corp election.

Liquidation is the more complicated of the two. In a nutshell, the process begins with a unanimous vote to close the business. Once that decision is made, it's a complicated process of contacting creditors, assessing receivables, distributing or selling property and closing up the books.

Termination, moderately more elegant. Terminating the S Corp election can happen one of two ways. Preferably by revocation, or the next best alternative, violating one of the S Corp rules. Violating one of the S corporation rules is not an elegant option however.

Therefore, revocation is the preferred direct route and is as simple as writing a statement to the IRS revoking your S-Corp election. In this manner, obtaining written consent from more than 50% of your shareholders is required. Simple for one or two owner S Corps, but community property states, tenants in common, and majority shareholders could complicate that. Again, if the underlying entity is an LLC then the members will be bound by the operating agreement in terms of voting and other requirements.

When your S corporation election is revoked, either intentionally or not, your company will more than likely revert to a C Corp for taxation. We can then file a Form 8832 which will reclassify your business back to an LLC or partnership, again for taxation. Remember, the underlying entity does not change with the Secretary of State. There might be some accounting headache and subsequent tax consequences with capital accounts or other assets, but we can advise you on those concerns once all the details are vetted out.

Why would you want to revoke your S Corp election? There are many reasons- business closed or is shrinking to a point where it doesn't make sense, lost the contract gig, got converted from 1099 to W-2, foreign investors, etc. are among the most frequent. We can help guide you as these situations arise.

Notice how making too much income wasn't on the list of possible reasons. Of course there are exceptions, but generally speaking if you make $30,000 or $300,000 or even $3,000,000, the S Corp election is going to be your friend.

Distributed Assets

When you revoke S corporation status, you will trigger a taxable event. A potentially big one. Upon revocation, assets are distributed to the S Corp shareholders at fair market value. Cash is easy. An automobile is generally not a big deal. But real estate can kick your butt. Therefore, before we put out the flame a review of the assets and fair market values must be done. To pay capital gains on appreciated assets when you have cash from a transaction is easy. To pay capital gains on appreciated assets when a cashless revocation occurs is brutal.

5 Year Rule

S Corps that lose their "S" status must typically wait five years before being able to re-elect it. As mentioned, deliberately violating one of the rules, such as transferring stock to an ineligible shareholder, is not a good thing. What happens if it was unintentional? The IRS in private ruling letters has on a case-by-case basis allow S Corps to remain as such if the event causing termination was not reasonably within the control of the owners. Hard to demonstrate and private letter rulings (PLRs) can cost thousands of dollars.

In other cases, the IRS has relented and allowed an S Corp to continue when there is a more than 50% change in ownership. Details. Details. So, a company becomes an S Corporation. Revokes the election. Then has a greater than 50% change in ownership within five years. Begs to the IRS. Perhaps is granted an early S Corp election.

Life Cycle of an S Corporation
Here is a summary of the life cycle of an S Corporation in terms of startup and shutdown-

▲ LLC Formed

▲ S Corp Election Made, Form 2553

▲ Payroll Accounts Opened

▲ S Corp Revoked, Letter to IRS

▲ Reverts to C Corp for Taxation

▲ Form 8832 (Entity Classification Election)

▲ Distributions and Tax Consequences Dealt With

▲ Payroll Accounts Closed

▲ Final S Corp Tax Return Filed, Form 1120S

Chapter 6
Operating Your S Corp
(updated December 23, 2017)

Section 199A S Corp Considerations
Section 199A deduction also known as the Qualified Business Income deduction arises from the Tax Cuts & Jobs Act of 2017. This is a significant tax break for small business owners but there are rules and limits of course.

As with any major revision to the tax code, there will be modifications and interpretations which will change how Section 199A can be used for pass-through businesses. Stay tuned to updates as additional guidance is released.

Calculating the Qualified Business Income Deduction
The basic Section 199A pass-through deduction is 20% of net qualified business income which is huge. If you make $200,000, the deduction is $40,000 times your marginal tax rate of 24% which equals $9,600 in your pocket. Who says Obamacare isn't affordable now?

Here is the exact code-

(2) DETERMINATION OF DEDUCTIBLE AMOUNT FOR EACH TRADE OR BUSINESS. The amount determined under this paragraph with respect to any qualified trade or business is the lesser of-

(A) 20 percent of the taxpayer's qualified business income with respect to the qualified trade or business, or

(B) the greater of-

    (i) 50 percent of the W-2 wages with respect to the qualified trade or business, or

    (ii) the sum of 25 percent of the W-2 wages with respect to the qualified trade or business, plus 2.5 percent of the unadjusted basis immediately after acquisition of all qualified property.

There are some devils in the details of course. The best way is to show some examples which we do later in this chapter.

Takeaways

No entity is penalized under the new tax law. Some entities and situations might not qualify or be limited in some fashion, but the high-water mark in terms of taxation is the old crummy 2017 tax law.

Taxable income becomes a big deal for two reasons! First, $1 over $157,500 or $315,000 starts the specified service business disqualification and W-2 limitation (and there is also a depreciation component that we are glossing over in this summary). Second, the Section 199A deduction is limited by 20% of taxable income from all sources (what would be reported on your tax returns).

W-2 wages include all W-2 wages, not just those paid to the owner(s). Converting a 1099 contractor to a W-2 employee might be beneficial.

It appears that self-employment taxes will still be calculated on the net business income before the Section 199A deduction since the deduction is taken "below the line" on Form 1040. Therefore, you could earn $100,000 and deduct $20,000 under Section 199A, but still pay self-employment taxes on $100,000. This remains unclear however and we will await further IRS guidance.

S corporations remain a critical tax saving tool for two reasons. First, the usual self-employment tax savings remains intact for all business owners including specified service trades or businesses. Second, a business owner might need to pay W-2 wages to himself or herself to not be limited by income, and only corporations can pay W-2 wages to owners (in other words, an LLC cannot without an S Corp election).

Section 199A Pass-Thru Optimization

There is some optimization that is necessary for a small business owner to get the most from the Section 199A deduction. On one hand we want to reduce W-2 salaries to shareholders to minimize self-employment taxes. On the other hand, we want to increase W-2 salaries so they do not limit the amount of Section 199A that is deducted.

This seems straightforward since payroll taxes are 15.3% plus some unemployment and other insidious stuff and the Section 199A Qualified Business Income deduction is 20%. However, the 20% Section 199A deduction must be multiplied by the marginal tax rate to obtain the true tax benefit. Even at a 37% marginal tax rate, the additional payroll taxes might exceed the Section 199A deduction tax benefit. Again, optimization is important.

Section 199A Deduction Decision Tree

Remember that taxable income is all income for the household.

Specified Service Trade or Business

▲ If taxable income is less than $157,500 (single) / $315,000 (married) then the 20% deduction for your pass-thru entity is fully available.

▲ If taxable income is greater than $157,500 / $315,000 but less than $207,500 / $415,000 then a partial deduction is available. The phase-in of the limit is linear.

▲ If taxable income is greater than $207,500 / $415,000 then you are hosed. Sorry.

All Others

▲ If taxable income is less than $157,500 / $315,000 then the 20% deduction is fully available.

▲ If taxable income is greater than $157,500 / $315,000 but less than $207,500 / $415,000 then a partial deduction is available with the W-2 and depreciable asset limit calculations phase in.

▲ If taxable income is greater than $207,500 / $415,000 then the 20% deduction is compared to the full W-2 and depreciable asset limit calculations (see Betty in Chapter 1).

We know... we know... you want to see the money! Just Cuba Gooding Jr, we get it. Let's crawl before we walk, and let's walk before we run. We want to discuss the operational hassles of an S corporation plus the reasonable shareholder salary theories.

Or you can say forget this, and flip ahead.

The S Corp Grind, Operational Hassles

You're probably thinking that running an S-Corp adds all kinds of burdens. Not true. When we ask the appropriate questions and recommend an S Corp election, some clients will say, "Sounds like a lot of work." There are very few additional hassles with an S corporation as compared to other entities. All the things you do now to maintain your financial records remain the same. Determining your business income and expenses remains the same. Whether you compile data to put on a Form 1040 Schedule C or Form 1120S (corporate tax return), the effort from you is identical. Additionally, the things you do in terms of corporate governance such as meetings, minutes and voting, also remain the same.

The two other requirements are paying a reasonable salary to S Corp shareholders through payroll and preparing a corporate tax return. If you use the Watson CPA Group (and you should), then this hassle is ours not yours. Well, not entirely true- we are attached at the hip if we prepare your tax returns, and while we can be demanding for a comprehensive tax return the hassle is mostly ours.

S Corp Salary

The bulk of this chapter is devoted to reasonable S corporation salary theory and calculation. We only mention it here since calculating a reasonable salary and processing payroll is a hassle as a business owner.

Corporate Tax Return

An S Corp must file a corporate tax return by **March 15** and there are additional financial reporting requirements. Since an S corporation is a pass-thru entity whereby the tax consequences are passed through to the shareholders, the personal tax returns of the shareholders cannot be completed until the S Corp tax return is completed (both can be filed simultaneously). However, if you use the Watson CPA Group to prepare your tax returns, we'll make it seamless and pain free. Ok, taxes and pain free don't really go together, but you get the idea.

S corporations file a Form 1120S and this in turn creates K-1s for all the shareholders. Unlike many other tax professionals, we always create a balance sheet and we always reconcile equity accounts (capital stock, additional paid in capital, retained earnings, shareholder distributions and basis). This can be challenging for us, but we feel it is important for you, the client, and for long-term reporting accuracy.

When you own an S corporation, you are both employee and investor. If you invested $100 into Google, you could only lose $100. Nothing more. The same with your S Corp as an investor. For example, if you invested $10,000 into your company, but your company lost $20,000, your K-1 will show a $20,000 loss but you are only allowed to deduct your basis which is $10,000. Without tracking this information, you could be incorrectly deducting losses in the current year instead of carrying them forward to future years.

More importantly, without shareholder basis information, there is no way to determine the gain on your future business sale. Just like stock sales, when you sell your company for a zillion dollars the IRS will consider all that to be capital gain unless you can prove otherwise.

Creating a balance sheet is also just good accounting practice, and it contributes to the overall tracking of your company's worth. Lenders and investors will also want to see this information if you need leveraged financial assistance for company growth. Recently, a business owner was gifting away chunks of her business to her sons, and her basis needed to be calculated and transferred for gift tax filings. Her balance sheet information was a mess and needed fixing. We are retained frequently to put humpty dumpty back together and build historical balance sheet information.

Business succession, exit strategies, asset sales, business valuation, buy-sell agreements, etc. are topics rarely considered by most small business owners, and that is Ok. But as accountants and business consultants, it is our job to keep you out of future trouble by putting things on the right track today. That starts with your corporate tax returns being comprehensively and accurately prepared, which includes Schedule L (the balance sheet). While we don't look for ways to complicate the heck out of things, demand that your tax professional prepare a balance sheet with your tax returns.

[Rest of this page blank for no other reason than pagination concerns]

S Corp Costs

People want to know costs and while this might seem like more shameless self-promotion, you still need to understand what you are getting into. The Watson CPA Group specializes in S corporations which have a small number of shareholders, and often just a one-person show. This is all we do.

Because it is a core competency for us, we have created an S Corp package that includes the following-

	Aspen	Vail	Breck	Keystone
S Corp Reasonable Salary Calculation	Yes	Yes	Yes	Yes
Section 199A Pass-Thru Optimization	Yes	Yes	Yes	Yes
S Corp Payroll Filings and Deposits	Yes	Yes		
Annual Processing (W2s, up to five 1099's)	Yes	Yes		
S Corporation Tax Prep (Form 1120S)	Yes	Yes	Yes	Yes
Individual Tax Prep (Form 1040), One Owner	Yes		Yes	
Estimated Tax Payments	Yes	Yes	Yes	Yes
2018 Tax Planning, Mock Tax Returns	Yes	Yes	Yes	Yes
Unlimited Consultation, PBRs	Yes	Yes	Yes	Yes
First Research Industry Reports	Yes	Yes	Yes	Yes
Small Business Tax Deductions Optimization	Yes	Yes	Yes	Yes
Solo 401k Plan	Yes	Yes	Yes	Yes
IRS Audit Defense	Yes		Yes	
Annual Fee	**$2,940**	**$2,640**	**$2,460**	**$2,160**
Monthly Fee	**$245**	**$220**	**$205**	**$180**

Couple of things to keep in mind- we make very little profits on payroll processing... we offer it as a convenience to our clients. One throat to choke with a single call can be reassuring but if you want to run your payroll, go for it! And... the benefit of the Watson CPA Group preparing both tax returns is that we slide things around depending on income limitations, phaseouts, alternative minimum tax (AMT), etc. Having our arms around both can yield some good tax savings!

Some more things to consider- Since only a partial year remains, our usual annual fee is pro-rated to not charge you for services you didn't use (like payroll and consultation). However, a large chunk of our annual fee is tax preparation which is typically a fixed amount of $1,300 (both corporate and personal). Whether we onboard you in January, July or December, we have to prepare a full year tax return. This increases the monthly fee for the remaining months of 2018 but the monthly fee will later decrease in January of 2019 to reflect the amounts above.

Break-even analysis is based on our annual fee of $2,940. If an S corporation saves you 8% to 10% (on average) in taxes over the garden variety LLC, then $2,940 divided by 8.5% equals $35,000 of net business income after expenses.

You can always find someone to do it for less- we know that. At the same time, we have a vested interest in your success and provide sound tax and business consultation as a part of our service. Here are links to our Periodic Business Review agenda and End of Year Tax Planning that we cover throughout the year so our consultation to you is comprehensive-

www.watsoncpagroup.com/PBR

www.watsoncpagroup.com/EOY

These general fees will cover most situations. However, depending on the number of transactions, accounts and employees, these fees might have to be adjusted to reflect additional complexities. The Watson CPA Group is not out to gouge anyone or do a quick money grab- we want to build relationships by doing things right for a reasonable fee. Check out our fee structure here-

www.watsoncpagroup.com/fee

No more shameless promotion... at least for a while.

Income Nomination

Another minor inconvenience. There are certain businesses such as insurance agents, investment advisors, realtors and consultants that might be precluded from receiving income and the subsequent 1099-MISC tax form in the business name and EIN. In other words, your Social Security number is being used to report the income to the IRS. Not to worry. We nominate this income to the S Corporation and all is good with the IRS.

Specifically, the 1099-MISC associated your social security number (SSN) is entered on your personal tax return. A reversing entry is made in the name of your S Corporation's employer identification number (EIN). Net zero on your personal tax return. The S Corp assumes the income and pushes it back down to you in the form a W-2 and K-1 after expenses, etc.

Follow these dots- 1099's SSN to S Corp's EIN to K-1's SSN and W-2's SSN. Full circle with the S corporation sanitizing the income (paint by numbers, fun!).

Salary First, Distributions and Loans Second

Shareholders must be paid a salary before any shareholder distributions are paid out or loans are advanced to shareholders. This is a technicality. You can take a shareholder distribution as an S Corp owner prior to paying a salary to yourself throughout the year. At the end of the year, however, you must have W-2 income if you received shareholder distributions.

If the business cannot afford to pay salaries, it is not necessarily required to do so. There is some gray area involving large depreciation expenses and other non-cash reductions in business income. So, if you have a pile of cash but experience a loss due to large depreciation, for example, you might still be required to pay salaries. If you believe your company won't be profitable, then we suggest deferring the S-Corp election to another tax year. Remember there are provisions allowing a late S Corp election beyond the customary 75-day limitation- take advantage of this option by delaying your election if you are unsure.

IRS S Corp Stats

Let's jump right into some numbers first before going through reasonable S Corp salary theory developed from IRS revenue rules and tax court cases. The following table is a summary generated from IRS statistics on S corporation tax returns for the 2013 tax year. Yes, this is the most current. No, we do not know why a room full of servers can't crunch this in real-time. So here we are-

Annual Receipts	Gross Receipts Per Return	Net Income Per Return	Officer Comp Per Return	Officer Comp % of Net Income
$25,000 to $99,999	62,552	6,672	8,871	57%
$100,000 to $249,999	168,051	22,194	22,786	51%
$250,000 to $499,999	365,476	37,732	43,158	53%
$500,000 to $999,999	720,013	58,351	67,474	54%
$1M to $2.5M	1,572,621	119,808	110,911	48%

First some quick observations. Officer compensation is added back to net income to determine officer comp as a percentage of net income. Next, this is all industries from capital intensive manufacturing to personal services business such as attorneys, doctors, consultants, engineers and accountants. Also, this includes S corps who lost money, and whether they lost money and continued to pay a reasonable shareholder salary (officer compensation) is unclear. In other words, if losses were teased out would officer compensation be reduced as a percentage of net income? We cannot quickly determine.

Here is the same data grouped by gross receipts but detailed by selected industries. First one is $100,000 to $249,999 in gross receipts-

$100,000 to $249,999	Gross Receipts Per Return	Net Income Per Return	Officer Comp Per Return	Officer Comp % of Net Income
Finance and Insurance	160,359	34,408	23,213	40%
Real Estate	165,375	38,231	28,193	42%
Professional, Scientific	163,151	32,910	35,404	52%
Health Care	174,383	24,622	36,026	59%

And now for $250,000 to $499,999 in gross receipts-

$250,000 to $499,999	Gross Receipts Per Return	Net Income Per Return	Officer Comp Per Return	Officer Comp % of Net Income
Finance and Insurance	366,533	77,518	62,329	45%
Real Estate	359,163	65,419	51,151	44%
Professional, Scientific	355,693	71,136	74,493	51%
Health Care	378,147	51,553	75,382	59%

There you go. Remember that officer compensation includes all fringe benefits such as self-employed health insurance and HSA contributions, and it might be influenced (increased) by those who want to maximize 401k deferrals and / or defined benefits pensions.

Reasonable S Corp Salary Theory

Determining a reasonable salary is the hardest part of running an S corporation. What the heck do I pay myself? Before we get into that, let's discuss why shareholder salary needs to be just above bar napkin quality and just below NASA precision.

Scattered throughout this book we've stressed that the only tax savings an S Corp provides is the reduction of self-employment taxes, and in the case of shareholder wages we are talking about Social Security and Medicare taxes (payroll taxes). When your company pays you $10,000 in shareholder wages, 7.65% is withheld from your pay check for the employee's portion of payroll taxes. This is broken down into 6.2% Social Security and 1.45% Medicare. The company also must pay 7.65% for a combined percentage of 15.3%. Since the company deducts its portion of payroll taxes, the effective tax rate is 14.1%.

Therefore, a $10,000 shareholder salary costs you $1,410 in additional taxes beyond income taxes. Said in a different way, if you pay yourself $50,000 when $40,000 could have been a reasonable shareholder salary, you just wasted $1,410. Even a $5,000 delta equates to $705.

Truth be told there is some philosophical issues with the reasonable salary element where your labor is the only material income-producing factor for the business. Some would argue that all the S Corp's income should then be considered shareholder wages and subjected to Social Security and Medicare taxes, since if you died the company would die. Do we see this "loophole" being re-defined and shrinking over the next several years? Yes. But at the same time, we say let it ride until we can't use it. The IRS and Congress move at glacial speeds- let's worry about next time, next time.

Conversely, there might be times where your business would continue without you. When the Watson CPA Group does business valuations, especially in divorce proceedings, we assign a value to goodwill. We do this by taking a number called seller's discretionary cash flow (SDCF) and we subtract the cash flow that is derived from tangible assets (cash, equipment, etc.). This leaves us with a theoretical number that is considered goodwill which can be used as a proxy to determine your "value" to the business.

We further tease out personal goodwill and enterprise goodwill since in some jurisdictions personal goodwill is not marital property. This might seem like an odd tangent, but a similar argument can be made for a business that does not rely on you. One great example is a financial advisor that has a small team supporting him or her- typically the fee income continues well into the future without the direct involvement of the advisor (enterprise goodwill). In this situation, an argument for a smaller salary could be warranted since enterprise goodwill exceeds personal goodwill. Consider this-

Business Type	Owner Participation
Software developer who has gone to market	10%
Amazon retailer, a lot of drop shipments, no inventory	20%
Financial advisor with small team	30%
Doctor who is a partner in an emergency clinic	40%
Consultant, Attorney, Accountant	90%
Actor with no endorsements or couch-jumping events	100%

Of course, this is all theoretical and is open to debate, but you get the idea.

Not to go too far into the weeds, but when performing business valuations we also consider investor value. What rate of return would an investor need to earn after paying you a reasonable salary? Naturally, a lower salary to you results in a higher rate of return for the investor. We also look at the earnings generated from capital investments such as machinery and other non-owner employees versus shareholder labor. We digress...

In this chapter, we will review-

▲ IRS Revenue Rulings and Fact Sheet 2008-25

▲ Tax Court Cases

▲ Risk Management Association (RMA), Bureau of Labor Statistics (BLS) and Salary.com

▲ Rules of Thumb, Jumping Off Point

IRS Revenue Rulings and Fact Sheet

In 1959, **IRS Revenue Ruling 59-221** held that amounts of S corporation undistributed taxable income which are required to be included in each shareholder's gross income do not constitute net earnings from self-employment to shareholders. However, in 1974, **IRS Revenue Ruling 74-44** stated that "dividends" paid to shareholders will be recharacterized as wages when such "dividends" are paid to shareholders in lieu of reasonable compensation for services performed for the S Corp. The word dividends is in quotations because in reality we call these shareholder distributions, but in 1974 they referred to them as dividends.

This makes sense. Dividends being used to pay for services are truly wages. If Google or Amazon pays out a dividend to its shareholders, it is considered investment income. If your S corporation does the same thing to its only shareholder without an accompanying shareholder wage, then it is considered self-employment income and subject to the gaggle of taxes with that type of income.

Moving on... There are several factors to consider when coming up with a reasonable salary. The IRS through **Fact Sheet 2008-25** released the following laundry list (last update was in 2008 when Flo Rida was singing Low... apple bottom jeans, boots with the fur, the whole club was looking at her. How time flies!)-

▲ Training and experience.

▲ Duties and responsibilities.

▲ Time and effort devoted to the business.

▲ Dividend history (IRS nomenclature, really this should be shareholder distributions-however back in the day it was C corporations who later elected to be taxed an S corporation, so dividend history still has some historical merit).

▲ Payments to non-shareholder employees.

▲ Timing and manner of paying bonuses to key people.

▲ What comparable businesses pay for similar services.

▲ Compensation agreements.

▲ The use of a formula to determine compensation.

Clear as mud. This is the best the IRS can come up with? What is even more frustrating or perhaps embarrassing is that this list was the final draft after probably several meetings and rough drafts. Having said that, this is how our tax system operates in many ways- leave lots of wiggle room for interpretation so the law and the standards can evolve to meet the needs of today.

This list actually has two applications. Since C corporations have a high tax rate including being double-taxed, many small C corporations want to drive corporate income close to zero by paying high salaries. The IRS and the tax court will use this list to say your salary is too high as a C Corp. Conversely, S corporations want to increase corporate income by paying small salaries. The IRS and the tax court will talk out of the other side of their mouths by using this list to justify a higher salary. Yes, they get to have it both ways.

Here is a link to IRS Fact Sheet 2008-25-

www.wcgurl.com/8247

Tax Court Cases for Reasonable Salary
The tax court has provided some guidance over the years in several well-known cases. Here is a quick reference bulleted list, and later we'll dive into the finer details-

Ulrich v. United States, 692 F. Supp. 1053 (D. Minn., 1988)
Sole shareholder of an accounting firm whose only income was dividends. The court held "Under both the weight of the case law and under the treasury regulations, a corporate officer is to be treated an employee if he renders more than minor services."

Spicer Accounting v. United States, 918 F.2d 90 (1990)
Spicer was the only accountant working for the firm and it was owned 50-50 with his wife. He only received dividends, and claimed to donate his services to the S corporation. The court held "The Federal Insurance Contributions Act and Federal Unemployment Tax Act both

define 'wages' as 'all remuneration for employment... that the form of payment is immaterial... [therefore] the only relevant factor being whether payments were actually received as compensation for employment."

Watson v. Commissioner, 668 F.3d 1008 (8th Cir. 2012)

No relation to the Watson CPA Group! In this case, Watson was an accountant in a firm he owned. He drew a salary of $24,000 even though the firm grossed nearly $3 million in revenue. Watson was a Certified Public Accountant with advanced degrees. The 8th Circuit Court ruled that a reasonable person would consider the dividends paid to Watson to be "remuneration for services performed" as opposed to a return on investment. To support its position, the IRS successfully asserted that the $24,000 shareholder salary was not enough to support Watson's lifestyle. As such, his dividends were reclassified as wages and the firm was assessed huge employment taxes plus penalties and interest.

JD & Associates, Ltd. v. United States, No. 3:04-cv-59 (District Court, North Dakota, 2006)

Dahl, an accountant and sole shareholder, paid himself a small salary. The IRS hired a valuation expert who used Risk Management Association (RMA) data to determine what other accountants were paid for similar services. The RMA data was damning enough, however what really sent this case over the edge is the Dahl paid himself less than his staff including clerical positions. Admins cannot make more than you.

These darn accountants are out of control! Here are couple of "wins."

Davis v. United States, 1994 U.S. Dist. LEXIS 10725 (District Court, Colorado, 1994)

A husband and wife team owned a corporation. The husband worked elsewhere and the wife performed clerical duties (12 hours per month). Her accountant said her services were worth $8 per hour. The IRS did not challenge the value of the time commitment and therefore Davis won this case because the wife was able to prove her minimal hours.

Sean McAlary Ltd. Inc. v. Commissioner (Tax Court Summary Opinion 2013-62)

In a recent tax court case, the IRS hired a valuation expert to determine that a real estate agent should have been paid $100,755 salary out of his S Corp's net income of $231,454. Not bad. He still took home over $130,000 in distributions, and avoided self-employment taxes (mainly Medicare) on that portion of his income. Then again, this makes sense. Real estate oftentimes sells itself thanks to the internet, and the real estate agents are merely facilitators. In other words, the actions of the real estate agent were not solely responsible for $231,454 in income.

There are two tests that tax courts have used in the past. In **Label Graphics, Inc. v. Commissioner, Tax Court Memo 1998-343** which was later affirmed by the 9th Circuit Court in 2000, the court came up with-

▲ The employee's role in the company.

▲ A comparison of the compensation paid to similarly situated employees in similar companies.

▲ The character and condition of the company.

▲ Whether a relationship existed between the company and employee that may permit the company to disguise nondeductible corporate distributions as deductible compensation.

▲ Whether the compensation was paid pursuant to a (1) structured, (2) formal, and (3) consistently applied program.

In **Brewer Quality Homes, Inc. v. Commissioner, Tax Court Memo 2003-200**, the court re-iterated several points from another federal court case (**Owensby & Kritikos, Inc. v. Commissioner, 819 F.2d 1315 (5th Cir. 1987)**)-

▲ The employee's qualifications.

▲ The nature, extent, and scope of the employee's work.

▲ Size and complexity of the company.

▲ Comparison of the employee's salary with the company's gross and net income.

▲ Prevailing general economic conditions.

▲ Comparison of salaries with distributions to stockholders.

▲ Compensation for comparable positions in comparable concern.

▲ Salary policy of the company as to all employees.

▲ Amount of compensation paid to the employee in previous years.

Similarly to **IRS Fact Sheet 2008-25** no single factor controls. It really is a preponderance of the evidence as civil courts like to say. Tax court judges will go through these lists, depending on the case and the jurisdiction, and will apply the facts and circumstances to each of these factors, and essentially make a list of plusses or a minuses.

For example, the criterion might be "Payment to non-shareholder employees." The tax court will analyze the evidence to determine the plus or minus. Let's say the S corporation owner provides evidence that her star employee is the rainmaker and therefore the employee's salary including bonuses exceeds the S corporation shareholder. Let's also say that the tax court finds this argument to be compelling. This would a "plus" for the S corporation owner since the criterion of "Payment to non-shareholder employees" favors the S Corp shareholder.

Continuing with this example, assume the owner had $300,000 in net income after expenses, but only paid $30,000 to herself as an S corporation salary. The IRS and tax court would place a "minus" next to the "A comparison of salaries paid to sales and net income" criterion as they did in **K & K Veterinary Supply, Inc. v. Commissioner (Tax Court Memo 2013-84)**.

Reasonable Salary Labor Data

The tax court and the IRS will attempt to support a reasonable salary based on your peers and colleagues. They will use an expert who specializes in vocational valuations, and this person might use Risk Management Association (RMA) and Bureau of Labor Statistics (BLS) data, including local and regional data.

Our previous real estate agent benefited from this type of valuation since his S corporation earned significantly more than the average real estate agent's salary. But what if the opposite was true. So, instead of earning $231,454 and only paying out $100,755 in salary, what if you earned $110,000. Would you have to pay out $100,755 in salary just because you are a real estate agent in an area where other agents earn $100,755?

The answer is a true accountant or lawyer response- it depends. There are several factors that mitigate this. Perhaps you work part time. Perhaps you simply are not as good as your peers. Perhaps you focus on a different type of customer. Review the previous laundry lists, and as you go through each item ask yourself if you could safely use that to justify a lower salary than your peers- we bet you can find several instances.

Statistics attempt to homogenize a population so we may draw correlations and eventual conclusions. Certain professions that appear to be slam dunks are not as they appear. Attorneys and accountants come to mind- we know some attorneys that make $100,000 a year while others make $250,000. It is very tough to jam these two square pegs into the same round hole. Accountants, same thing. IT consultants, same thing. Even physicians doing the same line of work (such as anesthesia) range between $80,000 and $400,000. Same work, at least on paper, yet wildly different incomes!

There is another lesson to be learned here. As your S Corp income increases, the reasonable salary paid to the shareholders do not necessarily increase on a pro rate basis. In other words, if you peg your salary at $60,000 and that is supported with labor data, your salary does not double just because your net income in your S corporation doubles. Your salary is based on you, and the data surrounding you. Yes, the courts look at distributions and net income, and Yes, your salary would probably be increased if your net income doubles, but it is not tethered in a lock-step, $1 for $1 pattern.

Salary.com and the like also do a great job of compiling labor data. RMA and BLS is going to be much more authoritative in court, but RMA (as an example) requires an expensive subscription and is usually reserved for valuation experts who rely on it multiple times to warrant the cost.

RCReports

Recently we have started using RCReports or Reasonable Compensation Reports which is a consulting firm out of Denver, Colorado. They send out a survey to you which asks a bunch of questions about qualifications, time spent on various tasks, regional data, etc. From there, and in their words, "RCReports synthesizes a proprietary blend of IRS criteria, Court Rulings, geographic data and our EXCLUSIVE database of wages to accurately assess Reasonable Compensation for S Corp, Small & Closely Held Business Owners." Cool!

You can view a sample here-

www.wcgurl.com/8257

If you visit this link and read the report, RCReports does a wonderful job coming up with a number and then putting a bunch of data behind it. The report looks official and uses sources; this is a critical consideration since reasonable compensation is such a squishy thing. In other words, the IRS might challenge your reasonable S Corp salary much like a mall cop with a badge but no gun, and certainly no evidence. When you roll up with a 7-page document that has numbers, data and sources scattered about, it is super hard for the IRS to say No. For lack of better evidence, the IRS would be forced to use your evidence.

Two more considerations with RCReports. A large part of the calculus is predicated on the business owner wearing multiple hats. At times you are a janitor cleaning your office. At times you are a bookkeeper balancing your checkbook. At times you are performing clerical duties. These tasks might have a lower salary than your primary task, which creates a blended rate for an overall officer compensation.

The other consideration is that just because RCReports comes up with a salary does not mean you must pay that salary. There might be circumstances which would drive down a reasonable salary such as rapid growth, unsteady earnings, etc. There might be circumstances, such as 401k and other external reasons, to increase your salary.

Please keep in mind too that reasonable compensation includes self-employed health insurance and HSA contributions. Therefore, if RCReports comes up with $80,000 but your health insurance is $10,000, then your salary should be $70,000.

The Watson CPA Group can do a reasonable compensation analysis for you. Yeah, we have to charge you about $250 but it gives you a defensible salary and some peace of mind. Bargain!

W-2 Converted to 1099 Reasonable Salary

So you are bumping along and one day your employer decides to convert you from a W-2 employee to a 1099 contractor. Aside from this being a load-shedding sham that the IRS and most states believe to be an end-around, several large companies continue to reduce their workforce in favor of contractors.

You say, no problem, and eventually create an LLC taxed as an S corporation. Now what? Do you peg your salary to the same salary you had before? Hardly. Labor burden rates for companies can vary from 1.4 to 2.0. What does this mean? This means if a company is paying you a $100,000 salary, your actual cost to the company might be as high as $200,000. Why?

Health insurance, dental insurance, paid time off, vacation, sick pay, holiday pay, payroll taxes, workers' compensation insurance, disability, group life insurance, office rent (smaller workforce smaller office footprint), etc. Yeah... read that again. There is a ton of overhead that gets tacked on to you as an employee. No wonder the company just converted you from W-2 to 1099. Mo' money! Just not for you.

How does this factor in the reasonable salary conversation? Let's say your company's labor burden rate is 1.8 which is not far off most big, fat corporations. This would suggest that a $100,000 salary costs the company $180,000. If you are paid $100,000 as a contractor (which would be a crummy deal), then your relative salary could be $55,000. You shouldn't get penalized if you run a leaner operation than your former employer.

What about the risk of this new arrangement? As a shareholder in an S corporation you are assuming a ton of risk- equity risk, industry risk, small business risk and company-specific risk.

If we perform a business valuation where the business has a singular client, the risk of the future economic benefit (income stream) is huge.

As risk increases we demand a higher rate of return, or increased distributions. Makes sense, right?

Mini recap- labor burden rate plus increased risk of singular client can suggest a lower salary than the old W-2 job. And... being converted is not a bad deal- company car, your own 401k, business casual means PJs, etc.

S Corp Salary Starting Point

There are plenty of professions that have great data from the Bureau of Labor Statistics (BLS), Risk Management Association (RMA) or RCReports. But let's say your job is some odd-duck, whacky thing for which comparable data doesn't exist. Where do we start quantitatively? At the end of the day, we need a number!

One argument that we and others have made is the concept of 1/3, 1/3, 1/3-

▲ 1/3 paid as shareholder salary, plus

▲ 1/3 distributed as return on investment (distributions), plus

▲ 1/3 retained for company growth (if necessary, otherwise flushed out at end of year)

This is great starting point for a growing S corporation since most businesses need to finance growth from leftover cash after salaries and distributions. For a one-person show that is in a steady state of business, a good starting point is 40% of your net profit. So, if your net profit after expenses is $50,000, a $20,000 salary would be reasonable. Again this is a jumping off point. You must be able to justify the number, and this number could increase or decrease depending on you.

Using the 1/3 concept or the 40% concept is just a starting point- since we have to start somewhere, using a mathematical formula makes it easy. From there, similar to the "plus" and "minus" approach by the IRS and tax court judges, we massage this salary to be reasonable for you and your company's situation.

Reasonable Salary Recap

Keeping your salary low is what drives the savings in an S corporation. Recall that $10,000 in salary costs you about $1,410 in payroll taxes. However, through the IRS Fact Sheet and several tax court cases, the assignment of reasonable shareholder salary becomes qualitative in relation to several factors such as your role and qualifications, and the relationship to net income and distributions (just to name a few).

Labor data such as Risk Management Association (RMA) and Bureau of Labor Statistics (BLS) including RCReports can be hit or miss. Homogenized populations cannot definitely tell the IRS or the tax court what you should be paid. It could be a tool in your toolbox, or it could be one of the many nails in your coffin.

Also recall that self-employed health insurance and Health Savings Accounts (HSA) add to your Box 1 wages on your W-2. Let's say your reasonable salary is $60,000 and you pay $12,000 in health insurance premiums. You would pay yourself a $48,000 salary but your W-2 Box 1 and Line 7 (Officer Compensation) on your S corporation tax return would show $60,000, but only $48,000 is subjected to Social Security and Medicare taxes.

One of the best ways to win an argument is not have the conversation in the first place. The IRS is focused on S corporations who do not pay any salary, or who pay a ridiculously low salary. For them, it is an easy analysis. Line 7 versus Line 21 of the S Corp tax return (Form 1120S). They can also look at the K-1, Box 1 (ordinary income) and compare this to Box 16, Code D (distributions).

IRS scrutiny will only increase over time, but they also want winnable cases. The low hanging fruit is the S Corp without any reasonable shareholder salary. Why go after someone who is paying themselves $50,000 in salary just to settle on $60,000 after negotiation? An extra $1,410 in the IRS pocket for arguably a tough audit might not be worth it to them. This is contrasted to the person who pays themselves $10,000 and it should be $60,000. There's some cash in that IRS challenge!

There is a calculated risk when determining reasonable compensation for S corporations. You can eliminate the risk by paying yourself 100% of the net business income but then again that completely defeats the purpose of an S Corp. You can pay yourself 0% and wait for the audit. Or... ideally... you can operate in the soft middle.

Take Money Out of the S Corp

Remember, payroll taxes (Social Security and Medicare taxes) are the same as self-employment taxes. But they also include unemployment taxes, state disability insurance (such as California's state disability insurance- CASDI) and other odd-duck local taxes. We discussed this in previous sections. As an S-Corp shareholder, you are taking money out of the business in four ways-

Source	Payroll Taxes	Income Taxes
1. Reasonable S Corp Salary	Yes	Yes
2. Shareholder Distributions	No	No*
3. Self-Rental (not home office)	No	Yes
4. Reimbursements (accountable plan, health expenses, education assistance)	No	No

Let's talk about everything except a reasonable salary for your S corporation first. When you write a check to yourself or transfer money from your business checking account to your personal checking account, you are taking a shareholder distribution. However you are not taxed on shareholder distributions nor are they a deduction to the business- you are taxed on income.

Here is a story to drive home this point- the Watson CPA Group has an S Corp client who had accumulated about $400,000 in her business checking account over the years. No big deal. Cash is king, right? Her husband called, and wanted to know the tax consequences of moving the $400,000 into their personal checking account since they were buying a house. We said None. You already paid taxes on the income that aggregated to $400,000 over the past three years.

Another way to look at this- cash that you take out (shareholder distributions, dividends, owner draws, whatever you want to call them) is not considered when determining your taxable income. Cash is cash and income is income. Sure, in most cash based businesses, cash will equal income and income will equal cash (or will be very close). But there can be a difference when factoring in non-cash expenses such as mileage and depreciation. The opposite is true with non-expense outflow items such as the principal portion of debt service.

Yet another example. Sorry to belabor this issue, but it appears this income versus cash continues to frustrate small business owners. Ok. Let's say your S Corporation earns $100,000 after shareholder wages and expenses, and you magically also have $100,000 in the business checking account. You transfer $60,000 to your personal checking account as a shareholder distribution. $40,000 is left behind in the business checking account.

What is your taxable income? $100,000. Good.

Next year, your business is a bit slower and you only earn $50,000 and therefore you have $90,000 ($40,000 + $50,000) in the business checking account. You transfer $80,000 to your personal account leaving $10,000 in the business account.

What is your taxable income? $50,000 even though you transferred $80,000 from the business to you. Cash is cash and income is income. Over time, aggregated historical cash should be very close to aggregated historical incomes but don't get too caught up on that. Same with accrual versus cash accounting- in looking back 20 years both accounting methods should converge in net incomes. We digress...

This is one of the dangers of owning a business- being taxed on reinvestments. For example, you have $100,000 left over at the end of the year and your taxable income is coincidentally $100,000. You took $70,000 in shareholder distributions as a return on your investment, leaving $30,000 behind for business growth (the reinvestment). If you are taxed at 30%, you will pay $30,000 (100k x 30%) in taxes on $70,000 worth of "cash flow" from your business- suddenly this becomes painful and a near-45% tax rate. Something to think about.

We've already discussed self-rentals and how you can pull money out that is only taxed at the income tax level (see Chapter 1). Expense reimbursements and fringe benefits are explored further in Chapter 7 (Accountable Plan) and Chapter 8 (Tax Deductions, Fringe Benefits). Before we turn to the calculus of a reasonable S corporation salary, let's briefly discuss the frequency of payroll.

Quarterly S Corp Payroll

Throughout this book we make reference to running payroll quarterly. Before we discuss the reasons why, if you have a staff where payroll is ran every two weeks the quarterly S Corp payroll concept might still apply so please keep reading.

The most important consideration is that you do not have to wait for payroll to get cash. Remember, as an S corporation owner you wear two hats- employee and investor. As an investor, you receive distributions from the company. As a controlling investor, you also dictate the frequency and amount of those distributions. Therefore, if you need cash from the company to pay for groceries, mortgages, diapers, etc., then declare a shareholder distribution.

A huge word of caution is in order however. The IRS and tax court do not like to see you use your business as an ATM machine. This is not because you just said automated teller machine machine. This is because the spirit of a shareholder distribution is to be a return on investment, and if it is magically tied to personal living expenses it looks bad. Think of it this way- you wouldn't call up Google and demand a dividend because baby needs new shoes. Same thing here.

Another perspective- Apple shareholders are routinely upset because of the cash that Apple hoards. There are two ways to get a return on investment- capital appreciation (and subsequent sale) and dividends. If there are piles of cash and there aren't immediate or mid-term needs for the cash, shouldn't that be returned to investors who helped build the cash to begin with?

What do you do? One option is to take systematic distributions throughout the year, and flush out the remainder once a quarter or annually. Another option is simply take large chunks periodically without any cadence or basis that can be tied to personal living expenses.

As a side note, lenders do not like to see a bunch of cash in your S corporation bank account. If you are looking to buy a house in the next six months, drain your business bank account down to the operational minimum. Lenders see $100,000 in the business account and they assume the business needs this. You roll up and say you are going to take it all out for a down payment. Now the sales prevention team (i.e., underwriting) thinks your business will suddenly fail which cuts off your ability service your debt. Next thing you know we have to write letters explaining that your business won't fail and it becomes a big headache for everyone.

Bottomline- do not leave cash laying around in your business. Put that money to use, or put it in your personal savings account or retirement fund. Business owners routinely use their business checking account as a personal savings account. Bad. Don't do it. Run your business like a business, and make sure retained cash has a purpose! Idle business cash has very little upside unless you have a capital expenditure or some other near-future use.

Some accountants will simply run S Corp payroll once a year. In our opinion, this is bad for three big reasons-

▲ This contradicts your intention to establish a salary based on your credentials, work patterns, complexity of the company, etc. All those theoretical things the IRS and tax court use to determine a reasonable salary- we discussed these earlier. To the best of your ability and circumstance, salaries should be forward-looking or at least have the appearance.

▲ Running payroll once a year is a horrible budgeting tool. By running payroll quarterly, the Watson CPA Group eases you into your tax obligations throughout the year. We also tie estimated tax payments into payroll which further helps you budget (more on that when we get into the nuts and bolts examples later in this chapter). A $60,000 one-time salary event in December could easily require over $25,000 in tax withholdings. We are all humans first, and budgeters second. Spreading the pain throughout the year helps your cash flow budget and subsequent decision-making like a new car versus a use car.

▲ Your tax obligations might require you to make payroll and income tax deposits once a quarter versus once a year. We take the mystery out of this by having all our S Corp clients follow the quarterly schedule from the beginning. In addition, some states require quarterly payroll filings regardless if payroll was processed- setting up quarterly payroll for yourself can kill this bird with the same stone.

Running payroll quarterly also helps us stay ahead of your potentially silly ideas. If we communicate on a quarterly basis, we can prevent you from buying a car in your personal name when it is 100% business use. Or we can talk you out of a SEP IRA when a solo 401k plan is preferred (you are permitted to have both in the same year if they are both sponsored by the same company). There are thousands of ideas that sounded great at the time just to find out later that there was a better option. Quarterly payroll and the client communication that goes along with that helps everyone.

Most importantly, we can help you understand your impending tax obligation as we gather your net income data each quarter. We tell people bad news all the time, especially around March. However, we never want you to be surprised by it. We do mid-course corrections in Q3 since we have enough history to predict the future, and clean-ups in Q4.

If you are already running payroll every two weeks because you have a staff (or you are considering getting a staff), there are two options. We can worm your salary into the frequency of everyone else's payroll, or we can inject your quarterly payroll into one of the normal payroll runs prior to the quarter end. More discussion is required, but it is simple either way. Next we turn to the computation of a reasonable S Corp salary.

Processing S Corp Payroll

We've discussed the theory behind calculating a reasonable salary. You are also aware of the benefits of an S corporation such as K-1 income being taxed at the income tax level only, and not subjected to payroll taxes such as Social Security, Medicare, unemployment or disability taxes. This is one of the reasons you are using an S Corp election.

But these benefits come with the price of having to pay a reasonable salary to the shareholders. Here are the nuts and bolts throughout the year-

As the theory of S Corp salary suggests, the amount to pay as a reasonable wage is dependent on you but also on the health of the business. Here's what we do at the Watson CPA Group-

▲ Review your qualifications and projected net business income for the subsequent year in December of the current year (yeah, it sounds crazy but we have to start somewhere). Several business owners routinely tell us the gross income for the year- no one cares. Quite literally. No one. We don't. The IRS doesn't. Your tax returns don't and you shouldn't either. We always deal in net business income after expenses but before shareholder salaries. If you start talking about gross income and trip the rambling breaker, we'll kindly listen and then ask you to rephrase your answer to only consider net business income after expenses.

▲ Establish a reasonable salary for the year based on several factors, and run Q1 and Q2 payroll at the end March and June respectively. At times we'll skip Q1 and even Q2 for seasonal corporations such as real estate agents. Again, a guess on net business income is fine at this point. We have a lot of time to adjust.

▲ In July and August, we re-review your qualifications and projected net business income prior to running Q3 payroll. We can re-assess the trajectory of salary and net business income, and make salary adjustments accordingly. Perhaps you aren't working as hard as you thought, and we should reduce your salary. Perhaps your distributions are higher than you thought, and a small increase is warranted. Perhaps everything is fine and changes are unnecessary.

▲ In November we tidy up any glaring discrepancies and run Q4 payroll. Remember, this is not an exact science, nor does it need to be. There aren't any needles to thread, or Brett Favre passes to make between three Bears on the way to Chmura in the end zone.

2017-2018 Calendar
For a complete 2017-2018 calendar of events for S corporations visit this link-

www.wcgurl.com/33

Good stuff! Really.

Additional S Corp Salary Considerations

Beyond the reasonable salary theories and jumping off points, there are some things to keep in mind as officer compensation is determined.

Competing Interests

As mentioned before, the 35-40% salary is just a jumping off point. There are several factors that need to be considered and they can be competing. For example, you might want a higher salary to add to your Social Security basis. The first bend point is about $56,000 and the second bend point is $94,000 which are indexed each year for inflation. The first bend point means that you are getting the most credit for the least amount of salary, and it decelerates after $56,000 and almost hits a cliff at $94,000. And as you recall, $128,700 is the maximum wage where Social Security is taxed (for 2018).

So a $56,000 salary might be a sweet spot for those wanting more Social Security basis or "credits." The Social Security's website calculators are shockingly helpful.

You also might want a higher salary to maximize your i401k plan or solo 401k plan. You can contribute up to $18,000 (plus $6,000 catchup if 50 or older). Therefore if you are 55 years old you might want your salary to be at least $24,000. There are instances where a $265,000 salary might be the best solution given age-based profit sharing and defined benefits pensions. These small business retirements plans are added to the traditional 401k plan to "turbocharge" them. It seems crazy to want to pay a $265,000 salary when one of the resounding themes is to have a low salary, but there could be significant tax savings. See Chapter 10 for more details or this link-

www.wcgurl.com/turbo

Another competing interest, or at least a factor, is health insurance and HSA contributions. If your self-employed health insurance is $15,000 per year, you must pay yourself at least $15,000 in salary to be able to fully deduct the premiums. Conversely, your health insurance premiums and health savings account (HSA) contributions get added to your W-2 as Box 1 Wages, and will contribute to your reasonable salary testing since they are lumped together to form Officer Compensation on Line 7 of your S Corp tax return. This was discussed in Chapter 3 and there are some examples of how this affects your salary below.

High, but not too high. Low, but not too low. Confused yet? Let's run through some examples.

S Corp Section 199A Deduction

We are going to walk you through a handful of examples comparing non-S Corp scenarios such as sole proprietorships, single-member LLCs (disregarded entity) and other pass-through environments to those same situations being taxed as an S corporation. We will demonstrate the benefits of the Section 199A deduction, and how it plays into the "should I elect S Corp?" question.

Aside from the usual suspects such as not earning more than $35,000 or operating in Tennessee or New York City, every scenario provides an additional benefit by electing S Corp status on top of the Section 199A deduction.

Section 199A Calculation

There are four variables you need to assign values to, a definition to consider, one tax bracket to memorize and two phase-out numbers to understand.

▲ Taxable Income- You need to determine the amount the entire household reports as taxable income, not just the business income. See Line 43 of your Form 1040 from 2017 to gain perspective of where you are. Write down 20% of this number.

▲ W-2 and Depreciable Assets- You need to calculate the total amount of W-2 wages the business pays including staff. Write down 50% of this number. You need to calculate the unadjusted basis (the value immediately after purchase before depreciation) of any depreciable assets the business owns. Write down 2.5% of this number (this becomes important for real estate investors).

▲ Qualified Business Income- Take your net business income after expenses, and write down 20% of this number.

▲ Specified Service Trade or Business- Does your business survive on the reputation or skill of its owner(s)? Are you an accountant, actuary, attorney, consultant, financial advisor, medical doctor, paid athlete or performing artist?

▲ End of 24%- The 24% tax bracket ends at $157,500 for single taxpayers and $315,000 for married taxpayers. The next tax bracket leaps to 32%. The 24% to 32% jump is clearly intentional and draws a line in the sand between middle class and upper middle class in our opinion. The Section 199A benefit might erode after the 24% marginal tax bracket depending on your situation.

▲ Phase Out- The income phase out period is $50,000 for single and $100,000 for married.

Section 199A Deduction Limits

We explained the decision tree elsewhere in our book, however we want to illustrate the iteration in a different way. The question becomes, "How do I figure out my Section 199A deduction?" Besides using expensive tax software and professional advice, you can consider this flowchart.

If your taxable income is in the 24% marginal tax bracket or less, stop. You are done and can select the lower of 20% of your qualified business income or 20% of your taxable income.

Assuming now that your taxable income is in the 32% marginal tax bracket or above, you must worm in some additional Section 199A limitations based on the following-

▲ Non Specified Service Business- You must now consider the Section 199A deduction based on W-2 wages or depreciable assets, and use the most restrictive of all Section 199A calculations. If you are in the income phase-out range (or the deduction limitation phase-in range, however you want to view the nomenclature), there is a linear, sliding scale of limitation based on W-2 wages and depreciable assets. In other words, the deeper into the phase-out range you are, the limiting effect of W-2 / assets becomes stronger. No need to hurt ourselves with the calculus at this point.

▲ Specified Service Business- You must now reduce your Section 199A deduction on a linear, sliding scale that reaches $0 as you move along the phase-out range (which is $50,000 for single taxpayers and $100,000 for married taxpayers). W-2 wages or depreciable assets come into play, but in a different way (near the end we provide an example of the phaseout). Your Section 199A simply ends after $207,500 (single) and $415,000 (married).

Section 199A Examples

We created a handful of examples on the follow pages with two intentions. One, to demonstrate how the Section 199A deduction is calculated and Two, to show that an S Corp remains a critical tax reduction vehicle. Brace yourself for nauseating spreadsheets that are only meaningful to the spreadsheet designer. We hope our commentary and explanations make sense, and that the logic of the step-by-step iteration becomes clear. We might be dreaming...

If you are reading this in a bound book, we have intentionally made it so the explanation is on the right side and the ridiculous explosion of numbers is on the left. If you are reading the PDF version you might have to print the pages or arrange for side-by-side viewing.

Section 199A Basic Comparisons

Joe Public earning $100,000 with and without additional taxable income.

ln		Vanilla		Other Income	
		No S	S Corp	No S	S Corp
1	Business Income	100,000	100,000	100,000	100,000
2	less W-2 Wages inc. SEHI, HSA, etc.	0	35,000	0	35,000
3	less Payroll Taxes	0	2,678	0	2,678
4	Net Business Income Section 199A	100,000	62,323	100,000	62,323
5	Adjustments to 1040 / NBI				
6	less Social Security Tax	5,726	0	5,726	0
7	less Medicare Tax	1,339	0	1,339	0
8	less SEHI, HSA, etc.	0	0	0	0
9	Other Taxable Income	0	0	60,000	60,000
10	Adjusted Gross Income*	92,935	97,323	152,935	157,323
11	Itemized / Std Deductions	24,000	24,000	24,000	24,000
12	Taxable Income Before Section 199A	68,935	73,323	128,935	133,323
13	Section 199A Net Biz Income	20,000	12,465	20,000	12,465
14	Section 199A W-2 Wage Limit	0	17,500	0	17,500
15	Section 199A Taxable Income Limit	13,787	14,665	25,787	26,665
16	Section 199A Benefit	13,787	12,465	20,000	12,465
17	Marginal Income Tax Rate	12%	12%	22%	22%
18	Income Tax Benefit from Section 199A	-1,654	-1,496	-4,400	-2,742
19	plus Self-Employment Tax	14,130	0	14,130	0
20	plus Tax on Line 12 Delta (above)	0	526	0	965
21	plus Payroll Tax	0	5,355	0	5,355
22	Net Tax After Section 199A Benefit	12,475	4,386	9,730	3,578
23	Net S Corp Benefit $		8,089		6,152

*includes the S Corp W-2

There are several notables, takeaways and explanations-

Assumptions are $100,000 in business income prior to $35,000 in reasonable officer compensation. Married taxpayer with $24,000 as a standard deduction (Line 11), with and without an additional $60,000 in taxable income (Line 9) such as a spouse or pension.

Notice how under an S corporation scenario (the second and fourth columns) the adjusted gross income (Line 10) is higher than a garden variety LLC or sole proprietorship. This is because issuing a W-2 is limiting the amount of Social Security and Medicare taxes paid, and subsequently deducted to ultimately determine taxable income. This has always been the case before and after the Tax Cuts & Jobs Act of 2017. No change.

Taxable Income Before Section 199A Deduction (Line 12) is used for illustration purposes only. The Section 199A deduction will eventually reduce adjusted gross income to arrive at taxable income for income tax purposes (a deduction from AGI). Our illustration is purely for the difference between a non-S Corp and an S Corp. It is not an income tax calculation.

Lines 13, 14 and 15 compute the various Section 199A calculations and will be used to determine any limitations. In this example, since taxable income is below $315,000 the only two limits are Section 199A based on business income (Line 13) and Section 199A based on taxable income (Line 15). The Section 199A based on W-2 limitation is not used.

Line 16 is the selected Section 199A benefit depending on the calculation and income limitation rules.

Notice that under a non-S Corp scenario the limiting factor (or as nerdy military types say, limfac) is Section 199A based on taxable income whereas the S corporation scenario the limiting factor is Section 199A based on net business income. This should make sense.

Line 18 is the income tax benefit based on the Section 199A calculation. Remember we are thinking in terms of taxes, so the Section 199A calculation must be put into an income tax savings context based on marginal tax rates.

Next, we add self-employment taxes to the non-S Corp (Line 19), and income taxes and payroll taxes to the S Corp (Lines 20 and 21) to arrive at the cash in your pocket difference by being taxed as an S corporation. In this example, an S corporation is saving $8,089 for no additional household income and $6,152 with $60,000 in additional income. Of this savings, the bulk remain because of self-employment tax savings.

Fun! Moving on...

Section 199A Health Insurance Comparison

Same situation as before, but with $10,000 in health insurance premiums (Line 8).

In		Vanilla		Health Insurance	
		No S	S Corp	No S	S Corp
1	Business Income	100,000	100,000	100,000	100,000
2	less W-2 Wages inc. SEHI, HSA, etc.	0	35,000	0	35,000
3	less Payroll Taxes	0	2,678	0	1,913
4	Net Business Income Section 199A	100,000	62,323	100,000	63,088
5	Adjustments to 1040 / NBI				
6	less Social Security Tax	5,726	0	5,726	0
7	less Medicare Tax	1,339	0	1,339	0
8	less SEHI, HSA, etc.	0	0	10,000	10,000
9	Other Taxable Income	0	0	0	0
10	Adjusted Gross Income*	92,935	97,323	82,935	88,088
11	Itemized / Std Deductions	24,000	24,000	24,000	24,000
12	Taxable Income Before Section 199A	68,935	73,323	58,935	64,088
13	Section 199A Net Biz Income	20,000	12,465	20,000	12,618
14	Section 199A W-2 Wage Limit	0	17,500	0	17,500
15	Section 199A Taxable Income Limit	13,787	14,665	11,787	12,818
16	Section 199A Benefit	13,787	12,465	11,787	12,618
17	Marginal Income Tax Rate	12%	12%	12%	12%
18	Income Tax Benefit from Section 199A	-1,654	-1,496	-1,414	-1,514
19	plus Self-Employment Tax	14,130	0	14,130	0
20	plus Tax on Line 12 Delta (above)	0	526	0	618
21	plus Payroll Tax	0	5,355	0	3,825
22	Net Tax After Section 199A Benefit	12,475	4,386	12,715	2,929
23	Net S Corp Benefit $		8,089		9,786

*includes the S Corp W-2

There are several notables, takeaways and explanations-

Assumptions are $100,000 in business income prior to $35,000 in reasonable officer compensation. Married taxpayer with $24,000 as a standard deduction (Line 11) and no additional taxable income.

$10,000 has been added as self-employed health insurance premiums. This could easily be $7,000 in health insurance premiums and $3,000 in health savings account (HSA) contributions too. Both are considered a taxable fringe benefit when paid by the company (but later deducted $1 for $1 on your individual tax return).

Note the decrease in payroll taxes on Line 3. This is because less wages are being subjected to Social Security and Medicare taxes when considering health insurance, HSA, etc. as a form of officer compensation (reasonable shareholder salary). As a result, Box 1 of the W-2 will show $35,000 but Box 3 and Box 5 will only show $25,000. Form 1120S, Line 7, Officer Compensation will also show $35,000.

In this example, having the S corporation pay for self-employed health insurance increases the savings by approximately $1,800. Recall the language from IRS Fact Sheet 2008-25-

> The health and accident insurance premiums paid on behalf of the greater than 2 percent S corporation shareholder-employee are deductible by the S corporation as fringe benefits and are reportable as wages for income tax withholding purposes on the shareholder-employee's Form W-2. They are not subject to Social Security or Medicare (FICA) or Unemployment (FUTA) taxes. Therefore, this additional compensation is included in Box 1 (Wages) of the Form W-2, Wage and Tax Statement, issued to the shareholder, but would not be included in Boxes 3 or 5 of Form W-2.

Note that the Section 199A benefit (Line 16) is higher with an S corporation versus a non-S Corp by leveraging the health insurance / HSA aspect of an S Corp.

Section 199A 200k Comparison

New day, different problem. This is an online retailer earning $200,000 in business income.

ln		Vanilla		Other Income	
		No S	S Corp	No S	S Corp
1	Business Income	200,000	200,000	200,000	200,000
2	less W-2 Wages inc. SEHI, HSA, etc.	0	70,000	0	70,000
3	less Payroll Taxes	0	5,355	0	5,355
4	Net Business Income Section 199A	200,000	124,645	200,000	124,645
5	Adjustments to 1040 / NBI				
6	less Social Security Tax	7,979	0	7,979	0
7	less Medicare Tax	2,678	0	2,678	0
8	less SEHI, HSA, etc.	0	0	0	0
9	Other Taxable Income	0	0	100,000	100,000
10	Adjusted Gross Income*	189,342	194,645	289,342	294,645
11	Itemized / Std Deductions	24,000	24,000	24,000	24,000
12	Taxable Income Before Section 199A	165,342	170,645	265,342	270,645
13	Section 199A Net Biz Income	40,000	24,929	40,000	24,929
14	Section 199A W-2 Wage Limit	0	35,000	0	35,000
15	Section 199A Taxable Income Limit	33,068	34,129	53,068	54,129
16	Section 199A Benefit	33,068	24,929	40,000	24,929
17	Marginal Income Tax Rate	24%	24%	24%	24%
18	Income Tax Benefit from Section 199A	-7,936	-5,983	-9,600	-5,983
19	plus Self-Employment Tax	21,315	0	21,315	0
20	plus Tax on Line 12 Delta (above)	0	1,273	0	1,273
21	plus Payroll Tax	0	10,710	0	10,710
22	Net Tax After Section 199A Benefit	13,379	6,000	11,715	6,000
23	Net S Corp Benefit $		**7,379**		**5,715**

*includes the S Corp W-2

There are several notables, takeaways and explanations-

Assumptions are $200,000 in business income prior to $70,000 in reasonable officer compensation. Married taxpayer with $24,000 as a standard deduction (Line 11), with and without an additional $100,000 in taxable income (Line 9) such as a spouse or pension.

Note the spreads in Section 199A deduction benefit on Line 16 and the subsequent income tax benefit from Section 199A on Line 18. This is an interesting example since the extra household income increases the Section 199A deduction significantly.

However, when self-employment taxes and payroll taxes are added back, there is still a material savings even when Social Security limits are reached under the non-S Corp scenario.

If this example had $10,000 in self-employed health insurance premiums the savings on Line 24 would be $9,483 without additional household income (Line 9) and $7,099 with additional household income of $100,000.

Section 199A 250k Comparison

Same online retailer (not a specified service business) showing single versus married.

		Single		Married	
In		No S	S Corp	No S	S Corp
1	Business Income	250,000	250,000	250,000	250,000
2	less W-2 Wages inc. SEHI, HSA, etc.	0	87,500	0	87,500
3	less Payroll Taxes	0	6,694	0	6,694
4	Net Business Income Section 199A	250,000	155,806	250,000	155,806
5	Adjustments to 1040 / NBI				
6	less Social Security Tax	7,979	0	7,979	0
7	less Medicare Tax	3,348	0	3,348	0
8	less SEHI, HSA, etc.	0	0	0	0
9	Other Taxable Income	0	0	0	0
10	Adjusted Gross Income*	238,673	243,306	238,673	243,306
11	Itemized / Std Deductions	12,000	12,000	24,000	24,000
12	Taxable Income Before Section 199A	226,673	231,306	214,673	219,306
13	Section 199A Net Biz Income	50,000	31,161	50,000	31,161
14	Section 199A W-2 Wage Limit	0	43,750	0	43,750
15	Section 199A Taxable Income Limit	45,335	46,261	42,935	43,861
16	Section 199A Benefit	0	31,161	42,935	31,161
17	Marginal Income Tax Rate	35%	35%	24%	24%
18	Income Tax Benefit from Section 199A	0	-10,906	-10,304	-7,479
19	plus Self-Employment Tax	22,654	0	22,654	0
20	plus Tax on Line 12 Delta (above)	0	1,622	0	1,112
21	plus Payroll Tax	0	13,388	0	13,388
22	Net Tax After Section 199A Benefit	22,654	4,103	12,350	7,021
23	Net S Corp Benefit $		18,551		5,329

*includes the S Corp W-2

There are several notables, takeaways and explanations-

Assumptions are $250,000 in business income prior to $87,500 in reasonable officer compensation. Itemized deductions are $12,000 as a single taxpayer and $24,000 as a married taxpayer.

Note the spreads in Section 199A deduction benefit on Line 16 and the subsequent income tax benefit on Line 18. In the scenario where the taxpayer is single, he or she is phased out of Section 199A deduction because of income and subsequent W-2 limitations (Line 14).

The example is used to show the limitations of Section 199A due to income based on marital status. However, note that by electing S Corp tax status the Section 199A benefit is identical (Line 16). The difference then becomes the income tax benefit of this deduction which is a factor of marginal tax rates (Line 17).

For couples who are not married, there might be a reason to be legally married without altering your relationship definition just to grab some additional Section 199A benefit.

Section 199A Specified Service Business Comparison Part 1
Same online retailer but compared to an attorney (specified service business). Yuck!

ln		Retailer No S	Retailer S Corp	Attorney No S	Attorney S Corp
1	Business Income	250,000	250,000	250,000	250,000
2	less W-2 Wages inc. SEHI, HSA, etc.	0	87,500	0	87,500
3	less Payroll Taxes	0	6,694	0	6,694
4	Net Business Income Section 199A	250,000	155,806	250,000	155,806
5	Adjustments to 1040 / NBI				
6	less Social Security Tax	7,979	0	7,979	0
7	less Medicare Tax	3,348	0	3,348	0
8	less SEHI, HSA, etc.	0	0	0	0
9	Other Taxable Income	0	0	0	0
10	Adjusted Gross Income*	238,673	243,306	238,673	243,306
11	Itemized / Std Deductions	12,000	12,000	12,000	12,000
12	Taxable Income Before Section 199A	226,673	231,306	226,673	231,306
13	Section 199A Net Biz Income	50,000	31,161	50,000	31,161
14	Section 199A W-2 Wage Limit	0	43,750	0	43,750
15	Section 199A Taxable Income Limit	45,335	46,261	45,335	46,261
16	Section 199A Benefit	0	31,161	0	0
17	Marginal Income Tax Rate	35%	35%	35%	35%
18	Income Tax Benefit from Section 199A	0	-10,906	0	0
19	plus Self-Employment Tax	22,654	0	22,654	0
20	plus Tax on Line 12 Delta (above)	0	1,622	0	1,622
21	plus Payroll Tax	0	13,388	0	13,388
22	Net Tax After Section 199A Benefit	22,654	4,103	22,654	15,009
23	Net S Corp Benefit $		18,551		7,645

*includes the S Corp W-2

There are several notables, takeaways and explanations-

Assumptions are $250,000 in business income prior to $87,500 in reasonable officer compensation. Itemized deductions of $12,000 and both taxpayers are single. Same as previous example, but now we are comparing a non-specified service business (online retailer) to a specified service business (attorney).

Observe the differences in Line 16. Recall the Section 199A decision tree from earlier-

▲   If taxable income is less than $157,500 (single) / $315,000 (married) then the 20% deduction for your pass-thru entity is fully available.

▲   If taxable income is greater than $157,500 / $315,000 but less than $207,500 / $415,000 then a partial deduction is available. The phase-in of the limit is linear (more explanation later).

▲   If taxable income is greater than $207,500 / $415,000 then you are hosed. Sorry.

The attorney should absolutely be an S corporation and enjoy the $7,645 in tax savings. He or she simply won't be enjoying the $18,551 savings of the online retailer. Surely the online retailer should be sued by the attorney to help equalize the balance of tax benefits and preserve the natural order.

Remember that if a specified service trade or business has taxable income that is equal to or less than $157,500 for single taxpayers and $315,000 for married taxpayers, there is no phase-in of the limitations (or Section 199A phasout). Said in another way, if the online retailer and the attorney both earned $150,000 from their respective crafts, the Section 199A savings would be identical.

Let's do one more! Drool...

Section 199A Specified Service Business Comparison Part 2

Big shot surgeon compared to the lowly goat herder (non-specified service trade).

In		Surgeon		Goat Herder	
		No S	S Corp	No S	S Corp
1	Business Income	600,000	600,000	600,000	600,000
2	less W-2 Wages inc. SEHI, HSA, etc.	0	210,000	0	210,000
3	less Payroll Taxes	0	11,024	0	11,024
4	Net Business Income Section 199A	600,000	378,976	600,000	378,976
5	Adjustments to 1040 / NBI				
6	less Social Security Tax	7,979	0	7,979	0
7	less Medicare Tax	8,034	0	8,034	0
8	less SEHI, HSA, etc.	0	0	0	0
9	Other Taxable Income	0	0	0	0
10	Adjusted Gross Income*	583,986	588,976	583,986	588,976
11	Itemized / Std Deductions	50,000	50,000	50,000	50,000
12	Taxable Income Before Section 199A	533,986	538,976	533,986	538,976
13	Section 199A Net Biz Income	120,000	75,795	120,000	75,795
14	Section 199A W-2 Wage Limit	0	105,000	0	105,000
15	Section 199A Taxable Income Limit	106,797	107,795	106,797	107,795
16	Section 199A Benefit	0	0	0	75,795
17	Marginal Income Tax Rate	37%	37%	37%	37%
18	Income Tax Benefit from Section 199A	0	0	0	-28,044
19	plus Self-Employment Tax	32,028	0	32,028	0
20	plus Tax on Line 12 Delta (above)	0	1,846	0	1,846
21	plus Payroll Tax	0	22,049	0	22,049
22	Net Tax After Section 199A Benefit	32,028	23,895	32,028	-4,149
23	Net S Corp Benefit $		8,133		36,177

*includes the S Corp W-2

There are several notables, takeaways and explanations-

Well, that's a lie. There are only two. First, specified service trades or businesses got hosed in the Section 199A calculation. Being a goat herder raking in $600,000 as compared to a surgeon gets a $36,000 bump in tax benefit. If you give it careful consideration, how are these two businesses different? While we are being a bit facetious here, at the same time two business owners are experiencing different tax worlds based on titles. The goat herder could be operating with a staff and not relying his or her reputation or skill.

Second takeaway, although specified service industries such as accountants, doctors, attorneys, etc., are not enjoying the Section 199A deduction benefit, it still pays to be an S corporation. There is still a savings of $8,133 by being an S Corp for the big shot surgeon. You have an obligation as a citizen to reduce your taxes to the minimum allowed.

Recall the definition of specified service business or trade-

▲ Traditional service professions such as doctors, attorneys, accountants, actuaries and consultants.

▲ Performing artists who perform on stage or in a studio.

▲ Paid athletes.

▲ Anyone who works in the financial services or brokerage industry.

▲ And now the hammer… "any trade or business where the principal asset is the reputation or skill" of the owner. Why didn't they just start with this since everything else would have been moot? Oh well…

Interestingly, removed from the traditional service profession are engineers and architects. But an engineer operating a business based on his or her reputation or skill is still a specified service trade.

Section 199A Phaseout

We haven't had a chance to get this crude drawing to our graphic designer who can pretty it up, so please bear with us. We might lose our minds the next time Congress acts over the holidays and ruins our eggnog. At least Wisconsin won the Orange Bowl which is nice. How does the Section 199A phaseout work?

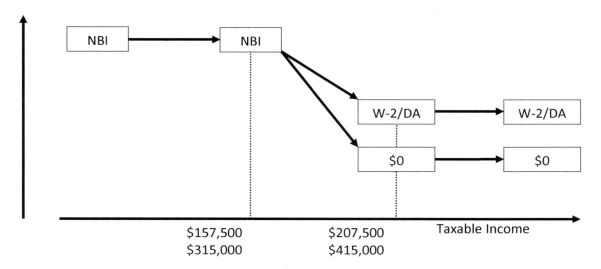

NBI is short for Net Business Income, and W-2/DA is the limit based on the greater of 50% of W-2 wages paid, or 25% of W-2 wages paid plus 2.5% of unadjusted basis for depreciable assets. The dashed arrow is a specified service trade or business. The Y axis is the Section 199A limit. The Section 199A phaseout should be viewed as where you are going to "end up." Quick example, step by step-

▲ Let's say your taxable income is $340,000 which is exactly 25% over the $315,000 income trigger when compared to $415,000. Again, the trigger of the phaseout is based on taxable income and not just net business income.

▲ We determine your Section 199A upper limit based on net business income, with an adjustment for specific service trades or businesses.

▲ We next determine your Section 199A lower limit based on W-2 / depreciable asset calculation from above, with a similar adjustment for service people.

▲ Next, we take the difference, multiply it by the percentage of taxable income that exceeds the trigger (in this example, 25%) and reduce the Section 199A deduction based on net business income by this amount. Huh? A table is coming up.

Here is table that attempts to summarize what the heck we are talking about.

Taxable Income	340,000
Phaseout Trigger	315,000
Amount That Exceeds	25,000
Phaseout Range	100,000
Percentage of Phaseout	25%

Since the taxable income trigger of $315,000 is exceeded by $25,000 and the phaseout range is $100,000 for married taxpayers, we are 25% into the phaseout range. We now have to split these up between non-service and service.

This gets really funky really fast. For the non-service people, the math is straightforward. For the specific service trade or business, we need to determine how much of the remaining phaseout range is available. In this case, 25% of the phaseout range is "used up" leaving 75% remaining.

	Non-Service	Service
Net Business Income	300,000	225,000
Section 199A on NBI	60,000	45,000
W-2 Wages Paid	100,000	75,000
Section 199A on W-2	50,000	37,500

Therefore, 75% of the NBI of $300,000 is $225,000. 75% of the W-2 wages paid of $100,000 is $75,000. These remaining amounts are the basis for the original Section 199A calculations of 20% of net business income, or $45,000 above... and 50% of W-2 wages paid, or $37,500 above. This creates an "upper limit" and a "lower limit" which further creates the difference to apply the phaseout range percentage (in this example, 25%).

	Non-Service	Service
Section 199A Upper Limit	60,000	45,000

Section 199A Lower Limit	50,000	37,500
Difference	10,000	7,500

Finally, we choose the greater of the Section 199A based on net business income and the Section 199A based on W-2 wages paid. In our example, $60,000 and $45,000 respectively. This is then reduced by the percentage of phaseout range multiplied against the difference. In this example, 25% of $10,000 and 25% of $7,500 for the specified service business.

This summarizes the Section 199A reduction and ultimate deduction.

	Non-Service	**Service**
Section 199A on NBI	60,000	45,000
Section 199A Reduction	2,500	1,875
Section 199A Deduction	57,500	43,125

This should make sense. Another way to look at this- let's say your taxable income was exactly $415,000. You would be 100% into the phaseout range, so your Section 199A deduction would be reduced by $10,000 (100% of the difference of $10,000) for a non-service trade or business. This would also magically equal the Section 199A limit set by 50% of your W-2 wages paid or $50,000.

Extending this logic would suggest that a specified service trade or business who has $415,000 in taxable income would have his or her Section 199A deduction reduced by 100% since the remaining amount of the phaseout range is 0%.

Section 199A Recap

Hopefully you are still with us and not in the fetal position sucking your thumb. To hammer these points home, the Section 199A won't help everyone and the S corporation still has some shine (although perhaps less in some situations) as an overall tax reduction mechanism.

Here is a summary of the previous examples-

Business	Status*	Biz Income	Other Income	Health Ins.	199A Benefit	S Corp Savings
Consultant	Married	100,000			1,496	8,089
Consultant	Married	100,000	60,000		2,742	6,152
Consultant	Married	100,000			1,496	7,518
Consultant	Married	100,000		10,000	1,514	9,786
Retailer	Married	200,000			5,983	7,379
Retailer	Married	200,000	100,000		5,983	5,715
Retailer	Single	250,000			10,906	18,551
Retailer	Married	250,000			7,479	5,329
Retailer	Single	250,000			10,906	18,551
Attorney	Single	250,000			0	7,645
Surgeon	Single	600,000			0	8,133
Goat Herder	Single	600,000			28,044	36,177

Missing Guidance for Schedule C

There are some things we are unsure about. One example is 401k or defined benefits contribution. This is typically an adjustment on Form 1040 separate from Schedule C. Will these amounts get filtered back into the Section 199A calculation when basing it on Schedule C net business income? Probably... since this would be a double dip. Same with self-employment taxes and health insurance We'll have to wait and see on handling the C.

Missing Guidance for Mixed Income Sources

What happens if big shot surgeon owns a gaggle of rentals which throws off $100,000 in net business income? Assume that he or she is phased out of the Section 199A deduction based on the specified service trade of being a doctor. Can he or she still get the Section 199A deduction based on the rental income? We would like to think so, but we'll have to wait and see.

Thank you for hanging in there!

Revoke S Corp

The hot question since the passage of the Tax Cuts & Jobs Act of 2017 and Section 199A is, "Should I revoke S Corp status and go to C Corp?" The answer is No.

Quick Numbers-

S Corp Income	100,000	200,000	300,000
Salary	40,000	80,000	120,000
Payroll Tax	6,120	12,240	18,360
Income Tax	6,980	24,150	44,266
Total Tax S Corp	13,100	36,390	62,626
C Corp Income	100,000	200,000	300,000
C Corp Tax	21,000	42,000	63,000
Dividends	79,000	158,000	237,000
Dividend Tax	0	23,700	44,556
Total C Corp Tax	21,000	65,700	107,556
S Tax Rate	13.1%	18.2%	20.9%
C Tax Rate	21.0%	32.9%	35.9%
Delta	7.9%	14.7%	15.0%

Assumptions included Section 199A deduction for the S corporation's shareholder plus $24,000 in standard deduction, in addition to the 3.8% surtax on top of the 15% capital gains tax rate for the $300,000 column. As you can see, a C Corp does not make sense after you add in capital gains tax on the dividends. This in turn makes sense- the lawmakers didn't set out to kill S corporations. They set out to give every business owner a tax break. Geez... half of Congress (535 doesn't divide evenly, we get it) probably run S corporations on the side.

So, please pump the brakes on the "I wanna dump my S Corp for the magical tax arbitrage offered by a C Corp" nonsense.

Multiple Shareholders Payroll Split

Many S corporations have multiple shareholders, and several are husband and wife teams. In these cases, we determine a starting point as a collective and then massage from there. For example, using our example above with the $42,000 salary. Perhaps one spouse should be paid $30,000 and the other spouse be paid $12,000 commensurate to his and / or her individual worth to the company. In other words, don't double the salary once you determine your starting point because you have two shareholders. The starting point is for all aggregated shareholders, and from there you can divvy it up, massage it, increase it, etc.

Remember, this would only be for active shareholders. Please recall from Chapter 1 that you could have your spouse be an inactive investor in your S corporation at 20% and you would remain at 80%. As we've mentioned previously, one of the reasonable salary tests is the relationship between salary and shareholder distributions. Therefore, if you own 80% of a business taxed as an S corporation, you are receiving 80% of the distributions. Subsequently, your salary could be possibly reduced (but your salary is still ultimately dependent on you and your value to the company).

Here is a table assuming a 35% jumping off point for salary with a column at 100% ownership and 80% ownership to further explain-

Income	Salary at 100%	Salary at 80%	Payroll Tax Savings
30,000	10,500	8,400	321
50,000	17,500	14,000	536
75,000	26,250	21,000	803
100,000	35,000	28,000	1,071
150,000	52,500	42,000	1,607
200,000	70,000	56,000	2,142

To reiterate, the $100,000 line above would 100,000 x 80% x 35% = 28,000 resulting in a payroll tax savings of $1,071. Note that is a savings of payroll taxes, and not income taxes since the 80% and the 20% would flow presumably onto a jointly filed individual tax return.

Estimated Tax Payments, Withholdings Issues

Estimated tax payments change as well when you have an S Corp, especially the first year. Generally speaking, you are required to pay at least 100% of your prior year tax liability or 90% of your current year tax liability whichever is lower. If you earn over $150,000, you must pay 110% of your current year tax liability. How do you keep that straight?

Here is some more Watson CPA Group elegance- we calculate and pay your quarterly estimated payments through payroll. No more writing separate checks and tracking due dates. We do this by manually entering your Federal and State withholdings accordingly to reflect the tax liability for your W-2 income and your K-1 income. Beauty!

For example, we will use a net business income before shareholder salaries $150,000 and a reasonable salary of $54,000. We would also review your previous tax returns, determine the amount of income taxes you paid and deduct other withholding sources (spouse W-2, pension payments, etc.).

Here is a summary from our internal work paper-

Taxable Income	184,718
Tax Calculation	38,606
Less Other Withholding Sources	-8,000
Tax Deficit	30,606
Less W-2 From S Corp	-31,000
Less Estimated Tax Payments	0
April Tax Obligation (Federal)	**-374**

What the heck are we showing you here? The taxable income is making some assumptions such as spousal income, itemized deductions, exemptions, etc. The $184,718 is just a number. Please accept as is.

The tax related to this income is $38,606 according to a simple tax table and your spouse has withheld $8,000 on his or her W-2. The resulting deficit in this example is $30,606. If we simply entered $54,000 into the payroll system and let the computer figure out the withholdings it might come up with $7,000ish. This would be a tax surprise in April since you would owe $23,000ish. Yuck. Bad news is OK. Surprises are bad.

Therefore we increase your W-2 withholdings to account for your K-1 income, but this only fixes your income. It doesn't address the possible increased marginal tax rate when three sources of income (your W-2, your K-1 and your spouse's W-2) are combined. Individually each source of income is withholding correctly, but when aggregated it blows up.

Think of it this way- you make $150,000 and your spouse makes $60,000. When your spouse's employer computes tax withholdings, the payroll system does not understand that the household income is $210,000. It can only make basic assumptions. In this disparity, even if the $60,000 spouse claims 0 exemptions on a W-4, the taxes withheld will not be enough when combined with the $150,000.

As a result, we compute your household tax liability and subtract external withholding sources to determine the amount of tax to be withheld from your S Corp payroll. No more estimated payments (usually). No more underpayment penalties. This is a nice way of reducing some chores in your world.

Unemployment and Workers Compensation

We addressed these issues in Chapter 3. Please review. Here is a summary of the topics-

▲ FUTA and SUTA- unemployment tax. Unavoidable. You might be able to opt out, and as the Minnesota example in Chapter 3 illustrates, there is a tax savings.

▲ SDI- state disability insurance. Might be able to opt out for single-owner corporate officers such as California and New York.

▲ Workers Compensation Insurance- has nothing to do with unemployment or state disability insurance, and is not interchangeable with those terms. This is purely insurance coverage for on the job injuries and is provided by private insurance such as State Farm, All State, Farmers, etc. Ask your local insurance agent if you can opt out. Typically you can since you don't plan no suing yourself for a paper cut or a rogue paperclip stabbing.

Cash Needs, The $0 Paycheck

If you use the Watson CPA Group for processing your S corporation payroll, we work with you to determine the reasonable shareholder salary. About 3-4 weeks prior to the due date, we provide a "cash needs" email and a corresponding text message. As mentioned earlier, we have a calendar of events for S corporations-

www.wcgurl.com/33

Here is a sample email template that we used for Q4 payroll events (no need to read too carefully)-

--

Cash Summary-

Cash for Income Taxes	$6,200
Cash for Payroll Taxes	$2,000
Total Cash Needs	$8,200
Funds Drafted On	Thursday, December 28

This is based on the following assumptions-

Net Biz Income	$150,000 (after expenses before salaries)
Annual Salary	$50,000
Q4 Salary	$12,500 (which might not be evenly split up depending on previous quarters)
Health Insurance Premiums	$10,000 (for all of 2017, total)
Employer HSA Contributions	$0 (for all of 2017, total)

Salary is subjected to social security and medicare taxes. However, health insurance and HSA contributions (if paid by the company) will be added to this salary for total Officer Compensation (to be used for reasonable salary testing) but is not subjected to social security or medicare taxes.

Employee (you) 401k Deferral	$18,000 pre-tax (for all of 2017, total)
Employer (company) 401k	$5,000 pre-tax (for all of 2017, total, must be pre-tax)
IRA Contribution	$0 pre-tax (for all of 2017, total)

*** Please confirm the health insurance, HSA and 401k numbers ***

Since self-employed health insurance premiums, health savings account (HSA) and 401k numbers affect your W-2, we must have these numbers be confirmed by you. We cannot stress the mini-disaster that is created if we have to change these numbers after the Q4 payroll run.

Quarterly estimated cash requirement of $8,200 which includes-

1. Payroll taxes (Social Security, Medicare and Unemployment)
2. Federal income taxes, and
3. Any applicable state income taxes

This is based in part on last year's tax returns and 2017 projections. Of this amount, payroll taxes are $2,000 and represent the minimum amount of cash that is needed to run payroll each quarter- if you authorize an amount less than $8,200, the difference must be paid thru estimated tax payments, or due on your individual income tax returns plus underpayment penalties.

Please do not freak out. If none of these numbers make sense, please contact us. We will walk you through it. Your cell coverage is spotty on the ledge so contact us right away if this does not compute.

Cash of $8,200 will be drawn on or about Thursday, December 28 and sent to the IRS (and state if applicable). At this time, additional estimated tax payments are NOT necessary since all tax obligations are being handled through payroll. This might change as your circumstances change.

Your W-2 withholdings have been grossed up to plan for your K-1 income and associated income taxes by using your previous tax returns coupled with your projected business income. This is always our goal- compartmentalize your business and help you budget for the income tax consequence throughout the year. If you want more or less taxes withheld, please let us know. If you have major life events such as new home, new baby, marriage, divorce, changes in income, etc., please let us know so we can accommodate. The exact amounts will be on several payroll reports including your paystub which will be uploaded to your client portal shortly after payroll is completed.

We are computing an overall 2017 IRS income tax liability of $13,200. This is the total federal income taxes that will be due LESS estimated tax payments and withholdings, including any additional sources of income and withholdings (such as a spouse). Your cash needs above will commonly exceed this amount- this is due to payroll taxes (social security, medicare, etc.) and state taxes. We based this income tax estimate on a taxable income projection, and use your exemptions and deductions from your 2016 tax returns. Please review our S Corp calendar for other important dates-

www.watsoncpagroup.com/Schedule.pdf

If you have not told us about other household income such as a spouse's W-2 income or pensions, we are shooting in the dark in terms of computing your overall tax liability. Please provide us with paystubs or other documentation. Important!

Our goal is to put you into a tax neutral position for April.

Cash is required to be in your banking account on Thursday, December 28. Bank drafts for tax payments will take 1-2 days to complete. If the bank draft for tax payments does not appear within 72 hours , please notify us immediately.

If you are tight on cash, we understand- we can always reduce the cash needs to a lower number. Income taxes can be delayed until your personal tax return but you will incur underpayment penalties.

Your 2017 overall net business income after expenses, SEP/401k, etc. and before shareholder salaries are paid is projected to be $150,000.

Your S Corp is saving you over $10,200 in taxes. Yay!

--

You might have skimmed through all that gibberish. Here are some thoughts to ponder-

▲ We will provide cash needs well in advance of running payroll.

▲ We are flexible with the cash needs by either skipping a quarterly payroll or by reducing the amount of income tax withheld (we cannot go below the payroll taxes). Any deficiency between the cash needed and the cash you have will be flushed out on your individual tax returns, and become a tax due.

▲ A one-time deduction in the amount of the net check is made back to the company to reduce cash needs. In other words, if you had a $10,000 gross check that would have netted a $4,000 take home paycheck (after increasing your withholdings), we would deduct the $4,000 to create a net $0 check. You would only need about $6,000 on hand in cash versus $10,000. Why transfer money into your business checking account just to transfer it back?

Reclassify Shareholder Distributions

Since payroll is usually processed at the end of the quarter, at times we need to re-classify prior shareholder distributions as shareholder wages (and perhaps employee reimbursements).

Here is a sample journal entry for an S Corp shareholder who took out $20,000 as a shareholder distribution, but later re-categorized the transaction as distributions, wages and reimbursements.

	DR	CR
Shareholder Distributions		8,950
Shareholder Wage Expense	7,000	
Employee Reimbursements	1,950	
Totals	8,950	8,950

When the original distribution took place, there was a debit to Shareholder Distributions for $20,000 and a credit to Cash for the same. We are simply reducing the $20,000 by $8,950 so the actual distribution reflects $20,000 less $8,950 or $11,050.

In other words, Shareholder Distributions was a negative $20,000 in the equity section of your balance sheet. After increasing Shareholder Wage Expense by $7,000 and Employee Reimbursements by $1,950, net business income is reduced by $8,950. This naturally reduces equity by the same therefore Shareholder Distributions must be reduced so equity remains unchanged. No adjustment is made to Cash. Make sense? Don't worry… we can provide these journal entries as necessary. We are just geeking out on our own silly accounting fun. If we were putting this transaction into the books together from the start, it would look this starting with the shareholder distribution-

	DR	CR
Shareholder Distributions	11,050	
Cash		11,050
Totals	11,050	11,050

Then the Shareholder Wage Expense and Employee Reimbursements-

	DR	CR
Shareholder Wage Expense	7,000	
Employee Reimbursements	1,950	
Cash		8,950
Totals	8,950	8,950

Everything would end up in the same spot- Shareholder Distributions at $11,050, Owner Wage Expense at $7,000 and Employee Reimbursements at $1,950. Cash spent would be $20,000. The only difference is the first example is a correcting or reversing entry.

This is a slight over-simplification since there would also be a Payroll Tax Expense entry for the company's portion of Social Security, Medicare, Unemployment, etc. but you get the idea.

Comingling of Money
We've mentioned this previously, and we'll do it again here. Rule #1- Please get a separate checking account for your business, preferably with the same bank as your personal checking account so transfers (shareholder distributions) are easy. Rule #2- Do not pay for personal expenses or any mixed-use expense with business funds.

This is bad for several reasons- the IRS hates it. It erodes the corporate veil which is already dangerously thin since you are a closely held corporation. Lastly, if you need to re-construct your financials because of a QuickBooks disaster or some other disaster, having your business transactions compartmentalized within a bank account makes life better. All money coming in is income. All money going out is an expense or a distribution.

Read Rule #2 again. It is imperative to keep an arms-length perspective on you, the employee, and relationship with the S corporation. If you worked for Google or Ford, you wouldn't be able to get the business to buy your groceries or pay your mortgage directly. Same thing with your business. Please refer to Chapter 8 – Tax Deductions, Fringe Benefits for a nice table.

Other Tricks of the Trade with S Corps
The big theme with S Corps is payroll for shareholders, and what constitutes a reasonable salary. Here are some tricks that you can consider to help reduce, lower or avoid self-employment tax, or Social Security and Medicare tax burdens-

A Shareholder Who Has Other W-2 Income

If you have other W-2 income then you are that much closer to max'ing out your Social Security contributions. This in itself is not a trick. But, if you have a business partner who doesn't have W-2 income, then you can lop side the salary to the shareholder who does. This is especially helpful with a husband and wife team since office politics won't get in the way. For example, the wife has another job and earns $100,000. Her S Corp salary may be much higher than the husband's since she is closer to the Social Security cap (which is $128,700 for 2018).

Huh? Let's say the S corporation had to pay out $70,000 in shareholder wages. The employer portion of Social Security and Medicare taxes are a sunk cost regardless of who is paid. However, if the spouse with outside income is paid and he or she exceeds the Social Security limit for the employee's portion of Social Security taxes, that overage is returned to the taxpayer.

Of course salaries must be commensurate with each shareholder's skill level, hours worked, value to the business, etc. but there is some grey area to work with.

Husband and Wife Team with High Income

Let's say a husband and wife team work in the IT field, and combined they earn $400,000. The S Corp could have just one shareholder, let's say the wife, and the husband is merely a volunteer employee. The wife's salary could be higher than the husband's since she is running the business and is the only shareholder. She would reach the Social Security cap much sooner, but this only works if the husband's salary can remain below the cap. Again, salaries must be commensurate for the work performed. A cool thing about making the wife the sole shareholder is that the company could gain benefits from being minority owned or considered "disadvantaged" although those benefits are becoming more rare.

Be mindful of the possible reduction in future Social Security benefits from a smaller salary. The first bend point is around $56,000. And a spouse can either take half of the other spouse's benefit or his or her own whichever is higher. These calculations get exotic right quick, and more consultation and financial planning is usually necessary.

Put Your Kids on the Payroll

You can also reduce the company's overall profits by paying your children to work at the office and paying them a wage. You already have to perform payroll, so you can simply add them to the list. See Chapter 8 – Tax Deductions, Fringe Benefits for expanded information about putting your kids on the payroll.

Income Splitting as Gift

You can make someone in a lower tax bracket a shareholder in your S Corp to give them money. For example, you are taking care of your Mom and need to give her $10,000 each year to help with expenses. You would need to earn $13,000 or more just to be able to write a check for $10,000. However, if your Mom is in a lower tax bracket, as a shareholder she would pay fewer taxes to pocket the $10,000. And when your Mom eventually passes, her ownership can transfer back to you.

Yes, you could justify not paying Mom a reasonable salary since she is not performing any work for the company. She is simply an investor. However, just like paying your children to work for you, there might be a tax savings by having Mom work- her marginal tax rate could be dramatically lower than yours. Good luck with the "Hey Mom. Want a job?" conversation. What goes around comes around.

Just remember, putting family members on payroll is heavily scrutinized. Make sure the basics such as job descriptions, pay rates, time records, etc. are all in very good order. Memories fade, so document it today!

Health Insurance

Health insurance premiums paid by the company on behalf of a 2% or greater shareholder are reported as wages in Box 1 on your W-2, and therefore increase your salary. This increase is artificial however since as 2% or greater shareholder you are considered self-employed for the deduction of health insurance premiums. So your salary shows more which helps pass the reasonable test yet you receive a neutralizing deduction. As you recall, this deduction is a direct reduction in gross income as your individual tax return works towards an adjusted gross income figure (what we tax people call above-the-line deduction- the best kind since there aren't any thresholds or limits). Here is a summary.

W-2, Box 3 and 5	50,000
Health Insurance	10,000
W-2, Box 1	60,000
Wages, Line 7, Form 1040	60,000
Health Insurance Deduction, Line 29, Form 1040	-10,000
Adjusted Gross Income, Line 37, form 1040	50,000

Don't forget about HSAs. An HSA is a great way to save taxes today on money you need when you retire. It is a foregone conclusion that when you get older you'll need more medical attention. The benefit of an HSA over a 401k plan or an IRA is that you can take money out of an HSA prior to 59.5 years old for medical bills, but with a 401k plan or an IRA you would be penalized.

Remember that health insurance premiums and HSA contributions for 2% or greater shareholders are only reported in Box 1 of your W-2, and therefore not subjected to Social Security and Medicare taxes (Box 3 and Box 5 respectively).

Double the Retirement

Let's say you have $36,000 to blow on retirement savings and you are married. If only one person draws a salary, he or she can only contribute $18,000. But if a married couple pays an $18,000 salary to each person, then the total retirement contribution can be $36,000 without having to increase salaries to allow for a larger company contribution. More details in Chapter 10 on Small Business Retirement Planning.

Operating Your S Corp Recap

This chapter about operating your S corporation focuses mainly on payroll, and the reasonable S Corp salary determination. Here is a brief recap of some of the key points-

▲ Having an S corporation is very similar to an LLC in terms of hassles and headaches. If you think having an LLC is not a big deal, having an S corporation will be the same. If you consider having an LLC to be a pain in the butt, having an S corporation isn't going to make it easier.

▲ The savings can be huge. Most S Corps earning about $150,000 will see about $9,500 to $10,000 in savings. For kicks, please review Line 57 of your individual tax return and imagine reducing it by 60 to 65%.

▲ The break-even where an S Corp election makes sense is about $35,000 in net business income after expenses. This is determined by dividing the annual cost of our S Corp package ($2,940) by 8% to 10% in average savings.

Don't forget to review Chapter 8 on Tax Deductions and Fringe Benefits. Several business owners want to know which deductions they can and cannot take- we've included those lists in Chapter 8, but we've also listed a bunch of expenses that might become tax deductions if you position yourself carefully. Recall that the trick is to find ways to deduct money that is already budgeted to leave your person like trips to Vegas and fancy sports cars.

American Jobs and Closing Tax Loopholes Act of 2010 (HR 4213)

Here is some chin-scratching fodder for your day. Back in 2010, the House created a bill that would disqualify small professional service S corporations (attorneys, doctors, consultants, etc.) from benefiting from the S Corp "loophole." Thankfully the Senate saw this as discrimination since non-professional service businesses (construction, retailers, manufacturers, etc.) would still benefit from the "loophole." The bill was rejected naturally.

Tax Cuts & Jobs Act of 2017

It appears specified service trades or businesses dodged another bullet. There was chatter similar to 2010 but eventually it gave way. Yes, some of the tax breaks disappear for attorneys, doctors, accountants and anyone else whose reputation or skill is the material income producing factor. However, it could have been way worse. Instead the crummy laws of 2017 and earlier are simply the high-water mark, and if you are phased out of the Section 199A deduction you are no worse off. Yeah, it doesn't make you feel any better.

Chapter 7
Accountable Plan

Pull Money Out, Accountable Plan

One of the goals of any business owner is to be able to pull money out of the company without creating a taxable event. There are four big ways to accomplish this-

▲ Reimbursements for Out of Pockets Business Expenses (Accountable Plan)

▲ Fund Your Retirement Account

▲ Reimbursements for Self-Employed Health Insurance Premiums and HSA Contributions

▲ Paying for an Employee's Education (kind of rare)

We encourage businesses to create an Accountable Plan which allows employees to turn in expense reports for home office use, mileage, cell phone, internet, meals and travel. All these expenses have one thing in common- they are mixed used, both personally and business. Mixed-use expenses should be paid by the employee and later reimbursed. Conversely, anything that is 100% business use should be paid directly by the business. The same thing, but in bullet form-

▲ 100% business- Paid by the business, from the business checking account.

▲ 100% personal- Paid by you, from your personal checking account.

▲ Mixed- Paid by you, and reimbursed by the company for the business portion.

Of course if you are reaping some huge cash back or travel deals with your personal credit card, then by all means charge the 100% business use items to your personal card and run those expenses through an Accountable Plan. Quick warning- the IRS and credit card companies are butting heads over the rebate programs. It is an ascension of wealth and technically taxable income. Whoa! Yup, and the IRS would like 1099s to be issued to show the income. This will be battled for the next decade for sure.

Remember that as an S corporation owner, you are both a shareholder and an employee. Therefore, when you are being reimbursed you are being reimbursed as an employee and not as a shareholder.

The following table shows a quick comparison between reimbursing yourself through an Accountable Plan (**Scenario 1**) and deducting the expenses on your individual tax return on Form 2106 (**Scenario 2**). Form 2106 remains available for 2017 tax returns (but not 2018).

	Accountable Plan	No Plan
	Scenario 1	Scenario 2
Net Profits	100,000	100,000
less Home Office	1,500	
less Cell Phone	1,000	
less Internet	250	
less Mileage	6,000	
less Meals*	3,000	
Total Reimbursements	11,750	
less Employer Social Security, Medicare	2,080	2,640
Net Ordinary Business Income	74,420	97,360
Possible Reasonable Salary at 35%	26,000	33,000
Social Security, Medicare Tax @ 15.3%	**3,978**	**5,049**
Total Savings (per year!)	**1,071**	

* Meals and entertainment pose an interesting effect. The business profits on the books take the full deduction, but the business can only take a 50% deduction on the corporate tax returns. In theory, one could argue the basis for reasonable salary testing should be the "book net income" versus the "tax return net income." This certainly is splitting hairs. We say split away!

Ok. We seriously tried to keep the above table simple. Basically under Scenario 1 you are reducing overall company profits by paying out reimbursements for shareholder expenses. This in turn reduces the jumping off point of 35% for a reasonable salary, and in turn reduces the total amount of Social Security and Medicare taxes that are being paid out. The delta is $1,071 between the scenarios, and there are also income tax implications too not just self-employment taxes. If you want a better explanation or a walk-thru, please have an adult beverage and then contact us. Current suggestion is Absolut Vodka and Red Bull with a splash of Cranberry. Garnish optional. Yum.

Again, this is using a 35% reasonable shareholder salary. We had to jump off somewhere, but we also need to remind you that this number is not quantitative but rather qualitative based on several factors including shareholder distributions. For sake of argument, assume that shareholder distributions equal net ordinary business income.

If you reimburse yourself without an Accountable Plan, that money is considered taxable income. Therefore, you have to deduct those expenses as unreimbursed employee business expenses on Form 2106 subject to itemized deductions and income thresholds. Deducting and reimbursing are different, and can have sizable impacts on your taxable income and overall cash in pocket.

Also recall that with the Tax Cuts & Jobs Act of 2017, unreimbursed employee expenses and anything else that was deductible subject to the 2% adjusted gross income limitation are gone after 2017. Therefore, some of this argument is moot and essentially makes deducting expenses at the corporate level and getting reimbursed all that more important.

For 2017, deducting expenses on your personal tax return have a 2% of adjusted gross income threshold to get over- in other words, if you make $100,000 the first 2% or $2,000 is non-deductible. Accountable Plans avoid that. Wait! There's more. If you are a victim of the alternative minimum tax (AMT) where any additional Schedule A deductions are non-deductible, an Accountable Plan ensures that they are deducted at the S Corp level. Make life easy, get an Accountable Plan. Make life even easier, have the Watson CPA Group prepare this corporate document and the associated corporate governance documents (we charge about $150).

> **Another Side Note:** The processing of an Accountable Plan can be done at the end of each quarter to basically re-classify owner or shareholder distributions as employee reimbursements. For example, let's say you took out $20,000 over the quarter as distributions. But after completing the Accountable Plan Reimbursement, the company owed you $5,000. We would make an entry to reflect the reimbursement, and your shareholder distributions would be re-classified as a $15,000 distribution (taxable) and a $5,000 reimbursement (non-taxable).

The "look back" at the end of the quarter method might not work if you provide a stipend or some other advance to your employees throughout the period. This is due to the time limits imposed on the substantiation requests and returns of excess reimbursements. Try to avoid the advance or stipend approach.

We would prefer that employee reimbursements through an Accountable Plan be done as a single check or transfer from the business checking account into your personal checking account (as the employee). This makes the accounting very straightforward- you debit Employee Reimbursements and credit Cash. If you are using QuickBooks, you categorize the check or transfer as Employee Reimbursements with splits for each sub account.

Here is a sample journal entry for an S Corp shareholder who took out $20,000 as a shareholder distribution, but later re-categorized the transaction as distributions, wages and employee reimbursements.

	DR	CR
Shareholder Distributions		8,950
Owner Wage Expense	7,000	
Employee Reimbursements	1,950	
Totals	8,950	8,950

When the original distribution took place, there was a debit to Shareholder Distributions for $20,000 and a credit to Cash for the same. We are simply reducing the $20,000 by $8,950 so the actual distribution reflects $20,000 less $8,950 or $11,050. No adjustment is made to Cash. Make sense?

If we were putting this transaction into the books together from the start, it would look this starting with the shareholder distribution-

	DR	CR
Shareholder Distributions	11,050	
Cash		11,050
Totals	11,050	11,050

And then the Owner Wage Expense and Employee Reimbursements-

	DR	CR
Owner Wage Expense	7,000	
Employee Reimbursements	1,950	
Cash		8,950
Totals	8,950	8,950

Everything would end up in the same spot- Shareholder Distributions at $11,050, Owner Wage Expense at $7,000 and Employee Reimbursements at $1,950. Cash spent would be $20,000. The only difference is the first example is a correcting or reversing entry.

This is a slight over-simplification since there would also be a Payroll Tax Expense entry for the company's portion of Social Security, Medicare, Unemployment, etc. but this should be illustrative enough.

An Accountable Plan is easy to do, is a great way to pull money out of the business and reduces the amount of taxes paid. Keep in mind too that by reducing your overall net business income you are also reducing one of the criteria for the reasonable salary testing, and this in turn possibly decreases your salary (and subsequent Social Security and Medicare taxes). A win-win scenario.

Accountable Plan Provisions, Requirements

The plan is usually drafted as a company policy and later adopted through corporate minutes, and the plan satisfies three basic IRS requirements: a business connection; substantiation; and return of excess amounts-

▲ Business Connection: The expense must have a business connection. Typically expenses incurred by an employee while doing his or her job usually have a business connection. It might be a good idea to list some examples of such as home office, cell phone, internet, mileage and meals. Health insurance premiums should also be detailed.

You could also list conditions and parameters for reimbursement. Must answer phone calls outside the office to claim reimbursement. Or only mileage to and from client meetings, delivering product, running errands for supplies, etc. The more comprehensive the allowable business connections, the safer your plan will be.

▲ Proper Substantiation: The employee must adequately account to the company for expenses within a reasonable time. Adequate accounting means completing expense reports and providing the company with receipts, invoices, and other documentary evidence of the expenses. Using a separate credit card and requesting credit card statements is a great recordkeeping technique. For more information on recordkeeping, substantiation and documentary evidence, read our KB articles at-

www.watsoncpagroup.com/recordkeeping

There are special substantiation rules for meals, entertainment, business gifts and anything considered "listed property." We can help you these situations if necessary.

▲ Return of the Excess Reimbursement: The employee must return to the company any excess reimbursements within a reasonable time. While this is not an issue if you are reimbursed only for what you request, you should still detail this policy in your Accountable Plan. Many companies provide a monthly stipend to cover expenses, and employees are required to return unused portions.

Here is a timeline according to the IRS-

1. An advance may be received within 30 days of the time of the expense.

2. The employee furnishes an adequate account of expenses within 60 days after they were paid or incurred.

3. The employee returns any excess reimbursement within 120 days after it was paid or incurred.

The Accountable Plan should address the above issues, and it should be drafted as company policy for all employees. While different employee groups and individual employees can have different plans, you should draft this policy while distancing it from any favoritism towards the shareholder employees. The Watson CPA Group can help draft this corporate governance document for $150. Plus we teach you how to use it. Bargain!

Meals and entertainment pose an interesting scenario. They are 100% reimbursable to you, but only 50% deductible to the company. If you are an S Corp LLC then this 50% rule on meals and entertainment will increase your taxable income. Either way, the Accountable Plan is still the best option.

For a sample Accountable Plan reimbursement form that you can review please see-

www.watsoncpagroup.com/APlan

The company should buy the desk, office furniture and equipment used in your business, even if you use a home office. The cool thing is if the company buys this stuff, it can take an instant Section 179 depreciation deduction for the full amount. If you buy it directly, you might have to depreciate it over time on your personal tax return.

S Corp Accountable Plan Recap

In summary (sounds like a bad college paper at 3:00AM)... in summary, an S corporation with an Accountable Plan offers a great degree of flexibility to provide several options to minimize tax consequences and maximize your family's wealth. Some hassles, but manageable. We agree that it might not be simple and the rules can be onerous, so let the Watson CPA Group consult with you to review the bulleted points and determine a path that fits.

[Rest of page intentionally left blank]

Chapter 8
Tax Deductions, Fringe Benefits
(updated June 2016)

Ahh.. the good stuff. Yes, you work hard. Yes, you want to be able to get a little extra from your hard work and your business. Yes, you want this to be tax-advantaged. We get it. This chapter will discuss the 185 tax deductions you cannot take, explain how to position yourself on allowable small business tax deductions, and then get into hot topics such as automobiles, home offices, deducting MBAs, Cohan rule and other fun things.

Chapter 7 and Accountable Plans was a snap. Chapter 7 and Tax Deductions, Fringe Benefits is long.

We have not updated this chapter with the new tax laws. Frankly we have been a bit busy with the Section 199A deduction which is much more of a needle-push than other changes. And... we are a tiny 20-person firm gearing up for tax season. Two big notables- meals and entertainment has shriveled under the new laws, and automobile depreciation has increased. There are some other minor things and we'll update as soon as we can.

Four Basics to Warm Up To
Before we get into which tax deductions and tax moves you can take, there are some basic concepts to help formulate your thinking.

Marginal Tax Rate
Quick lesson on small business tax deductions. When you write a check and it has a tax savings element (office expense, 401k, IRA, charity, etc.) it is not a dollar for dollar savings. For example, if you are in the 25% marginal tax bracket, you must write a check for $4,000 just to save $1,000 in taxes. Keep this in mind as you read this information on tax deductions. Also keep in mind that cash is king, and that perhaps paying a few more taxes today with the added flexibility of cash in the bank can be comforting. More on this later in the chapter.

Cash Savings or Tax Savings
You can save $50,000 today! Yes, today! You just need to write a $150,000 check to your church. Huh? That might not sound like the best idea to a lot of people since so much cash is

leaving. Another way to look at this is this- most people say "I want to save taxes" but really what they are saying is "I want to save cash."

In other words, most people are in the cash-saving business not the tax-saving business. If we can do both, great. However, most tax-savings moves take cash, and cash is what you want to keep. So keep this concept in mind as you review business deductions below.

Building Wealth

At the end of your life, you'll measure your financial success on the wealth you built not the tax you saved. We agree that a part of wealth building includes tax savings, but be careful not to sacrifice wealth for the thrill of a tax deduction (or deferral). Here is an example- let's say you stuff all your available cash into a tax-advantaged retirement account such a 401k. A few years go by and a great rental comes on the market but your cash is all tied up in a 401k. So, you sacrificed potential building of wealth by not having an intermediate investment strategy for the sake of tax deferrals.

The Trick

Here's the trick. The Holy Grail if you will. You need to find a way to deduct money you are already spending. Read that again. For example, if you have a travel budget then you are already comfortable with a certain amount of money leaving your person. Let's find a way to deduct it through your business.

Automobile depreciation? Same thing. You are already comfortable with automobiles losing thousands of dollars in value especially in the early years, so let's a find a way to make this degradation in value a tax windfall.

The remainder of this chapter is written to help educate yourself so the money you are already spending can be positioned in such a fashion that it becomes a legitimate small business tax deduction. Remember that the greatest trick the devil ever pulled was convincing the world he didn't exist. The second greatest trick was finding a way to deduct the expense. You gotta love The Usual Suspects. Classic!

Section 199A Deductions – Pass Thru Tax Breaks

Section 199A deduction also known as the Qualified Business Income deduction arises from the Tax Cuts & Jobs Act of 2017. This is a significant tax break for small business owners but there are rules and limits of course.

Section 199, without the A, is the section covering Domestic Production Activities Deduction. Section 199A is seemingly modeled after this (or at least a portion was ripped off by legislators) since the mathematics and reporting is similar between Section 199A and Section

199. Recall that Domestic Production Activities Deduction was reported on Form 8903 and eventually deducted on line 35 of Form 1040 (rumor is it's now dead).

However, it appears that Section 199A Qualified Business Income deduction is a deduction from adjusted gross income to arrive at taxable income (what we nerds call a below-the-line deduction, from AGI). This is contrasted with an adjustment to gross income to arrive at adjusted gross income (what we nerds call an above-the-line deduction, for AGI).

Calculating the Qualified Business Income Deduction
The basic deduction is 20% of net qualified business income which is huge. If you make $200,000, the deduction is $40,000 times your marginal tax rate of 24% which equals $9,600 in your pocket. Who says Obamacare isn't affordable now? Here is the exact code-

(2) DETERMINATION OF DEDUCTIBLE AMOUNT FOR EACH TRADE OR BUSINESS. The amount determined under this paragraph with respect to any qualified trade or business is the lesser of-

(A) 20 percent of the taxpayer's qualified business income with respect to the qualified trade or business, or

(B) the greater of-

> (i) 50 percent of the W-2 wages with respect to the qualified trade or business, or

> (ii) the sum of 25 percent of the W-2 wages with respect to the qualified trade or business, plus 2.5 percent of the unadjusted basis immediately after acquisition of all qualified property.

There are some devils in the details of course. The best way to learn this is refer to the examples in Chapter 1.

185 Business Deductions You Cannot Take
Similarly to the 185 reasons to not elect S corporation taxation, there aren't 185 small business deductions that you cannot take. However, we want to start with the crazy things small business owners try to do since it is such a good springboard for discussion.

100% Cell Phone
Most small businesses operate on a cell phone. However, most small business owners also use his or her cell phone as a personal phone. The minute you get the "Hey honey... we need

milk and eggs" text message to your cell phone, it drops from 100% business use to something else.

If you attempt to deduct 100% of your cell phone as a small business tax deduction, the IRS will claim 0% and then force you to demonstrate why it should be something else. Conversely, if you approach this from a position of being reasonable it is extremely challenging for the IRS to argue otherwise. What is reasonable?

We usually start with a single phone line cost of about $120 to $140 per month in 2016 dollars. While it might only take $10 to add another line, you would still need to spend $120 to $140 for yourself. From there it becomes a preponderance of the facts and circumstances. Some people say there are 40 hours in a work week and there are 168 available hours (24 x 7).

However, this calculus assumes your personal use "density" is the same as your business use "density." For most business owners, this is not true. You probably talk longer with clients and business associates, than you do friends and family.

Anywhere from 50% to 80% is a good jumping off point. Since this is a mixed use expense between personal and business, the cell phone charges should be paid by you personally and then reimbursed by the company for the business use portion through an accountable plan. See Chapter 6 about Accountable Plans.

Automobiles

Automobiles will be discussed in nauseating detail later in this chapter, and there is a decision tree as well to help determine if you should own it or the business. In keeping with the business tax deductions that are disallowed, claiming your only automobile as 100% business use is a tough sell.

Home Office Improvements

You cannot spend $30,000, finish your basement, plop your desk in the middle of it and deduct the $30,000 for two reasons. First, the entire space must be regularly and exclusively used as a home office. This means the theater room must be a conference room, and the wet bar must be the office kitchen. Might be tough in the world of small business tax deductions.

Second, even if the entire basement is designated business use, the $30,000 represents an improvement. Therefore it must be capitalized as an asset and subsequently depreciated over 39 years. From there, only the business use portion of mortgage interest, property taxes, insurance, HOA dues and utilities are deductible. And if you have an S corporation, then this business expense is reimbursed to you by the company through an Accountable Plan (and therefore deductible by the company as an employee reimbursement expense).

Don't worry, the projection TV with the non-glare screen was still worth it. We'll talk more about home offices especially with multiple locations later in this chapter.

Food

More bad news. You cannot deduct your business meals unless you fall under one of two situations-

▲ You are entertaining a client, prospect or other business associate (or a small group such as 12), and discussing business matters, or

▲ You are away from your tax home where you require substantial rest (such as an overnight trip), and that trip has a business purpose.

So if you cruise through the Starbuck's drive-thru and grab your triple grande vanilla breve on the way to your day meeting, no good. However, if you are traveling away from your tax home when on a business trip, then order the venti.

Your small business tax deduction is limited to 50% under both circumstances.

The theory on this is straightforward- you have to eat regardless of owning a business or not. In other words, your meal is not contributing directly to the operations or success of your business. The IRS is clever- they don't mind giving you a tax deduction today on something that eventually will result in taxable business income through growth and profits in the future. Think of it this way- if you had a regular W-2 job, you wouldn't be able to deduct your meals. Why would that change with your shiny new business or S corporation?

Your tax home is the location where you earn income. Here is the word for word description from **IRS Publication 17**-

> To determine whether you are traveling away from home, you must first determine the location of your tax home.

> Generally, your tax home is your regular place of business or post of duty, regardless of where you maintain your family home. It includes the entire city or general area in which your business or work is located.

If you have more than one regular place of business, your tax home is your main place of business.

If you do not have a regular or a main place of business because of the nature of your work, then your tax home may be the place where you regularly live.

If you do not have a regular or a main place of business or post of duty and there is no place where you regularly live, you are considered an itinerant (a transient) and your tax home is wherever you work. As an itinerant, you cannot claim a travel expense deduction because you are never considered to be traveling away from home.

Main place of business or work. If you have more than one place of business or work, consider the following when determining which one is your main place of business or work.

▲ The total time you ordinarily spend in each place.

▲ The level of your business activity in each place.

▲ Whether your income from each place is significant or insignificant.

There you have it. Overnight travel away from your tax home will create a nice business deduction for that beer sampler with pretzels and mustard dip. Spicy of course. Here is a link to **IRS Publication 17 (Your Federal Income Tax)-**

www.wcgurl.com/5324

Tax homes can get tricky especially if you travel a lot or have multiple job locations. We can help sort through it and attempt to find the best tax position.

Per Diem

Sole proprietors including single-member LLC owners, and partners are allowed to deduct the federal per diem rate for meals. Lodging can only be deducted using the actual cost of lodging. Where are S corporations? You are not going to like this. Employees of corporations are eligible for per diem allowances, reimbursements and deductions **unless** this same employee owns more than 10% of the corporation.

This means that most S corporation shareholders are hosed, and can only deduct (or get reimbursed) for actual meal costs. **IRS Revenue Procedure 2011-47** has this limitation and

IRS Publication 463 states in part "A per diem allowance satisfies the adequate accounting requirements for the amount of your expenses only if...you are not related to your employer."

You are related to your employer if-

▲ Your employer is your brother or sister, half brother or half sister, spouse, ancestor, or lineal descendant,

▲ Your employer is a corporation in which you own, directly or indirectly, more than 10% in value of the outstanding stock, or

▲ Certain relationships (such as grantor, fiduciary, or beneficiary) exist between you, a trust, and your employer

So the question becomes, if you are an LLC being taxed as an S corporation, are you a corporation where you own stock or an limited liability company where you own a membership interest. We believe these are one in the same in this context. Don't fret. You can still deduct 50% of your meals when traveling; you just need to use actual expenses and not per diem allowances.

Country Club Dues

Nope. The IRS does not care how many times or how much you entertain your clients, prospects and business associates at your country club. The membership dues are not allowed. However, the specific out-of-pockets expenses associated with qualifying meals and entertainment incurred at your country club are deductible. There's some other devils in the details, but this is the general gist.

Don't confuse this with other types of dues such as Chamber of Commerce or other professional organizations such as BNI. Those dues are 100% deductible although there is some scuttle butt about BNI since a portion of the dues are for meals.

Client Gifts

Yuck, more IRS publications stuff on the way. In **IRS Publication 463**, here is the blurb on client gifts-

> You can deduct no more than $25 for business gifts you give directly or indirectly to each person during your tax year. A gift to a company that is intended for the eventual personal use or benefit of a particular person or a limited class of people

will be considered an indirect gift to that particular person or to the individuals within that class of people who receive the gift.

If you give a gift to a member of a customer's family, the gift is generally considered to be an indirect gift to the customer. This rule does not apply if you have a bona fide, independent business connection with that family member and the gift is not intended for the customer's eventual use.

If you and your spouse both give gifts, both of you are treated as one taxpayer. It does not matter whether you have separate businesses, are separately employed, or whether each of you has an independent connection with the recipient. If a partnership gives gifts, the partnership and the partners are treated as one taxpayer.

$25 is the maximum per year per person. The second paragraph explains you cannot give $100 to a family of four (as an example), unless you have a separate bona fide relationship with each family member. Here is the link to **IRS Publication 463 (Travel, Entertainment, Gift, and Car Expenses)**-

www.wcgurl.com/5330

In a recent IRS audit that we represented, the client presented a $1,000 receipt for forty $25 VISA gift cards along with forty names of clients, prospects and business associates, including the business connection to each. Excellent documentation frankly. The IRS agent accepted the business deduction as is, yet quietly we wondered if any of those names actually received the gift cards. We didn't bring it up. Interesting indeed.

Keep this in mind as well- note that the IRS refers to individuals in their little pontification above. Gifts to another business are limitless. So, if your client is a business and you want to express your gratitude, theoretically there is no limit provided an individual is not the designated recipient.

Promotional items that are under $4 in unit cost and have your company name or logo on them are not considered gifts and do not contribute to the $25 maximum.

Commuting Expenses

It is unfortunate, but expenses associated with your commute to work are not deductible. Tolls and parking are the common ones small business owners attempt to deduct. There is a subtle difference to be aware of- driving from a work location to your client's place of business is not commuting. Commuting is driving from your home to your office or client's place of business.

You can solve a lot of problems surrounding commuting expenses by qualifying for a home office. Then your commute is from the bedroom to the home office. And if you shower, then the commute is from the bathroom to the home office.

Professional Attire

The tax code is very clear on this. Anything that you can convert to everyday use is considered personal, and therefore not tax deductible. Many business owners want to deduct dry cleaning expenses or Men's Warehouse purchases, but they usually cannot. We know you are rocking it in the double-breasted vest without a coat look, but the IRS doesn't have fashion sense and therefore doesn't care. However, there are some exceptions (of course there are).

The Watson CPA Group prepares several tax returns for pilots, flight attendants, military personnel, nurses and firefighters. These uniforms are not suitable for everyday use and / or are protective in nature (such as steel-toed boots), and therefore are small business tax deductions. We also have a handful of models and actors as clients, and their clothing is considered theatrical costumes not suitable for everyday use.

Many small business owners will embroider a nice golf shirt or something similar. This can be deducted as either clothing not suitable for everyday use or advertising depending on the IRS agent who is bent out of shape about your tax returns.

The maintenance such as alterations and laundering of deductible clothing is also tax deductible. Shoes, socks, nylons, haircuts, watches and the like are all disallowed. Forget about it. In **Mary A. Scott v. Commissioner (Tax Court Summary Opinion 2010-47)**, a Continental Flight Attendant was denied shoes, socks, nylons and hair product as unreimbursed employee business expenses. Here is the link-

www.wcgurl.com/2010

It's a fun case and a quick read.

Loan Payments

Many businesses have loans, either for automobiles, business equipment or lines of credit. However, having an expense category of "Loan Payment" is a dead giveaway that the business owner doesn't understand that only the interest portion of the loan payment is deductible.

Think of it this way- if you lent your buddy $50,000 and he or she shockingly pays you back the $50,000 plus $10,000 in interest, only the $10,000 would be income to you. The $50,000 would be what we nerdy accountants call a return of capital.

Yet another way to look at this- your small business tax deduction must be recognized as income by another entity (either business or person), unless that entity is a charity. So, for the IRS to allow you to deduct mortgage interest on your home mortgage as an example, the lender must recognize the interest as income. Your deduction = someone else's taxable income.

Zeus and Apollo

Let's say you are a hotshot private investigator driving a red Ferrari 308 GTS in Hawaii. Can you deduct two Dobermans as business expenses? Possibly. We recently worked with a client who is a criminal defense attorney where we demonstrated that the need for security dogs was a bona fide occupational qualification. In other words, the dogs provided security to the criminal defense attorney so he was able to perform his job. Stop laughing, it was L-E-G-I-T. Not because of the creativity, but because of the argument's position.

Another way to look at these obscure examples- the IRS allows you to deduct most things if they eventually lead to the generation of taxable income. Think of investment fees. Think of Zeus and Apollo who allowed the attorney to continue taking on high-risk, high-profit (taxable) defense cases.

Conclusion

Enough about the stuff you can't do, or at least enough of the business deductions you need to carefully position yourself with, let's talk about the stuff you can do. There are several small business tax deductions that are common, yet overlooked or misapplied.

Depreciation

Before we get into the exciting world of automobiles, home offices and traditional business expenses, let's explore the concept of depreciation. How it works, how it can help, and how it can bite. There are three basic types of depreciation available to small business owners-

▲ Section 179

▲ Bonus

▲ MACRS (or other suitable schedules)

Section 179 of the tax code allows you to instantly depreciate assets up to $500,000. Each year this limit was reduced to $25,000. And every year Congress approves some sort of package that extends the limit to $500,000. However, the "Protecting Americans from Tax Hikes Act of 2015" (PATH Act) was passed by both the House and Senate and signed into law on December 18, 2015. The $500,000 limit is now as permanent as it can be.

Not all property qualifies for Section 179 depreciation, namely real estate. And some property is considered Listed Property which has special rules and limits, namely automobiles and computers. To deduct Section 179 depreciation, your business must have net income to absorb it, otherwise whatever is unused is carried forward to later years.

Bonus depreciation on the other hand does not require business income, and currently Bonus depreciation is 50% of Section 179 depreciation limits. The one caveat is that not all property qualifies for Bonus depreciation, and the property must be new, not just new to you. Under Section 179, you can buy the crustiest piece of machinery and deduct the whole thing in the first year (again, provided you have the income to absorb it).

There are all kinds of rules and interplay between Section 179 and Bonus depreciation. Please do your homework. **www.Section179.org** is a decent place to start.

MACRS is not a depreciation schedule designed for bourbons. Frankly, bourbon shouldn't be sitting around long enough to depreciate... or spoil as us accountants would say. At the Watson CPA Group, Maker's Mark seems to deplete long before it depreciates. All kidding aside, MACRS is Modified Accelerated Cost Recovery System which is the default depreciation schedule for most property. So, if you do not use Section 179 or Bonus depreciation, you will be utilizing MACRS depreciation (generally speaking). You can also elect other suitable schedules too but those choices and justifications get more complicated.

If you really want to complicate things, Generally Accepted Accounting Principles (GAAP) does not recognize accelerated depreciation. Therefore if you have audited financial statements, there will be a difference between "book" depreciation and "tax" depreciation. 99% of the small businesses out there don't have audited financial statements (or the need for them). But you might run across this if you are buying or selling a business. The Watson CPA Group also does business valuations for divorce cases or economic damages lawsuits, and the "book" to "tax" and vise-versa becomes an important valuation component.

Tax Planning with Depreciation
We are shocked every time a client walks into our office demanding to pay fewer taxes. We smile and tell them that they are the only one. Most people want to pay more taxes so we find it refreshing when someone wants to pay less. Yes, we're kidding.

Tax planning with depreciation must be carefully considered. Everyone wants the bird in the hand versus the two in the bush. We get it. But let's run through some scenarios which might expand your thinking and horizons.

Let's say you buy a piece of equipment for $200,000 and you deduct the whole thing in the first year using Section 179 depreciation. If your marginal tax rate is 15%, you saved yourself $30,000 ($200,000 x 15%). Nice job. In the next year, your business is growing and you find yourself in the 25% marginal tax rate but you don't have any depreciation left, so no savings.

Here is a table illustrating Section 179 depreciation-

	Allowed %	Depreciation	Tax Savings
Year 1, Savings at 15%	100%	200,000	30,000
Year 2, Savings at 25%	0%	0	0
Year 3, Savings at 28%	0%	0	0
Year 4, Savings at 28%	0%	0	0
Year 5, Savings at 28%	0%	0	0
Year 6, Savings at 28%	0%	0	0
Totals	**100%**	**200,000**	**30,000**

Here is the exact same scenario using MACRS as your depreciation schedule (as opposed to using Section 179)-

	Allowed %	Depreciation	Tax Savings
Year 1, Savings at 15%	20.00%	40,000	6,000
Year 2, Savings at 25%	32.00%	64,000	16,000
Year 3, Savings at 28%	19.20%	38,400	10,752
Year 4, Savings at 28%	11.52%	23,040	6,451
Year 5, Savings at 28%	11.52%	23,040	6,451
Year 6, Savings at 28%	5.76%	11,520	3,226
Totals	**100%**	**200,000**	**48,880**

That is an $18,880 difference! However, this is overly simplified comparison given that $200,000 spans at least two marginal tax brackets. We used this dramatic disparity to drive home the point that you might be leaving money on the depreciation table.

Before you call your tax accountant and franticly decline the Section 179 depreciation method, consider your income projections. The illustrations above only prove a point if your marginal tax rate is increasing. If you are experiencing an exceptionally good year, and the next few years will have less taxable income, then perhaps using the instant depreciation benefits of Section 179 make sense. Plan! Plan! Plan!

Tax Planning with Depreciation Recapture

Please understand that depreciation is a tax deferral system rather than a tax avoidance system. Huh? When you sell or dispose of an asset, you might have to pay tax on the portion that was depreciated.

For example, you buy a $200,000 piece of machinery and use Section 179 depreciation to deduct the entire $200,000 in the first year. Five years later you sell the equipment for $150,000 because you slapped some new paint on it and you are a shrewd negotiator with your buyer. You will now have to recognize $150,000 of taxable ordinary income. Yuck. But there is a silver lining- depreciation recapture is taxed at your marginal tax rate up to a maximum of 25% tax rate. So, you could have depreciated your asset during 39.6% marginal tax rate years just to pay it all back at 25%. Bonus. Tax planning is a must! How many times have we mentioned that?

You can kick this depreciation recapture can down the road with a Section 1031 exchange (also referred to as a like-kind exchange). Perform your favorite internet search on this topic- way too involved to explain here except that a Section 1031 exchange allows deferral of depreciation recapture and capital gains. And if you think you know what a 1031 exchange is, try learning about a reverse 1031 exchange- where you buy the replacement property first. Yup. It exists.

What if you think you can be clever, and not deduct depreciation on your asset? IRS is way ahead of you. Way ahead. There is a little known rule called the allowed versus allowable rule and it can bite you in the butt. And it's not a nibble, it is potentially quite the bite, like Jaws-size ("You're gonna need a bigger boat").

Several tax court rulings will have a statement similar to "Tax deductions are a matter of legislative grace." Nice. When have you ever felt the grace of a legislator as you pay taxes? Never. At any rate, let's extend this statement a bit, and one can infer that tax deductions are not required to be taken which is completely true. And some tax planning can involve not taking tax deductions on tax returns in certain cases (seems weird, but there are narrow examples).

But the IRS assumes that you have deducted depreciation expense in the past so when you dispose or sell your asset, you MUST recapture depreciation even if you didn't deduct it in the past. That is a big Yuck. The Watson CPA Group commonly sees this when taxpayers own rental properties and prepare their own tax returns. Tax preparation is a profession, not a hobby. Yeah, we said it! We have to, it's our chosen profession.

There are ways to fix this of course. One way is using Form 3115 Application for Change in Accounting Method. This form is used for a variety of things, and one of the things is to bring your depreciation current.

The IRS is becoming more flexible and has been allowing simple Section 481A adjustments without having to complete Form 3115. This gets complicated right quick, so if you need help contact your depreciation adjusting friends at the Watson CPA Group. One of the problems with slapping a whole bunch of depreciation in one tax year is revenue and expense matching- this is one of the cornerstones of accounting principles, so these adjustments need to be detailed correctly. And with rental properties specifically, you might get into passive loss limit problems.

We digress. Back to the chapter's topic- Tax Deductions, Fringe Benefits!

Small Business Tax Deductions Themes

There are some over-arching themes and concepts for all small business deductions. The business expense must be-

▲ Ordinary and necessary (IRS Publication 334), **and**

▲ Paid or recognized in the current tax year, **and**

▲ Directly related to your business, **and**

▲ Reasonable, and not lavish or extravagant (IRC Section 162 and IRS Publication 463).

Let's break these down. An ordinary expense is one that is common and accepted in your field of business, trade, or profession. A necessary expense is one that is helpful and appropriate, although not necessarily required, for your business. In **Samp v. Commissioner (Tax Court Memo 1981-706)**, an insurance agent had a handgun since he traveled to an area with a recent unsolved murder. The tax court responded with "A handgun simply does not qualify as an ordinary and necessary business expense for an insurance agent, even a bold and brave Wyatt Earp type with a fast draw who is willing to risk injury or death in the service of his clients."

You have appreciate a Wyatt Earp reference from a tax court judge. Ouch. Clean up on aisle Allstate.

The expense must be paid or recognized in the current year. Expenses that were paid but not deducted in previous years cannot be "caught up" by deducting them today without amending your prior tax returns (which are easy to do, and should be done if there is money to be had). There is some wiggle room by paying expenses in advance. Under the Code of Federal Regulations (CFR), Title 26 (Internal Revenue), Chapter 1, Subchapter A (Income Tax) or **26 CFR 1.263(a)-4** for short, there is a rule called the 12-month rule. This allows you to deduct in full an amount where the benefit received from paying the expense spans two tax years.

Here is the exact wording allowing the immediate deduction of prepaid expenses for "any right or benefit for the taxpayer that does not extend beyond the earlier of-

▲   12 months after the first date on which the taxpayer realizes the right or benefit; or

▲   The end of the taxable year following the taxable year in which the payment is made."

Here is the link to the Code of Federal Regulations on the 12-month rule-

www.wcgurl.com/5415

You'll need to search for Prepaid Rent, or scroll through a bunch of hoopla.

An example you see often is a one-year rental lease that starts July 1 and ends June 30 the following year. If you pre-paid the entire lease amount, you can deduct the entire amount since the benefit (the use of the rental space) is 12 months. However, let's say the lease term started February 1 of the following year, but you prepaid the entire amount December 31 of the current year. Since the benefit extends past the end of the following tax year, none of it is deductible in the current year and only a portion is deducted the following year.

Just because you can deduct an expense in one lump sum, doesn't mean that you should. Remember the conversation about depreciation, tax planning and increased marginal tax rates in the future? And, this small business tax deduction scheme is usually reserved for those using cash based accounting.

The expense must be related to your business- that seems obvious. Finally, the expense must not be lavish or extravagant. **IRS Publications 463** states "You cannot deduct expenses for entertainment that are lavish or extravagant. An expense is not considered lavish or extravagant if it is reasonable considering the facts and circumstances. Expenses will not be disallowed just because they are more than a fixed dollar amount or take place at deluxe restaurants, hotels, nightclubs, or resorts." The link for **IRS Publication 463 (Travel, Entertainment, Gift, and Car Expenses)** is below-

www.wcgurl/5330

So, your Board of Directors meeting might spend $500 on catering but a $5,000 expenditure to hold your board meeting in Fiji might be considered lavish and extravagant. Be reasonable out of the gate, and it will be hard for the IRS to knock you off your perch.

Value of a Business Tax Deduction

Here is another concept that small business owners miss. Tax deductions only reduce taxable income. If you spend $1,000 and your marginal tax rate is 25%, then you only save $250 by spending $1,000. Every December the Watson CPA Group fields hundreds of phone calls and emails from clients asking if they should buy something to save on taxes. Our response is a simple flowchart-

▲ Do you need the item you are considering? If No, then stop. Don't buy anything. If Yes, then continue to the next question.

▲ Is the current year's income unusually high, or do you expect to earn more next year?

Without sound snarky, why would you buy something on December 31 if your tax rate will only increase the following year? Wait 24 hours, buy the cool thing you need and get a better yet delayed tax deduction. And if you don't need it, why would you spend money unnecessarily only to get a portion of that back in tax savings? Another way of saying this is- keep some tax deductions in your pocket for next year. You don't want to be in a position where you ran out of perfectly good deductions in a year of increased taxable income.

Conversely, if your current taxable income is unusually high and you expect it to go down next year then perhaps you should accelerate your timelines for major purchases. The Watson CPA Group can help with the tax modeling and planning.

All too often we hear people at cocktail parties say something silly like "Don't worry, it's a write-off." Remember that money is still leaving your person, and the money you are getting back in the form of a tax deduction is substantially less. Just because it is a "write-off" or a business tax deduction doesn't mean that you are using Monopoly money.

Tax credits are in contrast to tax deductions. Tax credits such as $7,500 for buying a cool Tesla or $13,400 for adopting a child are a dollar for dollar reduction in your tax due. For example, if the computed tax liability is $20,000 and you max out your adoption credit of $13,400, you will only have a tax liability of $6,600. However, if you spend $13,400 in office furniture you will save taxes based on your marginal tax rate- 25% tax rate equates to $3,350. See the difference?

Tax deduction versus tax credit. There are very little tax credits for small businesses, but here are most popular-

▲ Alcohol Fuels

▲ Alternative Motor Vehicle (only the Honda FCX Clarity currently qualifies)

▲ Disabled Access

▲ Employer Provided Child Care

▲ Reforestation

▲ Qualified Research Expenses (models, patents, environmental testing, etc.)

▲ Pension Plan Start Up Costs (Watson CPA Group administers 401k plans, ask us!)

▲ Work Opportunity and Welfare to Work

Look these up. These are like college grants and other obscure things that most people don't chase down. There might be easy money for things you are already doing.

Deductions the IRS Cannot Stand

Here is a quick list of the small business tax deductions that the IRS cannot stand. That isn't phrased correctly. The IRS actually likes these tax deductions since most business owners either incorrectly deduct them or cannot substantiate an otherwise qualified deduction for lack of proper record keeping.

The IRS plays pot odds on the following business deductions since the recovery of taxes is probable and therefore profitable for the government. In poker, if it costs you $10 to bet and there is $100 in the pot, then you can be wrong 90% of the time and still break even. This is the essence of the pot odds: You're paying a fraction to win a larger sum, and the IRS is no different.

Here we go-

▲ Meals and Entertainment (shocker)

▲ Car and Truck Expenses, Mileage Logs (another shocker)

▲ Travel

▲ Home Office

There are others, but these are the biggies. We don't want you to have a chilling effect on these expenses. You should not be afraid of an audit. You should not be afraid of losing an audit. You should only be afraid of having an unreasonable or indefensible position. Sure, easy for us to say.

At the same time, if you have legitimate expenses and you can back them up with proof, then happily deduct them. Like Muhammad Ali once said, "It's not bragging if you can back it up." Well, the same can be said of small business tax deductions that are at higher risk of audit. If you can back it up then deduct it!

Automobiles and LLCs, S Corps

A question we entertain almost daily is "I want to save taxes. Should I have the company buy me a car?" Our auto-attendant replies with, "Do you need a car?" If you answer with "Yes" the auto-attendant replies with, "Hold please." If your "Yes" is not quick or mumbled, or if there is any recognition of hesitation, the auto-attendant is unhappy.

We digress. There are only a few questions you need to ask yourself when considering a car purchase. Are you the type of person who buys new? How long do you typically keep your cars? Is the car 100% business use? How many miles do you plan to drive? There is a decision tree at the end of the automobile section.

Back up for a bit. Remember our previous discussions about tax deductions, and how only a fraction of the money you spend is returned to you? So, back to our auto-attendant, "Do you need a car?" If the answer is "Yes" because your bucket of bolts is getting exceedingly dangerous, then Yes, buy a much-needed car out of a sense of safety. If the answer is "Not really, but I want to save taxes," then don't. Two rules to live by-

▲ Cash is King (keep it!)

▲ Depreciation is a tax deferral not a tax avoidance system (typically)

There might be some other external forces at play. For example, if you need a car next year but your income is ridiculously and unusually high in the current tax year, then reducing your income now makes sense. Again, tax modeling and planning is critical.

Ok, you've chatted with your car-loving buddies at the Watson CPA Group and we've determined that a car purchase should be in your near future, now what? There are all kinds of issues here, so, buckle up as we go through this stuff. There are four scenarios-

▲ Company Owned Vehicle (mixed bag)

▲ You Own the Vehicle, Get Reimbursed By The Mile (clean and elegant)

▲ You Own the Vehicle, Take a Mileage Deduction (silly in an S Corp)

▲ You Own the Vehicle, Lease it Back to Your Company (exotic)

We'll start with the crowd favorite- Company Owned Vehicle. Everyone's default favorite. As we go through these, please excuse our interchange of vehicle, automobile and car. They all mean the same thing. And if you are being chastised by Tina Watson's sister for bringing food into her Toyota 4Runner then she would use the word "vehicle," with stark over-annunciation of each syllable.

Company Owned Vehicle
If the company truly owns the car, then it must be titled in the company's name. The IRS is cracking down on this, and it makes sense. If the company is the owner, then the company must be on the title. This might be a challenge with car loans and leases, but for the company to claim it as an asset and subsequent expenses the title needs to be in the LLC or S-Corp's name. And if you buy the car yourself and then transfer it to the business, you might be on the hook for sales tax twice (technically).

This is a good example of rules getting in the way of common sense, so try not to freak out on the motor vehicles clerk when you are attempting to transfer title from you to the business. Another concern is higher insurance rates. It appears that most auto policies will charge a higher premium for cars owned by a business for business purposes. While the insurance companies are regulated and must demonstrate the need for the premiums being charged, the higher amount appears to be a money grab.

Depreciation
One of the main reasons to have the company or S corporation own the vehicle is the ability to take Section 179 depreciation. As mentioned earlier, this allows you to get an instant

deduction each year. Since automobiles are listed property, **IRS Revenue Procedure 2016-23** states that passenger automobiles can take $3,160 in depreciation the first year (for the 2016 tax year), $5,100 the second year, $3,050 the third year and $1,875 each year thereafter until fully depreciated. These are the same as 2015's numbers with the assumed continuation of $8,000 in the first year for bonus depreciation.

The numbers are slightly higher for trucks and vans. The depreciation numbers and revenue procedures are released in April for the current tax year. So, 2017 figures are released sometime in April 2017.

Vehicles that weigh more than 6,000 pounds but under 14,000 pounds may qualify for Section 179 deduction of $25,000 in the first year. Some medium-sized vehicles qualify for the full Section 179 depreciation deduction. These are non-SUV cargo trucks, vehicles that seat 9 occupants behind the driver's seat (e.g., hotel van) and classic cargo vans. In addition, vehicles that weigh over 14,000 pounds, ambulances, large moving vans, delivery trucks, law enforcement or fire vehicles, among many others, also qualify for the full Section 179 deduction.

To take Section 179 depreciation the vehicle must have a greater than 50% business use. This might be one of the major obstacles for shareholders especially if they do not have another car. Another concern is that the business must have sufficient income to absorb the deduction (in some situations there might be enough shareholder basis to absorb it beyond income- this is complicated but we can help).

Don't forget the other issue with depreciation is the recapture of depreciation- any gain on the sale of your vehicle (the difference between the original price less depreciation and the sale price) is taxable. The good thing is that most cars depreciate rapidly as they relate to fair market value or resale value. Work trucks and vans might not depreciate as quickly, so there might be some depreciation recapture on your gain when you sell the vehicle.

The depreciation issue has another element. One of the questions we asked previously was how often are you buying new cars. If you are the type of person who buys a new car every 2-3 years, then you know the pain of depreciation. The minute you drive the car off the lot it drops 10-15% in value. If you are automatically "losing money" by frequently buying a new car then deducting depreciation through your business is a huge windfall.

In the first two years you could deduct $16,260 (for the 2016 tax year). Your ownership model and level of comfort already allows for a loss, you might as well get the small business tax deduction. Said in a different way- you buy a new BMW 435 for $70,000 and two years later it is worth $54,000, and you sell it for $54,000. Since you've already taken $16,260 in depreciation you do not recognize a gain nor a recapture of depreciation. In this case your fickleness of needing a new car every two years put some money in your pocket via tax deduction.

But wait! There is a catch. A huge one that is a bit obscure. It is essentially an involuntary Section 1031 Like-Kind exchange where the second vehicle might not get as big of a deduction. See the Automobile Decision Tree later in this chapter for more details on involuntary 1031 exchanges.

Leasing
If your business leases the vehicle, the business portion of the lease amount is expensed. However, there are limits to how much can be expensed, especially for expensive or what the IRS would consider luxury vehicles. The disallowed lease payment is called a lease inclusion and is detailed in **IRS Revenue Procedure 2016-23**. The amount is added back into income and taxed, leaving only the IRS allowed portion as a deductible lease expense. So before you lease that brand new 911, call us. We'll determine a plan after the joint test-drive.

Liability
Another consideration- if you are driving the company car and get into an accident, the company might get into a liability rodeo just based on ownership. Proving that at the moment you were driving the car for personal reasons might not matter. We are not attorneys, but this scenario is not beyond possibility.

Personal Use
Lastly, and this is yet another big deal, any personal use must be considered taxable income as an employee of your S corporation. Don't laugh, it's true! How do you calculate the amount of imputed income? The easiest and most widely accepted way is to use the Annual Lease Value Table in **IRS Publication 15-B Employer's Tax Guide to Fringe Benefits**. For 2016, the lease value of a $50,000 automobile is $13,250 annually. If you use the company-owned vehicle for personal use 10% of the time, then $1,325 will be added to your W-2 and taxed as compensation (including Social Security and Medicare taxes, and all the taxes you would expect). Here is the link to **IRS Publication 15-B**-

www.wcgurl.com/5337

You can also use the mileage rate, but there are strong limitations such as the fair market value of the vehicle must be below $16,000 (for 2015). That will preclude most vehicles. But let's run the math anyways.

For example, you drove 15,000 miles and 5,000 miles were personal. You would need to add 5,000 miles x 54 cents (for 2016) which equals $2,700 to W2 income. And here's the personal use kicker- if you are operating your car for less than the standard mileage rate (and you usually do), you will artificially be inflating your income.

Having a mixed use (personal and business) automobile be owned by the company sounds like a lot of work. Everyone at the Watson CPA Group likes French fries, but we won't run a mile for just one. Let's make sure it's worth it. Will the tax benefit of depreciation in the first two years offset the additional imputed income? Perhaps.

Keep in mind that it is difficult to justify 100% business use of a vehicle if it is the only vehicle you own- perhaps in Manhattan, but not for most Americans. Even if you have another automobile at your disposal, it still might not make sense to have your company own it. The question boils down to how many miles you will drive versus your ability to accelerate your depreciation versus your marginal tax rate today and the following years. At the end of this section on automobiles is an overly simplified flowchart to help you decide (or confuse the situation more).

LLC Owned But Using Standard Mileage Rate
If you operating an LLC without the S corporation election, you might be tempted to use the standard mileage rate. Typically this would be ill-advised- if you are using the standard mileage rate you are probably better off owning the vehicle personally and be reimbursed by the LLC. However, there are situations where this might make sense.

Let's look at the myriad of rules where using the standard mileage rate method is not allowed. According to **IRS Publication 463**, you cannot use the standard mileage rate when you-

▲ Use five or more cars at the same time (such as in fleet operations), **or**

▲ Claimed a depreciation deduction for the car using any method other than straight line (such as MACRS), **or**

▲ Claimed a section 179 deduction on the car, **or**

▲ Claimed the special (bonus) depreciation allowance on the car, **or**

▲ Claimed actual car expenses for a car you leased, **or**

▲ Did not use the standard mileage deduction during the first year of use.

This makes sense. The IRS does not want you to exploit the system by claiming huge amounts of depreciation in the first year, and then switch to the possibly more lucrative standard mileage rate deduction. However, after the first year you can bounce back and forth depending on which method (standard rate versus actuals) gives your LLC a better small business tax deduction. Here is the link for the **IRS Publication 463 (Travel, Entertainment, Gift, and Car Expenses)-**

www.wcgurl.com/5330

Again, if your LLC owns the automobile but is using the standard mileage rate and your LLC elects S corporation status for taxation, this asset needs an adjusted cost basis for depreciation within the corporation. Why? As an S Corp where the company owns the automobile, the company can only use actual expenses and depreciation is a part of that.

The calculation for determining the basis of the automobile is quite simple since the IRS publishes the depreciation amount within the standard mileage rate. Here's the math-

Purchase Price, 2013	50,000
2013 Depreciation @ $0.23 per Mile for 10,000 Miles	2,300
2014 Depreciation @ $0.22 per Mile for 10,000 Miles	2,200
2015 Depreciation @ $0.24 per Mile for 10,000 Miles	2,400
Adjusted Cost Basis on 12/31/2015	43,100

In this example, if the LLC elects S corporation status on January 1 2016, an asset would be created on the S corporation's balance sheet with an adjusted basis of $43,100. The depreciation schedule for an automobile is typically five years, but when you switch from standard mileage rate to actual expenses (e.g., LLC electing S Corp status) the IRS requires you to estimate the remaining useful life. This is another conundrum. In this example, somewhere between two years and five years would be reasonable.

We just went over a ton of stuff under the Company Owns the Vehicle section. Please look at a quickie decision tree later in this section.

You Own the Vehicle, Get Reimbursed By The Mile

This might be the best option, especially if Section 179 depreciation is not going to benefit you much and/or you use the car personally more than you use it professionally. As the owner of the vehicle, you would submit expense reports in the form of mileage logs. If you are a smart vehicle owner, you would also use a smartphone app to keep track of your miles for you. Keep in mind that the IRS wants corroborating evidence to support your mileage logs, so keep those Jiffy Lube receipts or other service records showing odometer readings near the beginning and end of the year (so extrapolation can occur). Just whippin' out a pretty color-coded spreadsheet during an IRS examination is not enough.

The company would reimburse you according to your mileage log submission. This can be a great option for a lot of reasons. First, you are reducing the net income of your company, and if you are an S-Corp the lower business income could decrease the amount of reasonable salary you must take as a shareholder. Second, older cars generally operate for less than the Federal mileage rate.

Let's look at some numbers-

Business Miles	12,000
MPG	25
Gallon of Gas	$4.00
Cost of Gas	1,920
Maintenance, Biz Portion	3,000
Total Cost	4,920
Reimbursement at $0.575	6,900
Difference	**1,980**

So you just took home $1,980 tax-free. All legit. All legal. AAA might consider these operating costs to be too low, but then again this would be representative of an older or thrifty vehicle. Why is that? In 2015, the IRS designated $0.24 of the $0.575 standard mileage rate to be depreciation of your vehicle (almost half). Therefore, if you have a $5,000 POS which will be worth $5,000 ten years from now, you are getting reimbursed for depreciation that never happens. Cool! 10,000 miles would be $2,400 in your pocket free and clear.

Quick recap: you took money out of the business tax-free and you reduced your company's overall taxable income through legitimate small business tax deductions. And if we are using net business income after expenses as a jumping off point for determining a reasonable S corporation salary, that salary starts off at a lower number and subsequently reduces Social Security and Medicare taxes (among others). Win win!

Wait! There's more. Really, Jason? Really!

Third, this is better than simply taking the mileage deduction on your personal tax returns. Any mileage deduction is completed within Form 2106 (Employee Business Expenses) on Schedule A. So, first you need to be able to itemize your deductions by exceeding the standard deduction. Next, any Form 2106 expenses (such as home office, mileage, cell phone, internet, meals, etc.) must exceed 2% of your income, and only that portion that exceeds 2% is deducted.

So, if you make a $100,000 as a household, the first $2,000 in mileage is not deducted. If you get reimbursed from your LLC or S Corp, all the mileage expense is deducted at the corporate level. This directly improves your tax consequence as a shareholder.

Another consideration is AMT (Alternative Minimum Tax). AMT calculations are performed on relatively low income amounts and while you might escape it every year, there might be a time where your Form 2106 expenses on Schedule A are limited because of AMT. So you could claim 15,000 miles or 25,000 miles, and your itemized deduction might be the same. Bummer. Don't mess around with Form 2106 deductions when you own a business. **Reimbursements are always better than deductions.**

There is some confusion out there about getting reimbursed for actual expenses. For example, a business owner will own the automobile personally but wants to get reimbursed for actual expenses. This same business owner will use the company credit card for gas and oil changes. This is bad. If you want to get reimbursed for actual expenses, it must be a pro-rated amount. If you drive 18,000 miles and 12,000 are business miles, then the company should only reimburse 75% of all actual expenses.

If you have leased your vehicle and you use the standard mileage rate for reimbursement, you must continue with that method for the entire lease term. This is contrast to owning the vehicle where you can bounce and forth between actual expenses and standard mileage rate (subject to the rules previously discussed).

Your company must have an Accountable Plan to take advantage of the You Own the Vehicle, Get Reimbursed scenario. As a general rule, any payment of an allowance or reimbursement of business expenses for which the employee does not provide an adequate accounting (i.e., substantiation with receipts or other records) is considered to have been provided under a non-accountable plan and is required to be treated as taxable wages for purposes of federal, state, and local (if applicable) income tax withholding, Social Security and Medicare taxes, and federal and state unemployment taxes. Yuck!

You Own the Vehicle, Take Mileage Deduction

This might be the easiest option, but it truly can leave money on the table. First, if your LLC is being taxed as an S Corp then your reasonable wage figure could unnecessarily be higher if you are not reimbursing yourself through an Accountable Plan, and therefore you are paying more Social Security and Medicare taxes. Yuck #1.

Second, as mentioned earlier, you have to get over the 2% hump for deducting business mileage. To reiterate, any Form 2106 expenses (such as mileage, cell phone, etc.) must exceed 2% of your income, and only that portion that exceeds 2% is deducted. So, if you make a $100,000 as a household, the first $2,000 in mileage expense is not deducted. Yuck #2. Don't forget AMT. Yuck #2.5.

Lastly, you still need to maintain written mileage logs detailing odometer readings, date, business purpose or connection, etc. Why not just turn those in and get reimbursed from your company? Apps exist for both iPhones and Android to track your mileage via GPS, record the purpose and email the log. Pretty cool.

Seriously, if we catch you using this option we'll have a heart to heart conversation about the value of money. Of course we'll need to charge an obscene amount of consultation fees since apparently money is not that valuable to you. Yeah, that was snarky- sorry.

All kidding aside, there are narrow and ridiculously rare situations where you have multiple owners, and some owners are taking advantage of the reimbursement program so the mileage deduction on personal tax returns might be the only way to avoid office politics. For example, three owners at 50%, 30% and 20% each with a company car. The 50% owner might be tweaked with the 20% owner if they are each driving the same amount enjoying the same equal benefit of a company provided vehicle.

Therefore, the owners in this example would buy his or her own car personally, and take the mileage deduction. A middle ground might be to reimburse each owner for the miles driven up to a maximum amount based on ownership percentage. There are all kinds of solutions to help with the office politics.

We are not just accountants and business consultants, we are also counselors. Yes, we have couches and incense, and talk about feelings. Usually on mute so we can do other things with the keyboard clicking in your ear.

You Own the Vehicle, Lease It Back to Your Company

This might take a bit of getting used to so we will start with a similar situation. If you owned and operated a landscaping company, you might own the heavy equipment personally, and lease it back to the company. This is very common, and is considered a self-rental. Please refer to Chapter 1 to refresh yourself on self-rentals and the handling of the income. As you know, self-rentals are perfectly fine as long as the lease rates being charged are considered market rates and cannot be considered enumeration of services provided (i.e., owner compensation).

The same thing can be accomplished with your automobile. You would lease a car that you own back to your company. This is **not** considered the same as the company leasing the car from a dealer. This is creating a self-rental arrangement between you and your business. And why would you want to do that?

The usual reason- it might prove to be a better tax position since you are reducing the income of your LLC which is subjected to self-employment taxes. Since we also use the ability to pay salaries as one of components in determining a reasonable salary for you as a shareholder in an S Corp, the leaseback option might influence a small reduction in your salary.

The income tax angle is a wash. A big table is coming up. First, let's talk about some basic assumptions.

Keep in mind- this arrangement will benefit an LLC through the reduction of self-employment taxes much more than an S corporation. You might be asking why not just elect S corporation status to solve your SE tax troubles? Perhaps your LLC is not generating the $35,000 in net business income after expenses to warrant the S Corp election.

Every year, AAA publishes the annual cost of driving an automobile, and the costs are broken down by small sedan, medium sedan, large sedan, sport utility vehicle and a minivan. From there, costs are established for 10,000 miles, 15,000 miles and 20,000 miles.

Small sedans are Chevy Cruze, Ford Focus, Honda Civic, Hyundai Elantra and Toyota Corolla. Medium sedans are Chevy Impala, Ford Fusion, Honda Accord, Nissan Altima and Toyota Camry. No numbers for a Porsche 911. Sorry. We're sure the operating costs aren't too bad, and we've recently heard that 911s never depreciate and the service checks are free.

There are certain fixed costs such as insurance, registrations and financing. There are certain variable expenses such as gas, tires and maintenance. Then there are some quasi-variable expenses, namely depreciation. Depreciation accelerates as the mileage per year increases.

Think about Kelly Blue Book, Edmund's or lease rates- the reduction in value due to mileage gets more severe as the mileage exceeds 15,000. Sort of a curvilinear equation.

The lease rate needs some discussion too. If you have a newer, more expensive automobile, you might be able to fetch $600 per month. If you have an older car or a car that is more economical, a market lease rate might be $400. It a challenge to determine the market rate. Is it the rate a rental car agency would charge such as Hertz or Avis? Is it the rate a dealer would charge? Something in the middle? Don't forget the **IRS Publication 15-B (Employer's Tax Guide to Fringe Benefits)** where the lease value is determined by the IRS based on the value of the car. The benefit of ambiguity is the ability to pitch an argument on most numbers.

[Rest of this page blank for a ridiculous table on the leaseback option for you car]

More tables. More numbers. Yes, tables are only meaningful to the table designer yet consider the following in a non S Corp situation-

	5,000	10,000	15,000	20,000
Business Miles	5,000	10,000	15,000	20,000
Personal Miles	5,000	5,000	5,000	5,000
Total Miles	10,000	15,000	20,000	25,000
AAA 2014 Costs for Small Sedan	0.597	0.464	0.397	0.360
less Depreciation, Finance	0.288	0.204	0.161	0.106
Actual Operating Costs	0.309	0.260	0.236	0.254
Mileage Rate Method				
2015 IRS Mileage Rate	0.575	0.575	0.575	0.575
Mileage Deduction on Sched C	2,875	5,750	8,625	11,500
Savings of SE Tax	406	812	1,219	1,625
Savings of Income Tax @25% MFJ	719	1,438	2,156	2,875
Total Savings	1,125	2,250	3,375	4,500
Lease Method				
Annual Lease @ $400/month	4,800	4,800	4,800	4,800
less Depreciation ($3,160 Year 1)	-3,160	-3,160	-3,160	-3,160
Biz Use Expenses Using Actual Costs	1,545	2,603	3,544	5,076
Savings of SE Tax	897	1,046	1,179	1,395
Savings of Income Tax @25% MFJ	1,586	1,851	2,086	2,469
Gain on Net Rental Income @25% MFJ	410	410	410	410
Total Savings	2,073	2,487	2,855	3,454
Delta on Mileage Rate Method	**-948**	**-237**	**520**	**1,045**

Tilt!

The first question is the break-even. That number is **11,875 miles** for a small sedan. That means if you drive fewer miles, then a lease arrangement might be a good idea. Conversely, if you drive more miles than 11,875, then using the mileage rate deduction is better. Yes, this is a middle of the road number. Pun intended.

Second question is depreciation and finance. Since you are charging a lease to your company for the use of the automobile, you cannot also add depreciation and finance charges. Those figures make up a large part of AAA's cost of ownership. You can only pass operational costs proportioned to business use. However, those expenses might be deducted on Schedule E of your individual tax returns, similar to rental properties.

How does the break-even move around? Good question. Frankly, AAA tends to be heavy-handed on the costs. So, if the average costs to operate a vehicle go down or is less than what the AAA thinks, the break-even point decreases. If the market lease rate increases from the $400 used above, the break-even mileage increases.

In other words, as the mileage increases, you are amortizing the same fixed costs across more miles, whereas the IRS is giving you a flat rate of 57.5 cents for the 2015 tax year. Low miles? Lease arrangement might make sense since the mileage rate is lower than the actual costs. High miles? Your actual costs are being spread thinner, but the IRS still gives you 57.5 cents. Things to consider.

How does this arrangement reduce my self-employment taxes? Wow. Another good question- you are full of them. Leasing a car back to your company has the most benefit in the garden variety LLC or partnership where **all** the income is being subjected to self-employment taxes. As you know, an S Corp already sanitizes a bunch of income in the form of a K-1 which is not subjected to self-employment taxes.

So, to reduce your K-1 income in favor of non-passive self-rental income is basically moving money from your right pocket to your left pocket. Both income sources are only taxed at the income tax level. Net zero. But we've already discussed that reducing S corporation income through self-rentals might help reduce your reasonable salary. However, this is more apparent in self-rentals or lease arrangements that are not automobiles. The reimbursement allowances, depreciation limits and business use calculations on automobiles versus other self-rental items makes it less lucrative.

Conversely, in an LLC or partnership where self-employment tax is a concern, the vehicle lease arrangement is a business expense and directly reduces the income, and therefore reduces self-employment taxes. This arrangement might be a good idea if you are unable to use an S Corp election (foreign investor) or if it doesn't make sense to (below break-even income).

There is some danger with the lease back to your company option. The biggest challenge is estimating the actual costs to operate your vehicle, and the second challenge is estimating your mileage. So, if you are close to the break-even point it might not make sense. And engaging in revisionist history is not an ideal situation either.

Some more commentary. The AAA rate is published each year by the American Automobile Association and takes into account fuel prices, average insurance, registrations, etc.

The previous table assumes a 25% marginal tax rate. This is not a huge consideration, but as marginal tax rates increase the break-even point decreases. For example, on a small sedan, a jump from 25% to 33% in marginal tax rate increases your savings by $400 annually for a person who drives 15,000 miles for business **and** elects to use the mileage deduction and **not** the lease arrangement.

Medium sedans. With a slight increase in operating costs and subsequent market lease rates, the break-even is about 13,000 miles. Again, the might be low to some business owners. Hassle versus reward.

What is the net-net?

▲ The lease arrangement seems like an OK idea with low business miles.

▲ It seems exotic. It seems like a cool thing to drop at a party as a genius idea. But in the end, it might not be all that. But looking smart can be better than being smart.

▲ With one vehicle, it only works well in an LLC or partnership where self-employment taxes are being applied to all income.

▲ With several vehicles (fleet) or machinery, lease-backs can prove to be smart tax planning.

To confirm, however, the Watson CPA Group can model your specific situation.

Automobile Decision Tree

In deciding whether to own the automobile personally or through your S corporation, here is a simplified decision tree. It is not a hard and fast set of rules, but will provide some guidance.

▲ If you typically buy new cars every 2-3 years, can justify a business use above 80% and drive 15,000 miles or less per year, then have the company own it. The depreciation will be a great small business tax deduction.

▲ If you typically buy new cars every 2-3 years, but cannot justify business use above 80% **or** drive 15,000 miles or more per year, then own it personally and get reimbursed. At 15,000 miles the tax benefits of depreciation over 2-3 years becomes a wash.

▲ If you typically buy used cars that are 5 years or older, then own it personally and get reimbursed. The POS potentially becomes a huge money maker.

▲ If you buy a new car every 5-6 years, typically spending more than $60,000 and can justify business use above 80% then the question becomes more complicated and depends on miles driven. Fewer than 12,000 miles, have the company own it. More than 12,000 miles, own it personally and get reimbursed. At exactly 12,000 miles, flip a coin.

These are not hard and fast rules. These are rules of thumbs and generalizations. We always caution people trying to split the atom to save some money. At the end of day, most small business owners do what makes him or her feel most comfortable, and the few bucks that might be left on the table is overshadowed by the lack of anxiety and headache.

Trading in cars and buying new ones might create an involuntary Section 1031 Like-Kind exchange without you intending to. There is an IRS Revenue Ruling 61-119 and two tax court cases you can skim tonight in bed-

▲ Redwing Carriers, Inc. v. Tomlinson, 399 F. 2d 652 (5th Cir. 1968)

▲ Bell Lines, Inc. v. United States, 480 F. 2d 710 (4th Cir. 1973)

The IRS issued a Technical Advice Memorandum (TAM200039005) in May 31, 2000. In that memo they referenced the Redwing Carriers federal court case, and did a pretty good job of reiterating the finding. Here is the snippet-

> In Redwing … the Service [IRS] successfully argued that the taxpayer could not shape what was essentially an integrated purchase and trade-in transaction of new and used trucks into two separate transactions. The Fifth Circuit Court of Appeals agreed that the transactions constituted a like kind exchange, citing Rev. Rul. 61-119, 1961-1 C.B. 395. That ruling holds that where a taxpayer sells old equipment used in his trade or business to a dealer and purchases new equipment of like kind from the dealer under circumstances which indicate that the sale and **the purchase are reciprocal and mutually dependent transactions,** the sale and purchase is an exchange of property within the meaning of § 1031 even though the sale and purchase are accomplished by separately executed contracts and are treated as unrelated transactions by the taxpayer and the dealer for record keeping purposes.

Huh? If you own a vehicle and later trade it in for a new vehicle, and the purchase of the new vehicle was predicated on you trading in your current vehicle, the IRS forces you to assume this is a Section 1031 Like-Kind exchange. Why is this bad? This is bad because the basis in your new vehicle will be the basis of your old vehicle, and there is no tax deduction arbitrage in accelerated depreciation in the first year. Here's what you do to dodge the bullet-

▲ Buy your BMW 435 for $70,000. Grey or black.

▲ Depreciate $16,260 (using 2016 numbers) over the next two years. Upgrade the sound system, drive it very little and keep it in the garage.

▲ Sell it to Tina Watson, Senior Partner for the Watson CPA Group, who just loves that car for $54,000. Maybe a small discount, so $53,000.

▲ Buy a Porsche Panamera GTS for an obscene sum of money, but worth every penny.

▲ Depreciate $16,260 (using 2016 numbers) over the next two years.

Does this make sense? Hopefully.

Paying Rent, Home Office

Should I have my LLC or S Corp pay me rent is another daily question. No. Technically this is old school. When you own 2% or more of an S-Corp, the rules dramatically change when it comes to car ownership, paying rent for shareholder assets and home office deductions. These fringe benefits can be considered not so fringe, and therefore income.

What you might be asking is- Is there a way to have the company reimburse, compensate, or otherwise pay for my home office? Or, can I still take a home office deduction with an S corporation? Yes there is a way to claim a home office deduction with an S Corp.

Prior to the IRS making a recommendation to use the Accountable Plan and subsequent reimbursements to the employee (or shareholders), taxpayers would charge their corporation rent and declare the rent as income on Schedule E. Ok, but not elegant.

In the garden variety LLC world, the beauty of this was to take money out of the company as passive income. Since you were changing the color of money from earned income to passive income you were also sidestepping self-employment taxes. In the S corporation world, the beauty of this was to reduce the S Corp's overall income, and therefore reduce the reasonable salary thresholds for shareholders while still taking money out of the company as passive income (again reducing self-employment taxes).

The IRS got sick of this (among other things of course).

The new school way is to use an Accountable Plan and reimburse the employee (you) for expenses associated with the home office. Remember, if you are an S Corp owner, you are **both** shareholder and employee. Imagine yourself as an employee of Google- the relationship would be arms-length, and you would submit expenses to Google just like you should with your own S corporation. Maintaining an arms-length perspective in your dealings as an employee of your S Corp will help you in the long run.

Your company must have an Accountable Plan to take advantage of this scenario. And the basic housekeeping must be satisfied which is a home office must be exclusively and regularly used for business. The reimbursement calculation follows shortly.

Multiple Work Locations

You can have multiple work locations. The IRS states that if you use a home office as your primary location for substantial administrative activities you are allowed to essentially have two work locations. For example, you own a landscaping company and you have an office in your shop. You perform all your administrative activities such as hiring and firing employees, accounting, balancing your checkbook, talking to your attorney, chatting it up with your Colorado Springs CPAs at the Watson CPA Group, etc. in your home office, that office counts as a work location **in addition to** your office in your shop. Here is the play by play blurb from the IRS-

You can have more than one business location, including your home, for a single trade or business. To qualify to deduct the expenses for the business use of your home under the principal place of business test, your home must be your principal place of business for that trade or business. To determine whether your home is your principal place of business, you must consider:

1. The relative importance of the activities performed at each place where you conduct business, and

2. The amount of time spent at each place where you conduct business.

Your home office will qualify as your principal place of business if you meet the following requirements.

1. You use it exclusively and regularly for administrative or management activities of your trade or business.

2. You have no other fixed location where you conduct substantial administrative or management activities of your trade or business.

This also works well for the consultant who works out of his or her home office, but also spends a ton of time on site with the client.

Don't forget that commuting miles between your residence and your office **are not** deductible, but if you have a home office suddenly these miles become business miles and therefore deductible. Boom! The use of Boom! is apparently out of fashion. Whatever.

You can read the full **IRS Publication 587 (Business Use of your Home)** by using the link below-

www.wcgurl.com/5322

Get Reimbursed for the Home Office

The expense report should detail the space used as a home office or storage of business items (inventory, supplies, etc.) as a percentage of overall square footage of the home. This percentage is then applied against rent, mortgage interest, property tax, utilities, HOA dues, insurance and repairs to determine the expense amount to be reimbursed. The reimbursement can be monthly or quarterly or annually- your choice.

No depreciation or mortgage principal payments can be expensed and reimbursed. Depreciation would normally be allowed under the traditional home office deduction on your individual tax return. And you don't have to carry forward the depreciation schedule to recapture it when you sell. Makes life simple.

Keep in mind that two major expenses associated with a home office are mortgage interest and property taxes. These expenses are already 100% deductible on Schedule A, so for most taxpayers the home office deduction or reimbursement is relatively small. And you must reduce your mortgage interest and property taxes being deducted on Schedule A by the amounts reimbursed by your company. No double dipping.

[Rest of this page blank for a table to show the tiny amount a home office gives you]

Here is quick table on what we mean-

Total Home Size	2500
Home Office Size	150
Home Office %	6.00%

Expense	Amount	Reimbursed	Schedule A
Mortgage Interest	15,000	900	14,100
Property Taxes	2,500	150	2,350
Hazard Insurance	1,100	66	NA
Utilities	3,600	216	NA
HOA Dues	600	36	NA
Totals	22,800	1,368	
Total Non Sched A	5,300	318	
Savings @ 25%		**80**	
Savings @ 39.6%		**126**	

In essence with a home office you are only deducting the items that you otherwise cannot deduct on Schedule A of your individual tax return, such as Hazard Insurance, Utilities and HOA Dues. However, for those taxpayers who are seeing Schedule A deductions being phased out due to high income and / or Alternative Minimum Tax (AMT), using the home office reimbursement is a way to ensure these deductions are not reduced.

This can be a huge swing in taxes. This is one of the largest compelling reasons to have the Watson CPA Group prepare both your corporate and individual tax returns- we can move things around to ensure the maximum deduction is obtained.

There are other examples. A quick example would be where you own an office building 100% through an LLC and the business is operating as a separate LLC or S-Corp. The rent must be market rent- we suggest using Zillow or a realtor to periodically update your comparables for market rent analysis. This is outside the home office world (see Chapter 1 on self-rentals).

In our table above, the savings is $80 to $126. This depends on size of course and what you spend. Interestingly, a larger house will reduce your home office expense. The true savings of having a home office is found in deducting mileage from your home that would otherwise be considered non-deductible commuting expense.

Home Office Safe Harbor
There is a safe harbor provision for home office deductions where you can deduct $5 per square foot. This would be on Form 8829 for LLCs and Form 2106 for S corporation shareholders / employees.

If you choose to reimburse yourself for the use of the home office, you **cannot** use the safe harbor method. You must use actual expenses! This is in stark contrast to the mileage reimbursement since the IRS simply gives you a rate per mile regardless of what you spend.

For non S Corps, there are some real advantages such as being able to use all mortgage interest on Schedule A instead of a proration. But there are also some limitations that need to be considered. The Watson CPA Group typically optimizes for both methods for non-S corporations.

Business Travel Deduction
Let's start off by saying the IRS despises business travel deductions. They view it as a way to rifle personal expenses through the business, and on some levels they are correct. But then again, the rules allow for it under some circumstances. The easiest way to explain business travel as a small business tax deduction is to run through some examples.

You travel to Tahoe to look at rental properties. None of the expenses associated with this trip is deductible. If and when you purchase a rental property in Tahoe, the expenses associated with your travels will be considered an acquisition cost and added to the basis of the purchased property. Upon sale you will realize the tax benefit of your travels through a smaller capital gain.

You travel to Las Vegas on Tuesday for a conference. At night you take in the sights, attend the conference on Wednesday and return home the same day. Travel is deductible at 100%, hotel is deductible at 100% and meals are deductible at 50% (the normal deduction).

Same Las Vegas trip but you return on Friday, with Tuesday and Wednesday being the only days you attend the conference. Since the business portion of the trip did not exceed half of the overall trip, none of the travel is deductible. However, Tuesday's and possibly Wednesday's hotel and meal costs are deductible.

Same Las Vegs trip, but the conference is from Tuesday to Thursday, and you still return home on Friday. Travel is deductible at 100%, and hotel is deductible at 100% provided you demonstrate that returning home on Thursday was not economically feasible. Meals would follow suit with the hotel but at 50% (the normal deduction).

You travel to Miami on Thursday for a conference that starts Thursday and ends on Friday. You also schedule business meetings on Monday. You do not return home on Saturday since it was not economically feasible. Travel is deductible at 100%, hotel is deductible at 100% (including the Saturday and Sunday stay) and meals are deductible at 50%.

This is a generalization, but you get the idea. There are additional exceptions for travel outside the United States and additional rules about side trips (such as seeing Mom on the way home from a business trip). See your Mom (that's important) we'll worry about the deduction later!

If your spouse and / or children are employed by the S corporation, and have a genuine need as you for business travel then he or she follows the same rules above. Where business owners get into trouble is the employment part. Your spouse and / or children must have a legitimate position with the company, and a genuine reason for business travel.

Having Junior stuff envelopes is fine, but bringing Junior to a conference on the "evolution of the market economy in the early colonies" probably won't work. Or have Junior attend a seminar where Vickers argues that Gordon Wood "drastically underestimates the impact of social distinctions predicated upon wealth, especially inherited wealth." Gotta love that epic bar scene from Good Will Hunting.

Deducting Business Meals

We chatted about business meals earlier in the chapter. To reiterate the two themes, you must be either-

▲ Entertaining a client, prospect or other business associate (and small groups of the same), and discussing business matters, or

▲ Away from your tax home where you require substantial rest (such as an overnight trip), and the trip is for business purposes.

Your small business tax deduction is limited to 50% under both circumstances.

The theory on this is straightforward- you have to eat regardless of owning a business or not. In other words, your meal is not contributing directly to the operations or success of your business. The IRS is clever- they don't mind giving you a tax deduction today on something that eventually will result in taxable business income through growth and profits in the future.

To deduct a meal or entertainment as a business expense that was shared with a client, prospect or other business associate, there are two scenarios to consider.

For business discussions during a meal, you must have a clear business goal in mind, the discussion must be substantive beyond casual conversation, and you must have an expectation of income or benefit to your business from the meeting. The meeting's main purpose should be business related with the eating of food being incidental or secondary.

Here is a short list of the entertainment activities the IRS will categorically deny a business conversation effectively took place- nightclubs, theaters, sporting events, large social gatherings, hunting or fishing trips, pleasure boating, and Yes, golf outings. The theory is simple- you must be discussing business matters, and in the eyes of the IRS these activities don't allow for that. Not our argument, so don't blame us.

However, and this is a big however, these expenses can be deducted under "associated entertainment" also referred to as "goodwill entertainment." If the entertainment precedes or follows a substantial and bona fide business discussion or meeting, then sporting events, golf outings and the like are deductible.

This also leads to larger groups. For example, the Watson CPA Group has a client appreciation party. Last year, we had over 250 people show up for a baseball game. We could not discuss business matters with each person- impossible. And the IRS would not allow a meals and entertainment deduction for the same reason. However, we deducted the client appreciation party as a promotional expense and maintenance of our goodwill, booked under Advertising.

You may also deduct as a business tax deduction the cost of meals and entertainment for business discussions that occurred before or after the meal or entertainment. For example, after a length day of negotiating a business transaction you take the associate out for a nice dinner to relax. While eating your dinner nothing is discussed about business. Since these two events are so closely related, the cost of the dinner is deducted as a meals and entertainment expense. The business discussions before or after the meal or entertainment must be substantial and closely connected (nexus).

What happens if your spouse tags along to a business meeting over dinner? Or if the client or business associate brings his or her spouse? Do you have to split the bill up between business and non-business participants? No. The IRS considers the spousal attendance to the meeting to be incidental.

Can your spouse be considered a business associate as an employee? Of course. Before you get all excited about trips to Gallagher's in Time Square with your spouse to discuss business, we encourage restraint and reasonableness. If the occasional business discussion occurs during a meal, and the meeting's original intent was business, then this becomes a small business tax deduction at 50%. Position yourself carefully, and Yes, your spouse needs to be an employee or shareholder.

You can deduct 100% of the meals you provide your employees in social settings such as parties or picnics, or if the meal is for the convenience of the employer such as working lunches. This is called de minimis, and here is the blurb form the IRS-

In general, a de minimis benefit is one for which, considering its value and the frequency with which it is provided, is so small as to make accounting for it unreasonable or impractical. De minimis benefits are excluded under **Internal Revenue Code section 132(a)(4)** and include items which are not specifically excluded under other sections of the Code. These include such items as:

▲ Controlled, occasional employee use of photocopier. "Bob, making copies."

▲ Occasional snacks, coffee, doughnuts, etc. Glazed only.

▲ Occasional tickets for entertainment events.

▲ Holiday gifts

▲ Occasional meal money or transportation expense for working overtime

▲ Group-term life insurance for employee spouse or dependent with face value not more than $2,000

▲ Flowers, fruit, books, etc., provided under special circumstances such as your 103 year old grandmother died.

▲ Personal use of a cell phone provided by an employer primarily for business purposes. Don't even go there on this one!

In determining whether a benefit is de minimis, you should always consider its frequency and its value. An essential element of a de minimis benefit is that it is occasional or unusual in frequency. It also must not be a form of disguised compensation. Therefore, routine dinners with your business partner are not de minimis. It might not qualify for the 50% either unless a business purpose is germane to the meal.

Sutter Rule

The Sutter rule allows the IRS to disallow a portion of your business meals when they consume a large part of your normal living expenses. In other words, if every meal you eat is a justifiable business meal, it might not matter under the Sutter rule. This rule was created in **Richard Sutter v. Commissioner, 21 Tax Court 170 (1953),** where Sutter expensed his lunch every day but the court found that "the deduction for the cost of lunches was apparently almost entirely payment for petitioner's own meals when he attended such functions as meetings of the Chamber of Commerce. There is no evidence that these costs were any greater than expenditures which petitioner would have been required to make in any event for his own personal purposes. They must consequently be disallowed."

Sutter was audacious- he deducted everything he could think of. It is a great read.

Again be careful. Business meals and entertainment are low hanging fruit for the IRS. We've seen thousands of dollars in tax savings disappear before our eyes during an examination because the client could not demonstrate the business purpose. To not lose an audit, make sure you keep receipts beyond relying on the credit card statement. In addition, keep a log or journal of the person(s) you met with and the topics of discussion. Be very specific. Memories fade, so if you intend to reconstruct this evidence upon receipt of your examination notice from the IRS, think twice. IRS agents are no dummies on meals and entertainment.

Cohan Rule

Let's briefly discuss record keeping, and then jump into a famous New York entertainer named Cohan who ultimately provided a nifty rule that can be used during an IRS audit. To be able to demonstrate a business deduction you need to show the date, the amount and the person or business you paid. A bank or credit card statement, or canceled check, satisfies this. The second element is the business purpose must be documented either through a logbook, planner or accounting software. Proof of payment plus business purpose equals tax deduction.

Do you need receipts? Yes and no. For travel, gifts, meals and entertainment, if the amount is under $75 then you only need to document the event and business purpose in a logbook or planner. However, if you spend $10 at Costco for some paper, then you need proof of payment plus business purpose documentation. Seems a bit onerous and even contradictory, but it is true.

Enter **Cohan vs. Commissioner, 39 F. 2d 540 (2d Cir. 1930)**. Yes, 1930 and we still use it today. George Cohan gave us "Yankee Doodle Dandy" and "Give My Regards to Broadway", and he gave us a tax deduction rule. His rule is simple- you can approximate your business expenses and ultimately your business tax deduction. What?! No, it is not that simple.

You must have corroborating evidence that demonstrates your expense. For example, as a Colorado Springs CPA firm, the Watson CPA Group can demonstrate that we prepare so many tax returns which are so many pages in length, and therefore we can approximate our paper costs. **Temp. Regs. Sec. 1.274-5T(c)(3)** also gives latitude to the IRS to allow substantiation of a business expense by other means.

The Watson CPA Group has successfully used the Cohan rule in IRS examinations. We have also implemented it during tax preparation when records are incomplete or missing (i.e., one hot mess). Having said that, using estimates and approximations looks bad. Keep good records, please. Do not rely on the Cohan rule or some treasury regulation to save your butt.

The Cohan rule or any type of estimation cannot be used for travel, business gifts, meals and entertainment. All the good stuff need strict record keeping habits. **Section 274(d) of the U.S. Tax Code** also states that listed property must be substantiated with proper documentation. Listed property includes vehicles, equipment generally used in entertainment such as cameras and stereo equipment, and computers. Seems a bit out dated, but there you go. So, if you are a photographer who drives a car for business while entertaining guests, you will be a master at record keeping.

A logbook or planner is very influential during an audit. When a client can show contemporaneous records in a planner that coincides with travel, meals and home office use, the audit lasts about 90 minutes as opposed to four hours with a deficiency notice at the end. Contemporaneous comes from Latin, and means existing or happening during the same period. In other words, as things happen in your world, write them down in a logbook or planner.

Girls are better at this than boys because of purses which is why we now have European shoulder bags for boys. Yet boys still stink at record keeping. If you are a boy, keep in mind that your DNA precludes you from multitasking. You might be doing two things at once, but that in no way is multitasking. Your contemporaneous record keeping might be more sequential.

Capital Leases versus Operating Leases

One of the problems facing small business owners is disguised purchase payments. This happens often when a business leases a copier (for example) for 60 months and then has an option to own the equipment after the lease term expires. A true lease payment is deductible in full each month, but an installment purchase payment is only deducted to the amount of finance or interest charges.

Here is the blurb from **IRS Publication 535**-

Lease or purchase. There may be instances in which you must determine whether your payments are for rent or for the purchase of the property. You must first determine whether your agreement is a lease or a conditional sales contract. Payments made under a conditional sales contract are not deductible as rent expense.

Conditional sales contract. Whether an agreement is a conditional sales contract depends on the intent of the parties. Determine intent based on the provisions of the agreement and the facts and circumstances that exist when you make the agreement. No single test, or special combination of tests, always applies.

However, in general, an agreement may be considered a conditional sales contract rather than a lease if **any** of the following is true.

▲ The agreement applies part of each payment toward an equity interest you will receive.

▲ You get title to the property after you make a stated amount of required payments.

▲ The amount you must pay to use the property for a short time is a large part of the amount you would pay to get title to the property.

▲ You pay much more than the current fair rental value of the property.

▲ You have an option to buy the property at a nominal price compared to the value of the property when you may exercise the option. Determine this value when you make the agreement.

▲ You have an option to buy the property at a nominal price compared to the total amount you have to pay under the agreement.

▲ The agreement designates part of the payments as interest, or that part is easy to recognize as interest.

There's no real value added by exploding all these factors into drawn out explanations. The most common lease problem is the $1 buyout or something similar- be careful what you are getting into with leases that might be disguised as purchases. Not a huge deal, but the accounting and subsequent business deduction will be different.

In the accounting world we call this example a capital lease (as opposed to an operating lease). Here are some more signs of a capital lease to noodle on-

▲ The ownership of the asset is shifted from the lessor to the lessee (you) by the end of the lease period; **or**

▲ The lessee (you) can buy the asset from the lessor at the end of the lease term for a below-market price; **or**

▲ The period of the lease encompasses at least 75% of the useful life of the asset (and the lease is non-cancellable during that time); **or**

▲ The present value of the minimum lease payments required under the lease is at least 90% of the fair value of the asset at the inception of the lease.

Note all the "or's". Again, don't get too caught up in the technicalities. Just understand that you might have a capital lease that needs further investigation and special handling for your accounting records. Operating leases are simple, and deducted in their entirety (such as office rent). Here is the link to the **IRS Publication 535 (Business Expenses)-**

www.wcgurl.com/5334

Putting Your Kids on the Payroll
Should you pay Junior to vacuum? Perhaps. While most parents can't get their kids to clean a counter or put away dishes, perhaps putting kids to work at the office is a good option.

Tax Advantages
There are some minor tax advantages to paying your children- for example, you can pay your child $6,300 in wages, and since the standard deduction for 2016 is $6,300 the child will have not have any taxable income. This will not affect your ability to take the tax exemption for your child. If you pay yourself this income through a shareholder distribution and you are in the 15% tax bracket, you will unnecessarily pay about $885 in income taxes. Your kids are going to take your money anyways- might as well make it tax-advantaged.

You could also pay your child more money since their tax bracket is probably lower than yours. They can gift up to $14,000 per year back to you. Almost hard to say with a straight face.

For regular LLCs, if your child is under 18, the company does not have to pay employment taxes such as Social Security, Medicare and Workers' Compensation Insurance. You can also avoid Unemployment taxes until the child turns 21. But for S-Corps and C-Corps, Social Security and Medicare taxes are paid regardless of age.

Retirement Accounts

Your child can contribute to a retirement account and reduce your taxes. Seriously? Seriously!

For example, a 14 year old can have an IRA or a Roth IRA and contribute 100% of earned wages up the maximum contribution. And since the wages to the child are a direct business expense, this reduces your overall taxable income (lower S Corporation income, lower pass-thru income, and lower shareholder taxes).

IRA Scenario		Roth Scenario	
Junior's Earned Income	11,800	Junior's Earned Income	6,300
Junior's Standard Deduction	6,300	Junior's Standard Deduction	6,300
Junior's IRA Contribution	5,500	Junior's Roth IRA Contribution	5,500
Taxable Income	0	Taxable Income	0
Payroll Taxes @15.3%	1,805	Payroll Taxes @15.3%	964
Mom/Dad Savings @15%	-35	Mom/Dad Savings @15%	-19
Mom/Dad Savings @25%	1,145	Mom/Dad Savings @25%	611
Mom/Dad Savings @39.6%	2,867	Mom/Dad Savings @39.6%	1,531

There are several things at play here. First, Junior must actually work and this is the biggest bone of contention with the IRS. So, get that squared away. Second, Junior and the company will pay 15.3% in payroll taxes, which represent their portions of Social Security and Medicare. Non-refundable, can't avoid it. And therefore the 15.3% is a reduction in available cash and it decreases Mom and Dad's savings.

But since Junior's marginal rate is zero, the 15.3% might still less than Mom and Dad's marginal tax rate (25% and beyond). Wait! There's more! Mom and Dad still get the dependent exemption on their joint tax returns. A win-win. So, in using the above examples, the $35 or $19 you lose when in the 15% marginal tax bracket might not be a loss after all. On paper, Yes, but in the long-run, perhaps No.

Another issue to consider is support. If Junior is 18 or younger, it doesn't matter. But if Junior is going to college and Mom and Dad are paying him to work at the family business, in order for Mom and Dad to take the dependent exemption of Junior, they must provide over half of the Junior's support. This gets tricky, but there are easy arguments for it.

So, there is real savings **and** Junior is already saving for retirement.

A Roth IRA contribution is not deductible while an IRA contribution is, which is why the IRA scenario can have a higher salary. There is not a minimum age for an IRA or Roth IRA- you simply need to have earned income to contribute. And Yes, the money is the child's so when Junior turns 18 and wants to blow it on a new car, it's gone plus penalty. You can't fix everyone.

Company Sponsored Retirement Plan
A company sponsored plan could be a SIMPLE, SEP or 401k plan. The usual age for these types of plans is 21, but the plan may be created or adopted to be as low as 14 years of age. So if you hire your 14 year old and you also have a 19 year old working for the company, that 19-year old suddenly becomes eligible if your company sponsored plan allows 14 year olds. There are hours of service thresholds you could implement as well.

But setting up the plan correctly allows your child to contribute $18,000 to a 401k or the maximum limits on SIMPLE's and SEP's which can be significant. In turn the business gets an instant deduction and the kid gets your money albeit a bit early.

[Rest of this page left blank for a table on Junior's retirement plan]

Conceivably, your child could have a $29,800 salary and contribute all kinds of money to his or her 401k plan and IRA-

IRA <u>and</u> 401k Plan Scenario

Junior's Earned Income	29,800
Junior's Standard Deduction	6,300
Junior's 401k Contribution	18,000
Junior's IRA Contribution	5,500
Taxable Income	0
Payroll Taxes @15.3%	4,559
Mom/Dad Savings @15%	-89
Mom/Dad Savings @25%	2,891
Mom/Dad Savings @28%	3,785

So the rule is this- if you are covered by a retirement plan at work (what the IRS calls active participation), and you earn less than $59,000 adjusted gross income (which Junior does), you can contribute both to a 401k plan and IRA, and get the IRA deduction.

Let's not forget that your company could have a safe harbor 401k plan or some other profit sharing / matching system that increases Junior's retirement account and provides for an income reduction to the company. And lowering the business profits reduces your tax consequence at your marginal tax rate. Don't let this rock go unturned- there are several scenarios to explore and a lot of money to be saved.

Please refer to Chapter 9 of this book for more information on small business retirement plans. And of course, the Watson CPA Group can assist in setting these up. Here is a link about the various options for small business owners to set up retirement-

www.wcgurl.com/401k

IRS and State Concerns

You must be mindful of child labor laws, and as far as the IRS is concerned there are some rules too.

First, the child must actually perform work. Some argue that cleaning bathrooms and stuffing envelopes are different since cleaning bathrooms is non-essential to the business operations and therefore not qualifying. The counter argument is that having your child clean bathrooms replaces your third party janitorial expense. Our advice is to be as legitimate as possible- create a job description, list of expectations, etc. Ensure that the work they do has a business connection.

Also, the pay must be consistent and the pay must be reasonable relative to what you pay others for similar work. Basically you need to treat them like any other employee to avoid troubles. Lastly, you need to keep detailed records such as time cards and job descriptions (of course you do!). This must be a perceived as an arms-length relationship.

Many states have labor laws that dictate the age your child can work, even for Mom and Dad. For example, Indiana allows a 14-year olds to work with a permit. Minors under 14 may work as newspaper carrier, golf caddy, domestic service worker in a private residence (sounds like chores) or farm laborer. Minors under 12 in Indiana can only be farm laborers. Again in Indiana, there is no need for a work permit if the work is outside school hours of 7:30AM to 3:30PM. We bring these examples to light so you understand to check your state or local laws about hiring your kids.

Mom and Dad

The concepts above could also be applied to supporting your Mom and Dad. Aside from possibly making them minority owners and providing them with shareholder distributions, there could be some scenarios where a salary could make sense as well. Other sources of income and tax brackets of course all need to be considered.

Education Assistance with an S-Corp (Section 127)

There are two types of education- one that is open-ended and has no business connection to your trade or profession, and one that helps you improve a current work skill.

Open-Ended Education Assistance

Your LLC or S-Corp can pay up to $5,250 of an employee's tuition and education expenses including your children who work for you. But there are some rules for your child. He or she must-

▲ Be age 21 or older,

▲ Be a legitimate employee of the LLC or S-Corp,

▲ Not own more than 5% of the LLC or S-Corp, and

▲ Not be your dependent.

The Age 21 rule stems from attribution rules whereby a child under the age of 21 is deemed to own the same percentage as his or her parents. So, if you own 100% and your child is 20, your child is considered to be a 100% owner for this benefit (and many others), which obviously exceeds the 5% rule.

For your amusement, **26 USC 1563(e) Constructive Ownership** reads-

> *(6) Children, grandchildren, parents, and grandparents*
> *(A) Minor children*
> *An individual shall be considered as owning stock owned, directly or indirectly, by or for his children who have not attained the age of 21 years, and, if the individual has not attained the age of 21 years, the stock owned, directly or indirectly, by or for his parents.*

And, **26 USC 127(b) Educational Assistance Programs**-

> *(3) Principal shareholders or owners*
> *Not more than 5 percent of the amounts paid or incurred by the employer for educational assistance during the year may be provided for the class of individuals who are shareholders or owners (or their spouses or dependents), each of whom (on any day of the year) owns more than 5 percent of the stock or of the capital or profits interest in the employer.*

So, your kids essentially (a) have constructive ownership until 21 year of age, (b) are considered a 5% shareholder and (c) are ineligible for education assistance. And as mentioned through this book, special rules kick in for a 2% shareholder (or 5% shareholder in this case) triggering tax consequences for benefits received. Therefore the benefit might kick in around senior year in undergraduate school, and certainly for any graduate or post-degree education.

Under Section 127, reimbursable education includes any form of instruction or training that improves or develops the capabilities of an individual, and is not limited to job-related or degree programs. However, qualified expenses **do not** include meals, lodging and transportation.

A written plan must be drafted and employees must be notified of the benefit. Therefore we suggest having each employee sign a notice that explains the benefits, and that they have read and understand the benefits. And no other benefits can be offered as an alternative- in other words, you cannot provide additional pay or bonus for employees who do not use the educational assistance program.

Contact us if you want a sample Section 127 Educational Assistance Program plan for your company to adopt.

Improving Current Work Skills

To be able to deduct education expense as a small business tax deduction, the education must either-

▲ Maintain or improves skills required in your existing business, or,

▲ Is required by law or regulation to maintain your professional status through continuing education credits such as attorneys, accountants, real estate agents, mortgage lenders, etc.

So, can you deduct your MBA? Perhaps. In **Lori A. Singleton-Clarke v. Commissioner, Tax Court Summary Opinion 2009-182**, the court ruled in Lori's favor. She was an established nurse, and she went back to school to obtain an MBA in Health Care Management. She was already in charge of quality control from a management perspective, and the MBA did not lead to an additional and discernable skill. Additionally the court stated that the MBA improved her current work skill as a quality control coordinator. Subtle difference.

Before you drop $50,000 a semester for Wharton or Stanford, be careful. In our experience there is enough case law on either side of the MBA deduction issue to be wary. Having said that, get an MBA because you want the education, degree and ultimately more opportunities. If we can find a way to deduct it, great. If not, you still have improved yourself.

Summary of Small Business Tax Deductions

This chapter is huge, and has a ton of information in it and perhaps it is overwhelming. To reiterate information from the beginning of this chapter there are some over-arching themes and concepts for all small business deductions. The business expense must be-

▲ Ordinary and necessary (IRS Publication 334), **and**

▲ Paid or recognized in the current tax year, **and**

▲ Directly related to your business, **and**

▲ Reasonable, and not lavish or extravagant (IRC Section 162 and IRS Publication 463).

We want to give you this table to help summarize the business deductions that are clearly not allowed (black), the ones that clearly are allowed (white), and the gaggle of exceptions (grey).

Business Expense	Deduction?
401k Plan	Get $500 tax credit from IRS for starting one. Great way to defer taxes. We can set this up.
Advertising	Yes.
Automobiles	Business use only. Use decision tree to see if you should own it or the business. Depends on price, turnover, miles driven, business use and marginal tax rates. Personal use added to W2 Box 1, 3 and 5 using Lease Value rates in IRS Pub 15-B.
Business Travel	All kinds of rules. Mix pleasure with business under some circumstances.
Business Meals	50% if business discussion with client, prospect or associate. 50% if traveling away from your tax home on business. 100% for company social gatherings or convenience of the employer (lunch).
Cell Phone	Business use only. Never 100% unless you have second phone. Reimbursed through Accountable Plan.
Client Gifts	Max $25 per recipient per year.

Business Expense	Deduction?
Commissions	Yes.
Commuting Expenses	No. If you have a home office, then commuting becomes business travel and subsequently Yes.
Copier Lease	If the lease can be considered a capital lease, then No. If the lease is an operational lease, then Yes. Depends on the facts and circumstances.
Country Club Dues	No. Don't throw the book. Not our fault.
Defined Benefits Plan	Get $500 tax credit from IRS for starting one. Great way to defer taxes. We can set this up.
Education	Only if improves your current work skills or necessary for professional credentials.
Food	50% if business discussion with client, prospect or associate. 50% if traveling away from your tax home on business. 100% for company social gatherings or convenience of the employer (lunch).
Golf Outing	No. Seriously. Let it go. Unless you have a close nexus to a bona fide business meeting before or after (referred to as "associated entertainment").
Guard Dogs	If you are a high risk defense attorney on the East Coast and need a security detail, then Maybe. Must be a bona fide occupational qualification.
Health Savings Accounts	Company contributions, Yes. Added to your W2 Box 1.
Home Office	If regularly and exclusively used for business then Yes. Multiple locations OK provided home office is primarily used for substantial administrative activities. Reimbursed through Accountable Plan.
Insurance	Business liability insurance, Yes. Auto insurance, Yes if the company owns the car. Health insurance, Yes and added to W2 Box 1. Dental insurance, Yes and added to W2 Box 1. Eye insurance, Yes and added to W2 Box 1. Long Term Care insurance, Yes but limited. Disability insurance, No. Otherwise your benefits become taxable income. Life insurance, No. Only in C corporations where the corporation is the owner and beneficiary (no S corp election!).
Kids On Payroll	Great way of reducing tax liability for the same amount of cash. Must do it correctly and follow state child labor laws.

Business Expense	Deduction?
Legal, Professional Fees	Yes.
Merchant Card Fees	Yes.
Per Diem	Maybe. If employees own more than 10% of a corporation, then No. Sole proprietors and single member LLCs including partners in partnerships, Yes.
Professional Attire	If the clothing is suitable for everyday use then No. If the clothing is a uniform then Yes. Possible advertising expense. No dry cleaning unless clothing otherwise qualifies.
Profit Sharing Plan	Get $500 tax credit from IRS for starting one. Great way to defer taxes. We can set this up.
Retirement Plan	Get $500 tax credit from IRS for starting one. Great way to defer taxes. We can set this up.
Taxes	Sales tax, Yes. Payroll tax, Yes for company portion. Estimated tax payments, No. Nice try.
Utilities	No, unless you have a separate office location. If using home office, utilities is a part of the deductible basis.
Website	Yes.

There you go. There are tons of variations, exceptions, rules to follow, interpretations, positioning, and many more modifiers that we can't think of right now. Please contact us if you have any questions or concerns- we love to run through small business tax deductions with owners. And like a good parent, we try to find ways to say Yes. Yes, you can go to Johnny's house right after you clean your room. Yes, you can deduct that expense provided you document it this way.

Comingling of Money

We've mentioned this previously, and we'll do it again here. Rule #1- Please get a separate checking account for your business, preferably with the same bank as your personal checking account so transfers (shareholder distributions) are easy. Rule #2- Do not pay for personal expenses or any mixed-use expense with business funds.

This is bad for several reasons- the IRS hates it. It erodes the corporate veil which is already dangerously thin since you are a closely held corporation. Lastly, if you need to re-construct your financials because of a QuickBooks disaster or some other disaster, having your business transactions compartmentalized within a bank account makes life better. All money coming in is income. All money going out is an expense or a distribution.

Do you get the feeling that we've said these words before? Like déjà vu? Ever have vuja de? It is the feeling that this has never happened before- opposite of deja-vu. Yes, we did mentioned this before in Chapter 5 on Operating Your S Corp. Here it is again.

Read Rule #2 again. It is imperative to keep an arms-length perspective on you, the employee, and relationship with the S corporation. If you worked for Google or Ford, you wouldn't be able to get the business to buy your groceries or pay your mortgage directly. Same thing with your business. Here is another quick table to help you out with the "Which debit card should I use?" question.

Cash Outflow	Checking Account To Use
Car Lease	Personal, unless lease is in business name.
Gas for Car	Personal, unless owned / registered by business
Estimated Tax Payments	Personal, since an S Corp is a pass-thru entity
Cell Phone	Personal, reimbursed through Accountable Plan
Home Utilities	Personal, reimbursed through Accountable Plan
Home Office Renovations	Personal, possible partial reimbursement
DSW, Banana Republic	Personal, but it would be nice
Shareholder Distribution	Business
Self-Employed Health Insurance	Business
Out of Pocket Medical	Personal, unless you have an HRA
Accountable Plan Reimbursements	Business
401k Contribution	Business
SEP IRA Contribution	Business, but you should use a 401k instead

Read Chapter 6 about Accountable Plans for more information on getting reimbursed as an employee of your S Corp for those expenses that are both personal and business such as cell phones, home offices, internet, etc.

[Rest of page intentionally left blank]

Chapter 9
Health Care Options

Disclosure and Updates

There is no way around this. As you already know the Affordable Care Act has turned things upside down and inside out. Some things remain the same, some things have changed, and some things have yet to change.

There are third-party administrators (TPAs) who assist small businesses (and large businesses) in implementing plans to provide health care reimbursements and to allow for pre-tax deductions of certain expenses. And what makes things exceptionally challenging is that TPAs such as Zane, Base and TASC can disagree (imagine that- lawyers not agreeing). The IRS, DOL, ERISA, ACA and DUH, coupled with all kinds of other agencies both Federally and at the state level have chimed in.

DUH doesn't exist. We were just testing you.

The Watson CPA Group currently endorses TASC headquartered in Madison, Wisconsin (Go Bucky!). Their positions appear to be more in line with our interpretations, their legal team has successfully litigated cases in the past, and frankly their representatives are very talented.

This chapter was last updated **August 12 2014**. Be sure to contact the Watson CPA Group or TASC if you have any questions or concerns about the most recent updates. We are all in for a very long and bumpy ride.

Plans

Before we jump into the legalities of each plan for each business entity, let's first discuss the ins and outs of Health Reimbursement Arrangements (Section 105) and Cafeteria Plans (Section 125).

Section 105

Health Reimbursement Arrangements (HRAs), Health Reimbursement Plans (HRPs) and Medical Reimbursement Plans (MRPs) are all the same thing. Some TPAs attempt to repackage the guts of Section 105 under their own moniker for marketing purposes. Technically, Section 105 plans come from 26 CFR 1.105-11 titled Self-Insurance Medical Reimbursement Plan. For the exciting Federal Regulations, here is the link-

www.wcgurl.com/5405

An HRA (which is the most commonly heard name) allows a qualified business owner to deduct 100% of qualified long-term care insurance, out of pocket medical expenses, and several other related expenses. This is a great way for business owners to reduce their tax consequence. The costs of these programs from TASC is about $400 per year. The break-even analysis is-

15% Marginal Rate Break Even	2,667
25% Marginal Rate Break Even	1,600
28% Marginal Rate Break Even	1,429

If you are in the 25% tax bracket, for example, this means you would need $1,600 in recurring medical expenses to break-even with the cost of the Section 105 plan administration.

HRAs are ONLY available to sole proprietors, single-member LLCs and single owner S Corps, unless accompanied by a group health plan that meets minimum essential coverage requirements. This is called an integrated HRA and allowed by the Affordable Care Act, and clarified in IRS Notice 2013-54.

And as you will learn, Section 125 Cafeteria Plans are NOT available to this same group.

Section 125

Flexible Spending Arrangements (FSAs) and Cafeteria Plans are generally interchangeable from a naming convention. However it is listed under 26 U.S. Code Section 125 titled Cafeteria Plans. More exciting code at-

www.wcgurl.com/5406

A lot of people are familiar with Section 125 Cafeteria Plans since most companies offer them for their employees to deduct health insurance premiums, medical expenses and dependent care on a pre-tax basis. There is even an allowance for transportation expenses for certain commuting people. This is a huge savings since you get the tax deduction instantly, and there are no income limitations or thresholds. Here are some numbers that demonstrate the savings-

Medical Expenses	10,000		
Income	**50,000**	**80,000**	**100,000**
Marginal Tax Rate	25%	25%	28%
Savings with Section 125	2,500	2,500	2,800
Deduction on Schedule A	5,000	2,000	0
Savings without Section 125	1,250	500	0
Difference (again, real money)	**1,250**	**2,000**	**2,800**

By deducting the expenses through a Section 125 Cafeteria Plan, your savings are good at lower incomes and huge at larger incomes. However without a Cafeteria Plan you are relegated to deducting medical expenses on Schedule A, and subsequently the first 10% of your income is disallowed and only those medical expenses exceeding 10% of your income are deductible. That explains the difference show above.

Cafeteria Plans are not available to sole proprietors, single member LLCs, partners and S Corporation shareholders who own more than 2% of the company. However, you are entitled to hire your spouse who can enjoy this benefit subject to discrimination testing. Gotta love a good old fashioned loophole.

Administrative Costs

While you can probably administer your own Section 125 Cafeteria Plan, it is probably best left to the experts. Do you really want to keep up with regulations, compliance and filings? Yuck. TASC is our strong recommendation, and their fees are listed below-

Participants	Annual Fee
1-5	600
6-11	900
12-22	1,200

Note- participants are NOT all eligible employees. You only pay for those who are participating in the program.

Use or Lose It

All Cafeteria Plan payments for the prior tax year must be made by February 15, such as a medical procedure performed on December 31 yet billed in January of the following year. And the reimbursement request must be submitted by March 15 (this is a generalization depending on your plan provisions).

However, there is an interesting caveat to the use or lose it system- if you lose the money because you didn't have enough qualified medical expenses, the money is returned to the company as ordinary income. Whereas if you worked for a larger company that you did not own, the money would essentially be lost. But when you own the company the money returns to the company, is taxed (since it was once deducted), and it is yours to use.

Starting in 2014, Cafeteria Plans can either extend reimbursements until March 15 or allow you to rollover $500 to the next year. This is an either/or option within the plan covering all employees (not user selected).

Health Savings Accounts (HSAs)

Individuals and small businesses can make HSA contributions as allowed by a high-deductible health insurance plan. So you cannot have an HSA without a high-deductible plan. This acts very similarly to a Cafeteria Plan since you have an account that offers an instant tax deduction when you make contributions into your account. However, one major difference is that it is not a use it or lose it system- your money can accumulate, and you are allowed to invest it within the provision of the plan.

It is a foregone conclusion that when you get older you'll need more medical attention. When you need a new hip at age 72, you'll be drawing money from somewhere- either your 401k, IRAs or your HSA. So in some regards, your HSA becomes a tax-favorable retirement vehicle.

Dependent care benefits cannot be paid through your HSA, nor can an HSA pay for things like cosmetic surgery, fitness programs, maternity clothes, vitamins, etc.

Contribution limits for 2014 are $3,300 for singles, and $6,550 for family plans plus $1,000 each if you are 55 years or older (catchup).

Sole proprietors, single member LLCs and partners cannot have the company make a direct HSA contribution, yet are still allowed to take the deduction on Form 1040 (more on this in a bit).

Gaming the HSA System

As you understand, HSAs are only available in conjunction with a high deductible health plan. The term high deductible means any policy that exceeds $2,500 for a family plan. As you might not be aware, having kids is expensive. Expensive at birth, and it only gets worse- food, cars, house damage, college, etc. But the birth and post natal care is where you can get some HSA help.

Many people will pick a high deductible plan in their pre-children years. This is great. Max out your HSA each year that you can. When you are ready for a family, switch your insurance to a PPO or some other policy that is more robust and more expensive. This protects you during pregnancy, birth and the first 24 months where costs are the highest. Any out of pocket expenses can paid with your HSA funds. Beauty.

Then, when your family medical costs have stabilized, switch back to the high deductible plan.

Long-Term Care

You can purchase insurance policies that cover qualified long-term care services, and include those premiums when calculating your overall medical deduction. Qualified services include necessary diagnostic, preventative, therapeutic, curing treating, mitigating and rehabilitative services, including maintenance or personal care services. They must be required by a chronically ill person and provided by a licensed health care practitioner.

Big list, but this is referring to your typical nursing home and in-home care services usually reserved for the elderly who are unable to completely care for themselves. And Yes, we will all be there. This is probably the biggest overlooked retirement planning checkbox. Our physical longevity has outpaced our cognitive ability by several years. In other words, our bodies last longer than our minds. Here are the deduction limits for 2014-

Under 40	370
Age 41-50	700
Age 51-60	1,400
Age 61-70	3,720
Over 70	4,660

To deduct long-term care premiums you must have a Section 105 HRA or Section 125 Cafeteria Plan in place.

One Person Show or Husband/Wife Team, S Corporation

Generally speaking, for S Corporations with a single owner and therefore only one employee, the rules haven't changed. Business as usual. Remember, as a shareholder of an S Corp you are also considered an employee. If you hire your spouse or if your spouse is also a shareholder of the S Corp, this strategy blows up because you now have two employees.

Sole proprietors and single member LLCs will handle some of these issues differently, so we'll first tackle the S Corporation owner and how health insurance premiums and all the above-mentioned programs interact.

Health Insurance Premiums*

In **IRS Notice 2008-1** health insurance premiums including dental and vision, paid under individual medical and health insurance plans may be deducted as an "above the line" deduction (as opposed to Itemized Deductions on Schedule A) on your personal tax return if the following conditions are met:

▲ The S-Corp must establish an **Accountable Plan** for the payment of health insurance premiums on behalf of the shareholder.

▲ The S-Corp must either directly pay the premiums for the plan or reimburse the shareholder for the premiums paid. Proper recordkeeping habits must be followed. The Watson CPA Group strongly recommends that the company makes the premium payments directly.

▲ Here's the kicker- premiums paid or reimbursed must be included in Box 1 of the shareholder's W-2. The health insurance premiums are not included in Box 3 Social Security Wages and Box 5 Medicare Wages (thus they are exempt from employment taxes). This might take some payroll coordination, but it certainly is worthwhile.

* Sole proprietors, single member LLCs and partners are treated very similarly without the W-2 angle (see below).

By including the cost of health insurance as wages in Box 1 on your W-2, the S-Corp gets a "wage expense" deduction, which in turn reduces the K-1 income for all shareholders (but each shareholder gets comparable a bump in W-2 income as a part of his or her reasonable salary). On your personal tax return, you will get a dollar for dollar deduction for health insurance premiums paid.

You take this deduction on line 29 of Form 1040. This directly reduces your adjusted gross income, and is not a Schedule A itemized deduction (which is good). **If this procedure is not followed**, the premiums can only be deducted on Schedule A subject to the 10.0% income thresholds for medical expenses (which is not good). The quality and subsequent tax savings of this deduction is similar to the Cafeteria Plan example.

The policy can be in the name of the shareholder yet the S-Corp can make the premium payments directly. Or the shareholder can pay the premiums and be reimbursed- we suggest keeping the paper trail to a minimum and having the company pay directly.

Spouse Has Health Insurance
If your spouse has health insurance from another employer, the additional cost to cover the family or to cover you might be deductible, but probably not. The probably not part comes from the observation that most companies are already deducting health insurance on a pre-tax basis, and to take a portion of that as self-employed health insurance would be double-dipping.

So, if your spouse is spending $500 per month and $200 of that is additional premium to cover you, the entire $500 is probably being deducted pre-tax, providing an instant tax savings already. It was worth the thought though. No fault in asking.

Health Savings Accounts (HSAs)
These are treated similarly to health insurance premiums for the self-employed. Therefore, your company can make the contributions directly into your account, and add the contribution amounts to your W-2, Box 1 only. This in turn is deducted on line 25 of your Form 1040 just like health insurance premiums.

How Health Expenses Reduces Self-Employment Taxes
As mentioned earlier, self-employment taxes and Social Security / Medicare taxes are the same thing. When you pay health insurance and / or make health savings account contributions, this must be reported in Box 1 of your W-2. This income is subject to income taxes, but not Social Security and Medicare taxes since the premiums are not included in Box 3 and 5. And you get a $1 for $1 deduction as well on your personal tax return, so the income is a wash.

But extra savings kick in with the reasonable salary testing. As mentioned, 50% of net income is a jumping off point for a reasonable salary. But what if a big chunk of the 50% is actually health insurance premiums and HSA contributions? Example-

	With Health Insurance	Without Health Insurance
Net Income	100,000	100,000
Reasonable Salary at 50%	50,000	50,000
Health Insurance Premiums	12,000	0
HSA Contribution	5,000	0
W-2, Box 1 Income	50,000	50,000
W-2, Box 3 Social Security Income	33,000	50,000
W-2, Box 5 Medicare Income	33,000	50,000
Social Security, Medicare Taxes	**5,049**	**7,650**
Total Savings	**2,601**	

That's real money. In your pocket. Per year!

Section 105 Health Reimbursement Arrangements (HRA)
If you adopt an HRA, the S Corp can reimburse you directly for out of pocket medical expenses including long-term care benefits. This in turn reduces your business income and therefore your K-1 income and therefore your income taxes. Otherwise, to spend $10 on contact solution requires you to pay yourself $13. Silly. Get an HRA. But be careful as illustrated earlier with a 25% marginal tax rate you need $1,600 in out of pocket medical expenses and long-term care premiums (not including medical, dental or vision premiums) for it to be cost effective.

Husband/Wife Team
Not much is different with a husband and wife team operating an S Corporation. However, only one person can be an owner, and that same person can be the only employee. Heads or tails. The owner can obtain family coverage for health care services such as medical, dental and vision including family HSAs, and use the entire amount for computing the tax deduction. There is not a proration or limitation for an S Corporation shareholder with a family plan.

So, while it is not required to make your spouse an employee, it is also not advised since you will unnecessarily put yourself into a multiple employee scenario requiring a Section 125 Cafeteria Plan for these deductions.

Sole Proprietors and Single Member LLCs

As you know, single-member LLCs are disregarded entities meaning that the IRS views them as a sole proprietors. Each state might recognize the difference, but for health care purposes and illustration, we will follow the IRS perspective.

As a sole proprietor you do not earn a salary. There is not a W-2 issued to you. Therefore you take the self-employed health insurance premium tax deduction on Line 29 of Form 1040. But this is not always ideal or the most elegant because of self-employment taxes. Huh? Let's go to the numbers-

Premiums	10,000	
Net Business Income	100,000	

	No HRA Form 1040	With HRA Schedule C
Net Business Income	100,000	90,000
SE Tax Deduction (50%)	7,650	6,885
Health Insurance Deduction	10,000	0
Adjusted Gross Income	82,350	83,115
SE Taxes	15,300	13,770
Income Taxes	16,444	16,635
Total Taxes Paid	31,744	30,405
Savings (Real? Yes, real money)	**1,339**	

There's a lot of moving parts here. But two things to note- you pay slightly higher income taxes deducting the premiums on Schedule C, but you pay significantly lower self-employment taxes. If you have $15,000 in premiums, the savings is $2,008. Again, real money in your pocket.

What's the catch? With the IRS there's always a catch. To do this, you must adopt a Section 105 Health Reimbursement Arrangement (HRA), and as mentioned earlier the annual administrative cost is $400. Yet, the benefits exceed the costs. Economists love that scenario and you should too.

As a reminder, if you have an HRA you can lump a bunch more medical expenses including long-term care premiums as deductions to your business. So, the $90,000 figure you see above under Schedule C would decrease, and Yes, your savings would therefore increase. Beauty!

One thing to note. You must have enough business income to cover the cost of the premiums, otherwise they are limited.

Multiple Employees

If you have more than one employee, your world will be much different. Under the Affordable Care Act, or perhaps the Unaffordable Care Act, Section 105 HRAs are out unless you have an integrated HRA as described earlier. The only thing left is a Section 125 Cafeteria Plan (sometimes called Flexible Spending Arrangement or FSA).

If you attempt to reimburse your employees directly for their health insurance premium or provide any type of stipend toward that expense, you are violating IRS, DOL and ACA rules. The fines are big. Your only option is to adopt a Section 125 Cafeteria Plan, or gross up employee wages and pay all kinds of unnecessary taxes.

> **Note**: Section 125 Cafeteria Plans are the middle of some controversy right now. IRS Notice 2013-54 suggests that Cafeteria Plans **cannot** be offered without a group health insurance plan. However, some third-party administrators (TPAs) such as TASC are suggesting otherwise. The Watson CPA Group does not know which way this will go when litigated, so use caution if you decide to implement a Section 125 Cafeteria Plan without group health insurance.
>
> Read TASC's memorandum on the subject.

www.wcgurl.com/6555

If you offer group health insurance it also behooves you to adopt a Cafeteria Plan. This allows for the pre-tax deduction of health insurance premiums plus the benefits of flexible spending accounts for out of pocket medical expenses and dependent care benefits.

Remember, owners and partners are not eligible for Cafeteria Plans since they have other options. But this does not preclude you from hiring your spouse to enjoy in these benefits.

Combination Plans
There are advantages to adopting multiple plans, such as a Health Savings Account (HSA) and Section 125 Cafeteria Plan. Or, an HSA and Section 105 Health Reimbursement Arrangement. But there are some rules of course. When you do this, you are essentially creating a limited purpose plan.

Let's make some assumptions- you have $6,000 in your HSA and Junior needs $5,000 in orthodontics. Under the limited purpose plan arrangement, you would pay for the dental expenses through your Section 105 or 125 plan first, leaving your HSA intact. The same holds for $5,000 in Lasik. So, dental and vision expenses would be paid through the Section 105 or 125 plan first. Not required, but more ideal.

However, same scenario, but $5,000 in non-dental or non-vision expenses such as prescriptions. You must use your HSA first. No choice. Priority ordering.

Health Care Summary
Health care options within your small business are challenging. Expensive. Convoluted. What worked today might be wrong tomorrow. All kinds of stuff.

Section 105? 125? HSA? High-Deductible Plans? Reimbursing for health insurance? Hopefully all these elements to your health care options make sense now. If not or if you just want a warm fuzzy "you got it", please contact the Watson CPA Group for assistance.

And be sure to get your updates. Updates can be downloaded in PDF at-

www.watsoncpagroup.com/SubS-Chap7.pdf

Chapter 10
Retirement Planning
(updated March 11 2016)

Retirement Planning Within Your Small Business

Most people have a pretty good handle on personal finance and basic retirement savings, and while the principles are generally the same in the small business world, a lot of business owners have a deer caught in your headlights at 2:00AM look when it comes to leveraging their business for retirement. And there is good reason- retirement planning within your small business carries a bunch more options and potential pitfalls (sounds like life in general, doesn't it?).

Reasons for Small Business Financial Planning

There are three major wealth considerations for small business owners (or anyone for that matter)-

▲ Accumulation (fun and exciting part)

▲ Preservation (the tricky part)

▲ Transfer (the necessary evil part)

Each of these major wealth considerations are interwoven, and need comprehensive focus to ensure the necessary dots are connected, and no gaps or holes exist during transitions. That is where financial planning comes into play.

Accumulation is easy. Most people think if they toss some money at a mutual fund they are planning for retirement. Nope.

Preservation gets tricky since we need to have our money outlast our lives. And with people living well into their 90s, this can be tough. Let's put it another way- if you work for 40 years, from age 25 to 65, you need to save enough to live for another 25-30 years. That is incredible. If you are spending $100,000 at age 55, you better be making $180,000 and putting the $80,000 into a moderate growth retirement vehicle.

Preservation also includes proper insurance, asset protection through trusts, pro-active maneuvering and other tools in the toolbox.

Transfer of wealth is automatic. We have yet to see a hearse with a trailer hitch. Or, said in a completely more stark way, every life come with a death sentence. How it is executed is partially up to you. Did we just ruin your appetite? Sorry.

Transfer of wealth can also be tricky. Current federal estate tax exemption is $5.43M per person, and a passed spouse can posthumously port his or her exemption to the surviving spouse. Not bad. And most people don't have over $11.86M in estate value. Rich people problems (now referred to as high net worth).

These federal exemption amounts are indexed each year, and while Congress can always vote to repeal, this estate tax exemption was written in stone with passing of the American Taxpayer Relief Act of 2012. However, various states have much lower exemptions. Oregon for example is $1M and New Jersey is $600,000. Nebraska has a sliding scale. So, just because you are out of woods federally, doesn't mean the transfer your wealth is free of taxation. Get a plan.

What about your business? Does it have an exit strategy or wealth transfer strategy? Add this to the plan.

The reason for financial planning are-

Goals and Objectives
Define your goals and objectives, determine your current position and discover unmanaged risks. This sounds simple and makes sense, but defining goals and objectives is a fluid concept. They change. And as they change, the plan needs to be malleable enough to adopt. Financial plans are modified annually or whenever a major life change as occurred, whichever is more frequent. This is important.

The Plan
Financial plans also create a blueprint and chart a course on how to get reach goals and objectives while managing risk. Again, this sounds simple. But even the most basic house needs a blueprint for framers, plumbers, electricians and even inspectors to review and implement. And in the case of a financial plan, these same players are your financial advisors, tax professionals, attorneys and insurance specialists.

A financial plan brings these people together to work in concert. This is why the Watson CPA Group is a part of The One Call Team-

www.watsoncpagroup.com/toc

Accountability

Financial plans also provide confidence, measure success and hold everyone accountable. If everyone agrees that your financial plan will ensure financial security in your life, then it becomes a measuring stick for determining success along the way. Anyone can throw some money at an investment, but what does it mean? And does it fit the plan? And is the selection of that investment meet the plan's objectives.

The Watson CPA Group can always assist you with retirement and financial planning as it relates to your small business and taxation. And if you need a referral for a financial advisor we can offer that too.

Small Business Retirement Plans Comparison

We are going to put the carriage in front of the horse, and show you a comparison of basic small business retirement plans before explaining each plan. We cheated, and used Yahoo! Finance's online calculator to demonstrate these differences. Why re-invent the wheel? And frankly, Yahoo! Finance does a fantastic job at this type of stuff. Here is their link-

www.wcgurl.com/6103

[Rest of page intentionally left blank for really cool comparison table]

We took a handful of salaries (for corporations) and net incomes (for sole proprietors and partners in partnerships) and plugged them into Yahoo! Finance's calculator, and came up with the following table based on 2016 limits-

Salary/Income	Entity	Max 401k	Max SEP IRA	Max SIMPLE
40,000	Sole Prop	25,435	7,435	13583
40,000	Corporation	28,000	10,000	13,700
60,000	Sole Prop	29,152	11,152	14,124
60,000	Corporation	33,000	15,000	14,300
80,000	Sole Prop	32,870	14,870	14,665
80,000	Corporation	38,000	20,000	14,900
144,000	Sole Prop	44,837	26,837	16,408
144,000	Corporation	**54,000**	36,000	16,820
175,000	Sole Prop	50,954	32,954	17,299
175,000	Corporation	54,000	43,750	17,750
216,000	Sole Prop	**54,000**	41,044	18,477
216,000	Corporation	54,000	**54,000**	18,980

Note the underlined and bolded $54,000 number. This is the maximum defined contribution amount permitted in 2016 per plan (and Yes you can have two plans- we'll talk about Greg and his two plans in an example later).

Crazy! Some quick observations-

▲ In 2016, the maximum you can contribute to a qualified retirement plan is $53,000. You can go above this with a defined benefits pension (cash balance)- more on that later.

▲ Partnerships (those required to file Form 1065) follow the same limits as Sole Prop above.

▲ $140,000 in W-2 salary from your C Corp or S Corp is the magic number for maximizing your 401k. After that, any increase in salary does not help. Your fastest way to reach your contribution limit is through a 401k plan.

▲ $212,000 in Schedule C income from your small business or K-1 partnership income from your Schedule E as reported on your individual tax return is the magic number for maximizing your SEP IRA contribution. SEPs are old school and used for crisis management rather than planning (more on that too).

▲ Earned income from a sole proprietor is net profit minus 50% of your self-employment tax minus your contribution. Since the contribution actually adjusts the maximum contribution, this can be a circular reference. And No, 401k or SEP contributions do not reduce SE tax.

▲ 401k max is computed by taking $18,000 employee (you) contribution, plus 25% of your W-2 or earned income (as adjusted).

▲ SEP IRA max is computed by taking 25% of your W-2 or earned income (as adjusted).

▲ Max SIMPLE 401k is basically $12,000 plus 3% of your W-2 or earned income (as adjusted). Don't spend too much time thinking about SIMPLE 401k plans.

▲ You can add $6,000 for catchup contributions if you are 50 years old or older.

Let's talk about each of these qualified plans in turn, starting with the 401k. Out of the box, or non-traditional retirement plans will follow (profit sharing plans, defined benefits pensions, cash balance plans, Section 79 plans, etc.). Exciting!

Self Employed Retirement Plan Basics

There are two plan basics, either a defined contribution plan or a defined benefits plan.

A defined benefit plan is a benefit that is payable to you upon retirement. It is usually based on formulas to compute the periodic payments made to you during retirement. These are sometimes referred to as a pension or annuity since a benefit is defined, and the paid to you. For example, military personnel who meet certain obligations are paid a recurring benefit for the rest of their lives. It might be indexed each year for cost of living increases and it might have survivor benefits. Either way it is a guaranteed payment based on a formula. If you live to 100, you might "beat the system." If you die at 55, the pension payment ends and the money set aside for you is lost.

In contrast, a defined contribution plan specifies how much money will be contributed to a retirement plan today. This is precisely how 401k plans work. It removes a lot of the guesswork and risk from guaranteeing a certain defined benefit to you upon retirement. Rather, the risk is all yours- the amount you invest, how long you invest and how you invest it will dictate the retirement benefit. This benefit might be projected with planning software, but it is not technically defined or guaranteed.

Because of guaranteed payments and life expectancy issues, employers have scaled back on defined benefit plans. The cool thing is this- as a small business owner you are the employer and defined benefit plans might have a real place in your retirement planning. One of the examples is a cash balance account which is technically a defined benefits plan, but you can see the account balance like a defined contribution plan. More on that later.

Some terminology clarification. We use the word deferral when referencing employees and contributions when referencing companies. When an employee is putting money into a retirement plan, he or she is deferring a portion of compensation hence our use of deferral. This has nothing to do with deferring taxes since deferrals into Roth 401k plans do not reduce taxes.

As a side bar deferred compensation plans include pension plans, retirement plans and employee stock option plans. For now, let's go back to the defined contribution plan and run through some of the basics.

Retirement Questions to Ask

If financial planning is being skipped, and you need to boil things down a bit. There are three very simple questions that need to be asked and in most cases the last question is the most important.

Retirement Goals and Objectives

When do you want to retire? Will it be transition style or cliff style? Is it better to burn out than to fade away? And then all the issues of how much and for how long.

What type of legacy do you want to leave behind for your heirs? Do you want the check to the mortician to bounce?

Investment Risk

The quintessential question for all financial planning so retirement plans and products can be matched with the investor's level of risk tolerance.

Show Me the Money

How much money can you give up temporarily? This is the most important question. This will single handedly dictate 401k versus SEP IRA versus IRA versus defined benefits pension versus whatever. Perhaps not single handedly, but the amount of cash you can stomach separating from as a small business owner will be a compelling factor in your decision making.

For example, if only have $5,500 to spend, an IRA is all you might need. Having said that, a solo 401k plan which also has a Roth option to it, might be better even if you only put in $5,500. More on that in a bit.

And as any small business owner will explain, most extra dollars are invested back into the business. This is a simple math equation- many small business owners believe in and perhaps even realize a larger return on investment with a dollar invested back into the business versus the stock market or real estate.

In many cases, a small business will be a huge source of retirement income either through residual income (such as an insurance agent or a financial advisor), shareholder or partnership income such as guaranteed payments, or from the sale of the business.

This might not as true for the one-person consultant of course, but you get the idea of pressure between growth and retirement.

Are you worried about the stock market? Sure, it is natural. But there are plenty of reasons to chillax, and plenty of historical data to think about. For a recent post from the Watson CPA Group on the stock market volatility during 2015 and 2016, use this link-

www.wcgurl.com/6119

Tax Savings and Tax Deferrals

Many taxpayers walk into our offices at the Watson CPA Group and tell us they want to pay fewer taxes. Who doesn't? We usually chuckle, and tell the client that he or she is the only one and it is sooooo refreshing to hear someone want to pay fewer taxes. Sorry for being snarky, but taxes are a way of life. And Yes, our job is to have you pay your fair share of taxes and not a dollar more.

Tax savings comes in four variants- you can lie, cheat and steal, or you can understand the allowances and wiggle room afforded by the IRS code. We prefer the latter of course although the audit rate risk of 0.4% for S Corps makes it all too tempting. Darn laws and ethics!

However, notice how 401k plans, IRAs, and other tax-deferred vehicles are **not** listed as one of the four ways to save taxes within self employed retirement plans. A tax deferral is not automatically a tax-savings technique- it might be. It might not be. In true accountant fashion, it depends.

This is a real life case- we have two Boeing engineers who saved about $1 million in the company 401k plan. The employee deferrals were all pre-tax, so they avoided about $250,000 in taxes since they were in the 25% marginal tax rate. Not bad.

However, they currently have four children, a house mortgage, and the usual tax deductions of a household of this size and age. When this couple retires in 2025, their marginal tax rate will increase to 28% due to their pension income and other income sources, and the dramatic reduction in tax deductions and credits.

So, they save at 25% and they will pay it back at 28%. Bummer. But wait! There is more to the story. Just like Paul Harvey, there is a page 2, or in the case of this book, a page 147.

What about all tax deferrals? Where does that money go? Usually to buy stuff like cars, vacations, food, and other consumables which don't offer a return on investment. But what if this same couple invested the current tax deferrals into a conservative portfolio which yields a nice 5% rate of return (after tax consequence)? Things tilt in their favor- so we are back to having a tax benefit from tax deferrals. Huh?

The following is a ridiculously overly simplified table to demonstrate what we are talking about. Here are the assumptions-

▲ Defer $18,000 per year for 10 years

▲ Marginal tax rate is 25% during wage earning years

▲ Rate of return on investing tax deferral savings is 5% net of taxes

Year	Defer	Tax Savings	Growth
1	18,000	4,500	4,725
2	18,000	4,500	9,686
3	18,000	4,500	14,896
4	18,000	4,500	20,365
5	18,000	4,500	26,109
6	18,000	4,500	32,139
7	18,000	4,500	38,471
8	18,000	4,500	45,120
9	18,000	4,500	52,101
10	18,000	4,500	59,431
Totals	**180,000**	**45,000**	**59,431**

A quick recap- you deferred $180,000 and deferred $45,000 in taxes. That deferral grew to $59,431 because you invested it in a safe 5% investment portfolio. Great. What does this do?

28% Tax on Withdrawals	50,400
Growth on Tax Savings	59,431
Realized Savings	**9,031**

If your marginal tax rate increases from 25% to 28%, you still see a savings of $9,031 as shown above. Again, this is predicated on you taking the tax you normally would have paid, and investing it wisely. Not all of us are this disciplined.

But if your marginal tax rate increases from 25% to 33%, your savings is zero. Granted, to jump 8% in marginal tax rate between wage earning years and retirement years seems rare, but you get the point.

33% Tax on Withdrawals	59,400
Growth on Tax Savings	59,431
Realized Savings	**31**

The moral of the story is this. Yes, tax deferrals can lead to tax savings but you have to work the system and be disciplined. Not just today, but for several years. And you need a jump in marginal tax rate that is 8% or less (in general)- assuming you have an increase at all.

What should you do? Probably hedge your bet between pre-tax and post-tax retirement savings. At the end of the day, financial planning and tax projections can help in determining which way to go. The Watson CPA Group can help.

There is also the RMD angle. RMD is a common TLA (three letter acronym) tossed around at bingo parlors and country clubs, and stands for required minimum distributions. In a nutshell, the IRS forces you to take out a portion of your pre-tax retirement savings every year so they can collect on the IOU you gave them several years ago.

RMD calculations are simple. You take your age, find your life expectancy factor and divide that into your aggregate pre-tax account balance. Do you remember science class and discussing a molecule's half-life? RMDs are very similar- over the course of retirement, you must withdraw pre-tax retirement dollars, but the calculus doesn't force you to take it all out over your lifetime. It is always has some factor of your age, and depending on your frugality you might die with a pile of money since the minimum leaves behind a lot.

Here is snippet of the IRS RMD table-

Age	Factor	Age	Factor
70	27.4	80	18.7
71	26.5	81	17.9
72	25.6	82	17.1
73	24.7	83	16.3
74	23.8	84	15.5
75	22.9	85	14.8
76	22.0	86	14.1
77	21.2	87	13.4
78	20.3	88	12.7
79	19.5	89	12.0

So, if you are 75 years old and had $1M in pre-tax money, your RMD would be $43,668 ($1,000,000 divided by 22.9). Here is a link to FINRA's calculator-

www.wcgurl.com/6145

What does this have to do with tax deferrals becoming tax savings? At some point you die, and if you only take out the minimum amount from your accounts, you will die with money in the bank. And this now-inherited IRA, for example, is taxed at your heirs' rate. And there are similar rules where your heirs must take it out over time or within 5 years. The IRS wants to collect on your IOU to them, and they don't want to watch you keep kicking the can down the road.

So, for you there is tax savings built into the RMD system since not all the money is taken out and taxed. If you add in your heirs' marginal tax rates, perhaps this changes from a "family unit" perspective. Heck, you're the dead person- let your kids worry about your taxes by assuming them as their own. It takes a while to payback for all those sleepless nights and stinky diapers, but eventually it happens.

All kidding aside, here is something to consider- with life expectancy well into the 90s, your children might be retired too when you pass. Crazy but realistic, especially if you had kids before you had a career.

Using a 401k Plan in Your Small Business Retirement Options

A 401k plan is a defined contribution plan. Specifically, the name 401k refers to the section in the IRS code that allows for retirement plan contributions to give you an instant tax savings. Technically it is Title 26, Chapter 1, Subchapter D, Part I, Subpart A, Section 401, Subsection K.

Subchapter D deals with deferred compensation. Part I deals with pensions, profit sharing, etc. Subpart A deals with the general rule. Section 401 deals with qualified pensions, profit sharing, etc. And Subsection K deals with deferred arrangements. Who knew?

But from there, the 401k plan has several variants and options. We'll be exploring-

▲ i401k, Solo 401k, Solo K, Uni K, Exclusive K (Owners Only 401k)

▲ Traditional 401k (when you have a staff, yuck)

▲ Safe Harbor Provisions for 401k Plan Testing

▲ Roth Options with a 401k Plan

▲ Two Plans, Rolling Old Plans

▲ Loans and Life Insurance

▲ Age Based or Tiered Profit Sharing Add-On to a 401k Plan

▲ Defined Benefits Pension / Cash Balance Add-On to a 401k Plan

▲ SIMPLE 401k (**not** the same as SIMPLE IRA)

The Owners-Only 401k Plan

The i401k, solo 401k, solo k, uni k, Exclusive K or one-participant 401k is a great small business retirement plan for a one-person show, or a one-person show with a spouse who also works for the company (more on this in a bit). The Economic Growth and Tax Relief Reconciliation Act of 2001 modified the contribution limits and rules, and allowed for an emergence of the owners-only 401k plan.

Due to special tax rules, you can contribute more to this type of plan than other comparable retirement plans. The previous table in the beginning of Chapter 9 illustrated this point with real life numbers. Under the usual rules for defined contribution plans such as SEP IRAs and profit-sharing plans, the deductible contribution is capped at-

▲ 25% of your salary or 25% of your earned income (as adjusted), or

▲ $53,000 for 2016 (or $58,000 for catch-up) whichever is more restrictive.

But your deferrals as an employee into your solo 401k plan do not count towards the 25% cap, and this rule extends to your spouse. This is why the owner-only or solo 401k plan allows for the largest contribution because you have three sources of funding-

▲ You at $18,000 plus $6,000 for catchup (employee deferral), and

▲ Ditto for your spouse, and

▲ The company contribution up to 25% of your compensation, and

▲ The funding is independent of each other (deferrals are deferrals, and contributions are contributions).

Read that again. Let's say you have a $50,000 salary, $36,000 to invest into retirement savings and you are married. If only one person draws a salary, he or she can only defer a maximum of $18,000. But if a married couple pays a $25,000 salary to each person, then the total retirement deferral can be $36,000 without having to increase salaries to allow for a larger company contribution.

With a SEP IRA, in contrast, you would need a 4 x $36,000 or $144,000 salary to make the same retirement contribution. The increase payroll costs would wipe out your returns for at least two years. Not good. We'll talk more about why a SEP IRA is used for crisis management and not for self employed retirement plans.

Deferrals and contributions are discretionary, so you can cut back as cash flow and objectives change. The deadline for funding the employer matching or non-elective contribution to your solo 401k plan is the tax filing deadline for your company including extensions. So, if you are an S Corp, the business tax return (Form 1120S) is due March 15. But with a tax return extension you could delay the funding until September 15. However, sole proprietors have until April 15 (the tax return filing deadline) or October 15 (if you file an extension) to make his or her deposits.

Employee deferrals for corporations (such as an S Corp) must be deposited by the 15th of the following month. So, a March 27 paycheck for Q1 would require you to deposit employee funds by April 15, which is typically a slow day around the Watson CPA Group office (kidding).

These deadlines are true for all 401k plans (solo, company sponsored, Roth option, Safe Harbor provision, etc.). However, there is more wiggle room and less scrutiny for when employee deferrals are deposited since discovery is a challenge (in other words, you won't rat on yourself). To keep things and elegant, we recommend following the same schedule as "big boy" 401k plans.

As a side note, there is nothing saying you cannot wait until Q4 to make all your deferrals into your 401k plan, or any other quarter where perhaps a little bit of market timing or dollar cost averaging might be beneficial. Being the boss gives you flexibility with your small business retirement options.

Unlike company sponsored 401k plans, the individual or solo 401k plan does not need to perform discrimination testing of highly compensated employees (HCEs). More on that in a bit.

Solo 401k plans are also very economical to administer, allow for excellent retirement savings for you and your spouse, and remain simple enough to avoid all the hassles of a full company sponsored plan. A company sponsored plan (in contract to a solo 401k plan) will cost about $1,200 to $1,500 per year.

However, most solo 401k plans only charge for the commission or sales charge of the investments. For example, if you invest in A share mutual funds, there is a one-time sales load or commission of 5.75% (which might vary a bit between funds and fund classes). On that particular investment there are not any additional commissions, and the account fees are very small or non-existent. A shares (as opposed to C shares) are desirable for long-term investing since the commission paid is a one and done, and this cost is essentially amortized over several years.

The only downside is you cannot have this type of 401k if you have employees. Even one part-time admin might blow this up.

Having Staff with a Solo 401k Plan

If you have a staff, but you do not want to deploy a company sponsored 401k plan, you can still maintain an owners only self employed 401k plan by excluding employees.

▲ Your plan can exclude any employee who has not reached the age of 21.

▲ If the employee is 21 years old, and during a calendar year, the plan year (which is usually the calendar year) or any rolling 12-month period does not work at least 1,000 hours, he or she may also be excluded.

If one of these conditions is true, then you can maintain your solo 401k plan.

Don't go out and try to make your admin an independent contractor. In most states, to maintain independent contractor status, the person must hold themselves out to the public as a contractor in that trade of profession. We don't see too many admins running around with business cards and websites advertising admin services.

There is wiggle room. First, there are PEO (professional employee organizations) which allows you to hire the leased employees, but the PEO runs payroll and handles all the human resource functions. You now have an arms-length relationship with a person, and can truly call them a contractor. There is some mounting pressure on PEOs since they help small business owners avoid or reduce a lot of things such as unemployment compensation insurance, workers compensation premiums, fringe benefits, health care, and retirement plans.

You can also have everyone in your office be licensed. For example, insurance agents, financial advisors or real estate agents might work together as a team, but with revenue sharing capabilities an independent contractor status can be maintained while effecting certain "control." This gets tricky and is a narrow example.

Self-Directed 401k Plans

There are 401k plans that allow you to invest into non-traditional investments such as real estate or buying a business. It is beyond the scope of this chapter, and frankly it can be a very bad idea although it sounds hip at your next cocktail party.

A self-directed IRA is easier to setup and maintain, while a self-directed 401k plan is much more challenging. While these two self-directed vehicles, they share similar problems and gotchyas. Here is a recent post on the pitfalls of self-directed IRAs and 401k plans-

www.wcgurl.com/6133

If you want more information, we have coordinated with a company called Equity Trust who can create and help maintain these accounts and plans.

Traditional 401k (A Company Sponsored Plan)

Typically an employee must be allowed to participate in the 401k after obtaining 21 years of age and one year of service. One year of service is defined as 1,000 hours in any calendar year, plan year or rolling 12-month period of time.

Plans can be modified to have less restrictive eligibility requirements.

401k plans cost around $1,200 to $1,600 annually for the plan administration from a TPA (third party administrator) and there are asset management fees of 1.5% to 3.0% as well.

For example, the Watson CPA Group works closely with RPS out of Colorado and Polycomp out of California. These companies are TPAs who design the plan and defend the plan for compliance. From there, you also need an asset manager and custodian to handle the investments. We have experience with Nationwide, American Funds, Transamerica and Vanguard just to name a few.

So you will have two vendors with a traditional or company-sponsored 401k plan. You will have a self employed 401k plan administrator and you will have a custodian / asset manager.

Be very leery of ADP, Paychex and Wells Fargo. Those are the top 401k plans that are lost to competitors who offer better customer service, better choices and overall better plans for you and your employees. Wells Fargo is notorious for offering "free" 401k plans, and once you are committed, you discover that the plan is very limiting and underperforms. Free? Really? When is the last time you received something for free that was worth keeping? You don't work for free, so be careful of those who claim to.

401k Plan Safe Harbor Provision

Solo 401k plans do not need a safe harbor provision- this is reserved for company sponsored 401k plans. Regardless, we believe you should understand the rules.

Congress and the IRS want to ensure that self employed 401k plans do not favor highly compensated employees (HCEs). To be a highly compensated employee you must either own more than 5% of the company or earn more than $120,000 in salary (was $115,000 for a while until 2015). So essentially all small business owners are HCEs from an ownership perspective regardless of salary.

There are three tests-

▲ You cannot defer more than 2% above the average deferral of non-HCEs. Take a standard deviation curve, go out 2%, and draw a line in the sand. This is the ADP test (Actual Deferral Percentage).

▲ Another test looks at matching contributions from the employer (your company). This is the ACP test (Actual Contribution Percentage).

▲ Lastly, the top-heavy test ensures that HCEs don't have more than 60% of the entire plan's value.

As a small business owner, it is easy to fail any of these tests and more likely all three. A common example is where you have several plan participants, but only your HCEs are deferring close to the maximum. This creates a top-heaviness to your small business 401k plan, and the tax code will fail your plan by suggesting it discriminates in favor of a few highly compensated employees. Not your fault of course since you cannot force your staff to make deferrals into the 401k plan, but if the cookie crumbles that way the plan fails.

If your 401k fails the ADP or ACP testing, there are two methods to bring the 401k plan back into compliance. One method is to make an employer contribution for all non-HCEs. Second method is more individualized where each HCE is refunded a portion of their contributions and those amounts are also contributed by the employer to all non-HCEs. Messy and complicated. Read IRS Revenue Procedure 2013-12 for more information.

But isn't that the point? Isn't the point of a self employed retirement plan is to give the people who are worth the most, the most of the company's benefits and resources (i.e., the owners)? Of course it is. At the same time, we have to play by the rules. So help is on the way through the Safe Harbor provision. You can defer the maximum, and also have the company match it, without the HCE testing. What's the catch? There's always a catch in the "harbor."

A Safe Harbor plan must satisfy four requirements, with **required contributions** being the main one. This entails using one of the following formulas-

▲ Basic- Match 100% of the first 3% of compensation, plus 50% of the next 2% of compensation, **or**

▲ Enhanced- Match 100% on the first 4% of the compensation, **or**

▲ Non-Elective- Contribute 3% of compensation to all eligible employees

The first two options appear to be more in favor with small business owners than the third since you can take the chance that not all employees will contribute. In addition, the safe harbor 401k plan must have-

▲ 100% vesting for the required contributions,

▲ provide an annual notice to all participants, and

▲ contain withdrawal restrictions (no hardship withdrawals, for example).

However if the company contributes more than the safe harbor amount, that portion may follow a vesting schedule.

So, don't run out and make your 401k a 401k plan with safe harbor provisioning just because you think you need it. If you do not see a problem passing the discrimination tests, then skip it. For example, you have a small company, the disparity of salaries is low, everyone is participating pretty well and you as the owner are not overloading the plan. Your 401k plan might pass testing as is without having to add the safe harbor provision. Remember, under the safe harbor provision, the employer is **required** to make contributions according to one of the options above. So, there's your catch.

One planning strategy is that if you require a 401k with safe harbor, you could use the required contribution as a way to defer an annual raise. In other words, you could attempt to pass on an employee raise by contributing the obligatory 3% (for example) employer portion of a safe harbor 401k plan. Probably only one time though, unless you enjoy posting jobs and conducting interviews. Even the first attempt might be a bust.

As a side note, those employee groups that have a collective bargaining agreement can have a separate 401k plan. For example, airlines have pilots who are a large employee group and who have the most discretionary income among the other groups. Therefore, if the airline had one single 401k plan, it would probably fail ADP or ACP testing. Instead of electing safe harbor provisioning, the pilot group is able to have its own 401k plan under a collective bargaining agreement which isolates the plan from flight attendants, customer service, mechanics, etc. Who knew? I'll take 401k plans for $600, Alex.

401k Plans with Roth Option (Roth 401k)

If you want your retirement savings to grow tax free, you need a Roth IRA or Roth 401k. But don't get too hung up on the phrase tax free growth. Roth IRAs and Roth 401k's are not for everyone, and tax deferral today (non-Roth investments) might be the better answer as alluded to earlier (see Tax Savings and Tax Deferrals). Let's back up the truck a bit and chat about the Roth tag on an IRA or 401k. And Yes, a Roth IRA is different than a Roth 401k. The words have dramatically different meanings.

The 401k and traditional IRA came about because it was theorized that you had a much higher marginal tax rate during your wage earning years than you would during retirement. For example, you could easily be in the 28% marginal bracket when you are 55, but be in the 15% bracket when you are 70. So, you would save at 28% and pay back at 15%. Not bad. And this theory still holds true for hundreds of thousands of Americans. But, there have been some recent hiccups.

The data were shifting, and suggested that the delta between wage earning marginal tax rate and retirement marginal tax rate was waning. So, some smart people got together and passed laws allowing the Roth IRA. Specifically it was Senator William Roth from Delaware in 1997 who passed the legislation. Thankfully not much was going on in Delaware in the 90s and Senator Roth was able to create this excellent legislation. As you might be aware, the Roth IRA allows you to take after-tax dollars and invest it, and when you take the money out all of it is tax-free. Beauty!

So, the Roth IRA is not a tax deferral system like a traditional IRA. It is a pay tax now and avoid paying tax later system. But all that glitters is not gold as Robert Plant would say. A Roth IRA is only available to those who earn less than $193,000 per year for married filing joint taxpayers ($131,000 for single taxpayers) for the 2016 tax year, and a Roth IRA has very low contribution limits of $5,500. Yuck. Now what?

Enter the Roth 401k which is a hybrid of a 401k and a Roth IRA, and can be a great selection among the small business retirement options. All the taste of a Roth IRA without the calories. Starting January 2006, many companies amended their 401k plans and started introducing Roth options. So, even if your small business doesn't adopt a 401k plan, your spouse's job or your main job might benefit from the Roth 401k. Ask your benefits administrator to see if your other job or your spouse's other job offers the Roth 401k option.

A Roth 401k has no income limitations, and employees (you) can defer up to $18,000 (or $24,000 with catchup). But company contributions cannot be designated as Roth. Since the company matching or profit-sharing is a deduction to the company, these funds are considered pre-tax and will not enjoy tax free growth. In other words, your contributions as an employee may be designated as after-tax or Roth type contributions, and the company's contribution will be automatically designated as pre-tax or traditional type contributions.

In essence, the Roth 401k has two accounts which can be managed separately with the plan, one after-tax and another pre-tax.

Since the biggest challenge in deciding on using a Roth IRA or Roth 401k pivots on your marginal tax rate during retirement, and crystal balls don't have the accuracy they used to, a good plan is to hedge against both. A Roth 401k has this feature built-in. Your deferrals as an employee can be Roth (post-tax) which hedge against retirement tax rates being similar to wage earning tax rates. Conversely, company funds are traditional (pre-tax) and hedge against retirement tax rates being lower than wage earning tax rates. Got it? How about this-

Employee deferral into 401k	Pre-Tax (deduction to you)
Employee deferral into Roth 401k	Post-Tax
Company contributions into 401k	Pre-Tax (deduction to you vis a vis the company)
Company contributions into Roth 401k	Not allowed

The mix between the two is the challenging part. 80% Roth and 20% pre-tax? 60-40%? Truly depends on your vision of retirement and your income sources. Bunch of rental income and residual earned income? Rich parents leaving you with thousands of dollars in dividend income? Gotta coin? Two out of three? As mentioned earlier, financial planning and tax projections are the starting point for an answer that will unfortunately take a lifetime to validate. We can see your head stone now- "Her tax projections hit a 95% confidence interval. Kids are proud." Small font or big stone. You decide.

So be careful of anyone telling you to always max out your Roth contributions without at least asking questions. And Yes, there are zillions of calculators available on the internet- simply search for ira versus roth ira calculator and the inundation will be overwhelming. Or perhaps underwhelming.

Historically Roth options on a 401k plan used to be costly, but thanks to Adam Smith and his concept of economics, fierce competition has driven the pricing down. Down to zero, just ask eTrade, Scottrade, TD Ameritrade, or any other trade that comes to mind. Ironically, as far as we know today, Fidelity's self employed 401k plans do not allow for Roth option.

Two 401k Plans

Another twist. Let's say you have a side business and a regular W-2 job where you max out your deferrals into the 401k plan. You cannot make employee deferrals to your side business solo 401k plan since you are collectively limited to $18,000 (or $24,000 with catchup), but your business can make a profit sharing contribution up to $53,000. Here is the word for word example from the IRS (occasionally they illustrate things fairly well)-

Greg, 46, is employed by an employer with a 401(k) plan and he also works as an independent contractor for an unrelated business. Greg sets up a solo 401(k) plan for his independent contracting business. Greg contributes the maximum amount to his employer's 401(k) plan for 2016, $18,000. Greg would also like to contribute the maximum amount to his solo 401(k) plan. He is not able to make further elective deferrals to his solo 401(k) plan because he has already contributed his personal maximum, $18,000. He has enough earned income from his business to contribute the overall maximum for the year, $53,000. Greg can make a non-elective contribution of $53,000 to his solo 401(k) plan. This limit is not reduced by the elective deferrals under his employer's plan because the limit on annual additions applies to each plan separately.

Good ol' Greg. From the employer or company perspective, a non-elective contribution is in contrast to a matching contribution. This means that a contribution can be without the employee making a deferral. This is key since in the tidy IRS example above, Greg has max'd out his deferrals at his regular job, so he cannot make additional deferrals with his side business. However the company can make a non-elective contribution.

A non-elective contribution means that the company's contribution is not dependent on the employee's deferral. Seems counter-intuitive. In other words, you do not put anything into the 401k plan but your business can contribute up to 20% of your income from the business as a garden variety LLC (or 25% of your W-2 from your business if electing S Corporation status). These are also referred to as discretionary or profit sharing contributions.

In summary, the $18,000 limit is your limit as a person. But each 401k plan has a limit of $53,000 (see the last line of the IRS example on the previous page) which can add a lot of muscle to your self employed retirement plan.

No, you cannot add your W-2s together (main job and side job) and use that for the basis of your side job / business employer contribution. That would be nice though.

Rolling Old 401k Plans or IRAs into Your Small Business 401k Plan

Other benefits of having a 401k within your business include being able to consolidate other plan assets such as profit sharing, money-purchase plans, traditional IRAs and SEP IRAs into your 401k plan. And you can gain some elegance with this- for example, often times your IRA will have both deductible and non-deductible contributions. You could roll the deductible contributions into your solo 401k plan and roll the non-deductible contributions into a Roth IRA or Roth 401k (a Roth conversion). Ask us for help. No, Roth IRAs cannot be rolled into your 401k unless the 401k has a Roth option.

Some words of caution. Rolling old IRAs and such into your shiny new self employed 401k plan might not be the best idea. In some cases, the rollovers will be captive or trapped in the 401k plan. For example, let's say you have a $50,000 IRA and you move it into your 401k. Two years later you have a crisis, and need to access the $50,000. Your 401k plan might not allow you to withdraw this money without a hardship, have an in-service rollover or allow loans against the plan assets. These features or some would say poorly documented limitations vary among plan providers.

Also, 401k plans (beyond the solo 401k plans) might have higher fees and fewer options. In our observation, many 401k plans have an annual asset management fee of 1.5% to 3.0% of assets, whereas most IRAs (and solo 401k plans) operate for less than 1.5% annually.

401k Loans and Life Insurance

401k plans may have loan provisions. This means you can borrow up to 50% of the account balance with a hard ceiling of $50,000 (or 50% of $100,000+). You are basically paying yourself interest on the loan.

401k plans can also buy life insurance, which is a neat way of deducting your life insurance premiums since the money going into the 401k may be pre-tax. There are all sorts of rules and limitations, but you should be aware of this option.

Turbo Charged 401k Plans

Oftentimes business owners want to put away a ton of money in a small business 401k plan, but cannot due to inherit limitations within the plan. Or business owners want to keep most of the plan money for themselves, which is shocking yet natural. For example, to have the company make a 10% profit sharing contribution, every eligible employee will also receive a 10% contribution which is usually undesirable. You only thought having a staff was a pain because of drama and turnover. Add this dilemma to the list.

You work hard to make money, and you shouldn't have to work too hard to keep most of it. There are turbocharger kits you can add to your normally aspirated 401k plan. These usually work best with an underlying safe harbor 401k plan. Here we go-

▲ Age-Weighted / New Comparability Profit Sharing Plan, and

▲ Defined Benefits Pension / Cash Balance Plan

Age-Weighted

A profit sharing plan based on age allows older employees to receive more of the profits than younger employees (hence the tricky name of age-weighted). Another way to look at this is to consider those closer to retirement possibly needing the most assistance in saving for retirement. This also makes sense since older employees are usually more valuable, and therefore profit sharing plans can be used to discriminate in their favor.

Age-weighted profit sharing plans are designed to be top heavy, and two people earning the same salary can have very different profit sharing contributions simply based on age which is perfectly acceptable. No, there is a not a weight-weighted formula where older employees are usually heavier and therefore get more of the profit sharing. That would be fun though. Brings a whole new meaning to a top heavy plan. There are probably some more jokes in there, yet we digress.

How the formula works is beyond this book, but an age-weighted profit sharing plan allows a company to contribute more to those employees who are older **including owners**.

New Comparability
The new comparability profit sharing formulas take age-weighted formulas one step further by grouping certain employees together such as officers, executives, clerical, etc. Officers are given a higher portion of the profit sharing, and within the officer group the older employees are given a higher portion. A double shot. For example, a crusty officer will have a much larger contribution than a new administrative assistant.

The new comparability method is also referred to as cross-tested, and will normally have underlying actuary consulting defending the plan's provisions and discrimination. Remember, discrimination is not bad as long as it can be justified and supported. Yes, this adds to the cost. But let's look at a real life example that the Watson CPA Group worked on to see how this works first.

[Rest of page intentionally left blank for another really cool comparison table]

The following is a husband and wife business with over $600,000 in net profits.

Employee	Age	Salary	Deferral	NEC	Profit Sharing	Total
Mike	43	265,000	18,000	7,950	27,050	53,000
Susie	43	212,000	18,000	6,360	28,640	53,000
Linda	35	62,155	2,486	1,865	876	5,227
Aaron	29	39,868	1,595	1,196	562	3,353
Timothy	32	24,611	0	738	347	1,085
Blake	25	33,452	0	1,004	472	1,475
Jacqueline	31	34,411	1,376	1,032	485	2,894
Denise	23	27,529	0	826	388	1,214
Nate	32	22,104	0	663	312	975
Tony	26	22,086	0	663	311	974

Tilt. Here are some observations and clarifications-

▲ NEC refers to non-elective contributions, and in this example these are the contributions required under the safe harbor 401k plan provisions.

▲ Profit sharing is based on salary and age. Note the subtle differences for everyone except Mike and Susie.

▲ $53,000 is the maximum allowed under a 401k plan with tiered profit sharing.

▲ In this real case, the owners kept 75% of all monies put into the plan. Not shabby.

▲ The annual cost in 2016 to administer this plan was $2,500.

▲ The tax deferral savings was over $53,000 for these business owners including state income taxes too (based on 39.6% federal rate and 11% state rate). This was California, and the couple plan to retire in Nevada- instant 11% tax savings.

▲ Yes, those salaries for Mike and Susie are ridiculously high. So the increase in payroll taxes must be weighed against the savings and benefits. After $128,700 (for the 2018 tax year) only Medicare taxes are being "unnecessarily" paid at 2.9%. The benefits could outweigh this 2.9%.

Defined Benefits Pension / Cash Balance Plan

If the age-weighted or new comparability profit sharing plans supercharge a 401k plan, the defined benefits pension and cash balance plan turbocharges it. We can hear gear heads moaning all over the country above turbo and super charging your engine. Regardless, the defined benefits pension and cash balance plan adds a ton of meat to your 401k platter. Here we go.

A defined benefit is in contrast to a 401k plan since a 401k plan is a defined contribution. A defined contribution plan specifies the amount going into the plan and has nothing to do with how much will be available when you start taking withdrawals. It could be $0 or millions. A defined benefit is a calculus where some future benefit is defined, and is usually a stream of payments similar to an annuity.

A cash balance plan is a form of a defined benefits pension, with one major difference. The participant can see his or her account balance grow over time similarly to an IRA or 401k plan. A cash balance plan can be considered a hybrid since it does not rely on formulas and salary histories although it falls under a defined benefits umbrella by definition.

This is important. Since it is a defined benefit, the company has an obligation to fund the plan. Unlike a defined contribution, defined benefit is a 3 to 4 year commitment and a company cannot adjust contributions into the plan based on performance or cash flow needs. There are provisions allowing a company to pause the plan, but that gets tricky really fast. We have heard of cases where the IRS has seized a business owner's house and assets until the pension was correctly funded. Ouch.

A cash balance plan is usually piggybacked onto a safe harbor 401k plan, and it truly is a separate plan (the latter is a defined contribution and the former is a defined benefit). So why would a small business want a cash balance plan in addition to a 401k plan? The usual reason- put more money into a self-employed retirement plan for the owners' personal retirement and defer taxes.

Similar to age-weighted and new comparability profit sharing plans, cash balance plans use a person's age to determine the amount that can be contributed and use actuary consultation to defend the plan's discrimination.

Here is a quick list of the 2017 amounts that can be contributed into a cash balance plan based on age-

Age	401(k)	Cash Balance	Total	Tax Savings @ 45%
65	60,000	251,000	311,000	139,950
64	60,000	257,000	317,000	142,650
63	60,000	263,000	323,000	145,350
62	60,000	268,000	328,000	147,600
61	60,000	254,000	314,000	141,300
60	60,000	241,000	301,000	135,450
59	60,000	228,000	288,000	129,600
58	60,000	217,000	277,000	124,650
57	60,000	205,000	265,000	119,250
56	60,000	195,000	255,000	114,750
55	60,000	184,000	244,000	109,800
54	60,000	175,000	235,000	105,750
53	60,000	166,000	226,000	101,700
52	60,000	157,000	217,000	97,650
51	60,000	149,000	209,000	94,050
50	60,000	141,000	201,000	90,450
49	54,000	134,000	188,000	84,600
48	54,000	127,000	181,000	81,450
47	54,000	120,000	174,000	78,300
46	54,000	114,000	168,000	75,600
45	54,000	108,000	162,000	72,900
44	54,000	102,000	156,000	70,200
43	54,000	97,000	151,000	67,950
42	54,000	92,000	146,000	65,700
41	54,000	87,000	141,000	63,450
40	54,000	82,000	136,000	61,200

Before you lose your mind on the tax savings (which is assumed to be at 45% total), you need the cash to do so. To save $90,450 at age 50 you need to part ways with $201,000 in cash. And if your spouse is on the payroll, you can double it. There are data available for those under 40, we started there for simplicity. Observe that age 62, the amounts decrease.

Here is another real life example that the Watson CPA Group consulted on-

Employee	Age	Salary	401k Deferral	Profit Sharing	Cash Balance	Total Contribution
Betty	45	265,000	18,000	35,000	75,000	128,000
Fred	47	115,385	18,000	35,000	0	53,000
Subtotals		**380,385**	**36,000**	**70,000**	**75,000**	**181,000**
Wilma	43	70,181	9,825	4,562	500	14,887
Dino	25	23,109	693	1,502	500	2,695
Pebbles	29	22,892	687	1,488	500	2,675
Barney	23	13,908	417	904	500	1,821
Mr. Slate	23	13,444	403	874	500	1,777
Arnold	26	11,670	350	0	0	350
Tex	51	7,088	213	0	0	213
Daisy	18	713	0	0	0	0
Subtotals		**163,005**	**12,589**	**9,330**	**2,500**	**24,419**
Totals		**543,390**	**48,589**	**79,330**	**77,500**	**205,419**

It is a lot to absorb, and we could have cut off the example after Pebbles but we wanted to give you a real case. More notes and clarifications-

▲ Betty and Fred are the owners, and were able to keep **92.5%** of the money contributed to the 401k and cash balance plans. That is ridiculously good!

▲ Profit sharing can be on a gradual vesting schedule over 6 years (same holds true for standalone profit sharing plans without the cash balance piggyback).

▲ Cash balance contributions can have a cliff vesting over 3 years (remember the 3 to 4 year commitment previously mentioned).

▲ Total tax savings was 51% since this case was also in California, or about $92,000 combined for just the owners' portion.

▲ The annual cost to administer this in 2016 was $1,750 for the 401k plan portion and $4,300 for the cash balance plan. Cash balance plans are pricey since actuary consultants are used to defend the plan's discrimination. Worth every penny.

Ok, so we've covered the basics of how to turbocharge your 401k plan to allow for more contributions and tax savings. What are some of the downsides?

The plan costs are not low. Sure, the tax savings is much higher than the costs, but those tax savings are actually tax deferrals. And in most cases tax deferrals become tax savings, but you must be disciplined on using those savings to grow your business or invest wisely (which might be the same thing).

Asset management fees range from 1.5% to 3% for Vanguard, American Funds, Nationwide, etc. 401k plans and defined benefits pension plans have two cost elements- the direct plan cost including a per participant charge, plus the asset management fees. Granted asset management fees are everywhere you turn- but small 401k plans usually have the highest. Having said that, small 401k plans are also nimble and completely customizable so your investment options are vast.

The commitment on a defined benefits pension and cash balance can be huge. And there are some devils in details such as minimum interest rate credits and other things that can be challenging. This is not your problem- the people you retain to manage your defined benefits pension and cash balance plan take on this responsibility.

If a handful of employees are older than the owners, this will adversely affect how much the owners can contribute into the plan for themselves. As mentioned, profit sharing and cash balance plans are age-based. Ideally the owners are 8-10 years older than the rank and file for this to work well.

Total holdings in the defined benefits pension plan are limited to $2.3 million to $2.4 million, enough to cover the maximum allowed payment in retirement of $200,000 a year. The IRS also has strict required minimum contribution rules and a steady source of income is fairly important. Therefore, you cannot be a contingency based attorney with a huge stockpile of cash today without being able to demonstrate the ability to support the plan next year and the following years.

Let the financial team at the Watson CPA Group help with laying out your small business retirement options. Stay away from ADP, Paychex and Wells Fargo. Their low cost fee structure is for good reason- very little customer support and therefore the owner (you), spend too much time on HR functions. Poor investment choices so rates of return and performance are stunted.

In working with a handful of third party administrators (TPAs) they all have one thing in common- the plans they take over the most are from ADP, Paychex and Wells Fargo. Do you work for free? Of course not, so why do 401k plan and cash balance plan salespeople expect you to believe that they will? Certainly silly and almost insulting.

SIMPLE 401k

If you have employees beside your spouse, a SIMPLE 401k might be a good option. Under a SIMPLE 401k plan, an employee can elect to defer some of his or her compensation. But unlike a traditional 401k plan, the employer must make either-

▲ A matching contribution up to 3% of each employee's pay up to $265,000 (for 2016), or

▲ A non-elective contribution of 2% of each eligible employee's pay (non-elective means that the company must do it without fail to maintain the plan's integrity)

No other contributions such as profit sharing, can be made and the employees are totally vested in any and all contributions. You can only have 100 or fewer employees, and no other retirement plan is allowed. SIMPLE 401ks are also not subjected to discriminatory testing of highly compensated employees (HCEs) unlike traditional 401k plans.

Contributions are $12,500 in 2016 plus $2,500 for catch-up.

SIMPLEs have fallen out of favor recently since the only real benefits were no testing and low costs- that has changed a lot lately since the landscape of 401k plan providers is much more competitive (low cost) and lawmakers have given us 401k with safe harbor provisions so therefore no highly compensation employee (HCE) testing.

We haven't seen these plans get deployed with any kind of regularity since Bush was president. As in the first one.

SEP IRA

Simplified Employee Pension Individual Retirement Arrangement. Yes, the A in IRA does not stand for Account, it technically is Arrangement but if you say Account it's okay. We know what you mean. But if you call your IRA a 401k, our OCD does not allow us to let that one go. IRAs are not 401ks and 401ks are not IRAs. From what we understand, we can no longer say "our OCD." Our apologies.

How about this? Our super highly stressful and highly technical profession coupled with the desire to be hyper accurate cannot let you call your 401k and IRA and vise versa. Bagels and donuts are both breakfast foods, but that is where it ends. Hopefully that explanation is better than the OCD reference.

Back to business. As an employee, you do not make contributions to a SEP IRA, the company does so on your behalf. And Yes, it is a tax deduction to the company which is essentially a tax deduction to you. The company can contribute 20% of business income (for sole proprietors, single member LLCs and partnerships) or 25% of your salary (for corporations such as S Corps). There is no catchup provisions since the company is making the contribution.

All eligible employees must have a pro-rata employer contribution. So, if you make $100,000 and your assistant makes $30,000, if the company contributes 10% on your behalf it must do the same for your assistant.

Four reasons why these are fading (but there is a silver lining below)-

▲ SEP IRAs require much higher salaries to reach the $53,000 maximum retirement savings for 2016,

▲ Pro-rata contributions strictly based on salaries is no more beneficial or less restrictive than a 401k with Safe Harbor, and

▲ The administrative costs of 401k plans have been reduced to that of a SEP IRA.

▲ Another consideration is that the SEP IRA does not allow for plan loans whereas 401k plans do (up to $50,000 usually).

SEP IRA contributions are due with the associated tax return including extensions (similar to employer contributions in 401k plans). An interesting yet allowed tactic is to always file an extension for your tax returns. This allows you to file your tax returns any time up to the extension deadline, but not make the employer contribution until the extension deadline. Huh? Hang in there on this one. Here is another way of saying it-

You could file an extension on February 1. File your Form 1040 on March 1. And make the contribution on October 15. However, if you skipped the extension filing and simply filed your Form 1040 on March 1, your SEP IRA contribution is due April 15. Weird. Then again we don't make the rules, we just tell you about them.

SEP IRAs are old school in favor of the 401k plan. Unlike 401k plans which must be implemented before the calendar year is over, SEP IRAs can be used for crisis management after the fact. So December 31st can come and go blowing up your desire to have a self employed 401k plan, but a SEP IRA can be created after January 1 and allow for previous year contributions and tax deductions. Again, this is crisis management. Proper planning prevents the need for a SEP IRA.

SEP IRA, Roth IRAs and the Roth Conversion

If you want your retirement savings to grow tax free, you need a Roth IRA or Roth 401k. If tax-free growth is generally preferred, you can accomplish this outside of the company. However, there are some problems, or at least potential problems.

A quick recap of the limitations of a garden variety Roth IRA- a Roth IRA is only available to those who earn less than $193,000 per year for married filing joint taxpayers ($131,000 for single taxpayers) for the 2016 tax year, and a Roth IRA has very low contribution limits of $5,500. What can be done? Two things- a Roth 401k, which grows tax free, can accept company profit sharing and has much higher contribution limits of $18,000 (or $24,000 with catchup) as we've already discussed. That is option #1.

Another Roth like option involves two steps. You create a SEP IRA in 2015 and take your deduction. You convert the SEP IRA into a Roth IRA in 2016, and this in turn creates a taxable event but no penalty. You then create another SEP IRA in the same year to counter the tax consequence of the conversion. Imagine putting $53,000 into a Roth IRA each year- amazing. Frankly the ability to convert might not last long, but we'll take advantage of it as long as we can. However SEP IRAs can be viewed as the middle man, and we always want to cut out the middle man. Implementing a 401k plan cuts out the middle man.

If you have a regular IRA you can do the same thing. Be careful about shooting your income into the stratosphere in terms of marginal tax brackets. Too many financial advisors and taxpayers mess this up. Let us help. Let us model this taxable event.

Another option along the IRA lines is to make a non-deductible IRA contribution in 2015 and then convert that into a Roth IRA the following year. This has zero tax consequence since it was never deducted in the first place. So if you make too much money for a Roth IRA contribution you can contribute to a non-deductible traditional IRA and later convert it.

You are limited to one rollover or conversion per year per account (there is mild controversy within the IRS publications and industry practices on the number of allowed rollovers).

Controlled Groups

Another concern is controlled groups. If you think you are clever and create a holding company to only offer retirement savings plans to certain employees (like your family), the IRS says No. There are controlled group rules where a holding company that controls another company must offer the same retirement programs for both companies.

Two general types of controlled groups might exist- a parent-child and brother-sister. The parent-child is where one company owns another. That's simple. It gets a bit more complicated with brother-sister where various individuals own multiple companies. By definition, a brother-sister controlled group exists when five or fewer individuals, estates or trusts own a controlling interest (80% or more) in each organization and have effective control.

For example, you are smart and you connect with two other smart people to form a multi-member LLC. Since you have a revenue splitting scheme that varies from year to year, you use the multi-member LLC as a funnel and feed income to the underlying S corporations. So each person owns an S Corp that owns an equal interest in the multi-member LLC. Simple enough.

The following page has a pretty image that you might have seen in Chapter 1.

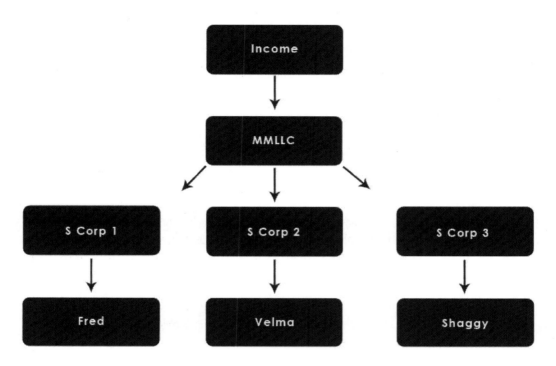

In this example, a 401k plan would be better implemented at the multi-member LLC level. Let's dive into the details shall we?

Affiliated Service Group Rules

Let's say a law firm is structured as a partnership similar to the schematic above. There are three partners. Each partner is separately incorporated as a professional corporation and taxed as an S Corp. Each corporation has a one-third partnership interest in the law firm (MMLLC). The sole employee and sole shareholder of each professional corporation is an attorney who would otherwise be an individual partner of the law firm if he or she were not incorporated. Easy so far.

All billings for legal services are done by the law firm and partnership income is distributed among the corporate partners according to the operating agreement. The law firm is the First Service Organization (FSO) and each of the three S corporations is an A-Organization (A-Org) with respect to that FSO. The four organizations constitute an Affiliated Service Group (ASG). This is the "classic example" of an ASG and can create all kinds of problems with retirement plans.

How did we go from easy to yuck in just a few sentences?

A business is automatically a First Service Organization (FSO) if it engages in one of the following fields-

▲ Accounting
▲ Actuarial Science
▲ Consulting
▲ Engineering / Architecture
▲ Health / Medicine
▲ Insurance
▲ Law
▲ Performing Arts

While you do not see certain professions called out, such as Financial Advisors, the IRS and ERISA are more concerned with function over form. Accounting + Consulting + Insurance might equal Financial Advisor. So be careful on trying to consider this list to be strict from a definitions perspective.

If you are an ASG, then the employees of all of the ASG businesses are deemed to be employed by a single employer for purposes of meeting the retirement plan provisions outlined below-

▲ Non-discrimination rules, IRC Section 401(a)(4)
▲ ADP/ACP testing for 401k plans, IRC Sections 401(k) and 401(m)
▲ Compensation limits, IRC Section 401(a)(17)
▲ Participation and coverage rules, IRC Sections 401(a)(3), 401(a)(26) and 410
▲ Vesting rules, IRC Sections 401(a)(7), and 411
▲ Limits on contributions and benefits, IRC Sections 401(a)(16) and 415
▲ Top-heavy rules, IRC Section 416
▲ SEP and SIMPLE rules, IRC Sections 408(k) and 408(p)

How does the IRS and ERISA find out? Challenging for sure! We've seen companies run around with an ASG for a decade without a problem. But let's say the IRS develops an app that allows them to peer over your shoulder. Aside from them telling you to floss more, they also notice your 401k plan.

Let's also go back to our example and say that Fred, Velma and Shaggy all had created solo 401k plans for each respective S Corp. Bad. Since this is an ASG, solo 401k plans will not work. A traditional or company-sponsored 401k plan would typically be implemented at the MMLLC level and all the S Corp entities would implement the 401k plan as an adopting employer.

This would allow Fred, Velma and Shaggy's S corporations to pay W-2 shareholder wages and make employer contributions at the S Corp level. Keep in mind that the 401k plan will be tested across all entities so discrimination rules would apply including top-heavy testing (which might require a safe harbor election).

Affiliated Service Groups and 401k plans don't defeat the beauty of the MMLLC – S Corp schematic, it just makes it a bit more complicated. There are more rules about FSOs, ASGs, A-Orgs and B-Orgs... nauseating. Just remember the possible issues and to do the homework. The Watson CPA Group works with a handful of Third Party Administrators (TPAs) who can give you deeper advice, and defend the 401k and profit-sharing plans. Here is a quick list-

polycomp	Pamela Stitt	916-773-3480 x2025	pstitt@polycomp.net
Barlow Consulting	Brad Barlow	412-498-6993	barlowconsultinginc@gmail.com
RPS	Sean Kadel	301-481-1575	seank@rpsplanadm.com

401k plans will range from $1,500 to $2,000 annually, and piggybacking a profit-sharing plan will be additional. You can custody the plan assets with any custodian who accepts outside retirement plans and TPA services such as American Funds, TD Ameritrade and Vanguard. Fidelity as of this writing is a No.

Spousal Attribution and Controlled Groups

Spouses generally have attribution to the other spouse by virtue of marriage. For example, a 5% shareholder cannot receive educational benefits from a corporation and by virtue of marriage neither can your spouse.

However, spouses may have separate companies with separate 401k plans without violating controlled group rules. This also allows each plan to be tested separately. For example, one spouse could have a business with employees and offer a 401k plan with safe harbor provisioning. The other spouse could also have a solo 401k plan for his one-person S Corporation.

Here is the snippet from 26 CFR 1.414(c)-4-

(5)Spouse -

(i)General rule. Except as provided in paragraph (b)(5)(ii) of this section, an individual shall be considered to own an interest owned, directly or indirectly, by or for his or her spouse, other than a spouse who is legally separated from the individual under a decree of divorce, whether interlocutory or final, or a decree of separate maintenance.

(ii)Exception. An individual shall not be considered to own an interest in an organization owned, directly or indirectly, by or for his or her spouse on any day of a taxable year of such organization, provided that each of the following conditions are satisfied with respect to such taxable year:

(A) Such individual does not, at any time during such taxable year, own directly any interest in such organization;

(B) Such individual is not a member of the board of directors, a fiduciary, or an employee of such organization and does not participate in the management of such organization at any time during such taxable year;

(C) Not more than 50 percent of such organization's gross income for such taxable year was derived from royalties, rents, dividends, interest, and annuities; and

(D) Such interest in such organization is not, at any time during such taxable year, subject to conditions which substantially restrict or limit the spouse's right to dispose of such interest and which run in favor of the individual or the individual's children who have not attained the age of 21 years. The principles of § 1.414(c)-3(d)(6)(i) shall apply in determining whether a condition is a condition described in the preceding sentence.

Drool. Let's cook the previous legalize down to two major bullets-

▲ Spouses don't have direct ownership in each other's business (mine is mine, yours is yours), and

▲ Spouses don't meddle in each other's business affairs.

Don't get too wrapped up in controlled groups or affiliated service groups- just understand the basic premise of what you offer in one must be offered in others if a controlled group exists. We can help identify the problem and then steer you to people smarter than us on this extremely narrow topic.

Non-Qualified Deferred Compensation Plan

We don't want to go too far down this road, but you should be aware of this option. It is usually reserved for highly compensated employees such as executives who can set aside more money, and it might allow a non-qualified deferral to help a qualified plan, such as a 401k plan, to conform to plan testing. 401k plans with profit sharing and defined benefits pension piggybacks usually eliminate the need for this.

Exotic Stuff

There are all kinds of exotic stuff out there. Be careful. If it sounds too good to be true, check it out. Do your research. Talk to us. Yes, there are several legitimate yet exotic plans out there. A lot of them use life insurance as the vehicle. Life insurance has many unknowns and can prove difficult to tease out the problems or issues. And with life insurance there must be an insurable interest by the policy owner and some of the life insurance-based plans cannot be used in a pass-thru entity such as S Corporations and disregarded entities such as single member LLCs.

Here are some things that might be a good fit for you and your business-

Self-Directed 401k Plans

Self-directed 401k plans allow you to invest into non-traditional investments such as rentals, other businesses, etc. This is very similar to self-directed IRAs (see Chapter 1) However, similarly to self-directed IRAs, self-directed 401k plans have several pitfalls such as unrelated business taxable income (UBTI) and unrelated debt financed income (UDFI). Please visit our website for more information-

www.watsoncpagroup.com/sdira

You can also review Chapter 1. Be careful with self-directed IRAs and 401k plans. Not always a bad thing, but being unaware can leave you with expensive lessons.

Employee Stock Ownership Plans

You can also set up an employee stock ownership plan (ESOP) where employees can purchase company stock over time, and the stock is held in trust. A cool feature is the tax deferral of this system- the employee-owned portion of the company profit's is added to the ESOP's overall asset balance, and is only taxed when the employee makes withdrawals similar to an IRA. Check out the National Center of Employee Ownership here-

www.wcgurl.com/6110

Section 79

Internal Revenue Code Section 79 offers huge deductions of policy premiums and instant tax savings. A Section 79 plan is where life insurance is offered as a group policy, but employees are able to obtain more benefits that are taxable as income. But, there is cash value to the policies that allow for borrowing in the future. There is one inherit problem- when a life insurance policy for a company under ten employees is underwritten, no medical exam is necessary which means the policy has high risk. And to balance that, the policy will have poor cash accumulation. Short-term gains, potentially long-term failures. Are all Section 79 plans bad? No. Just do your homework and ask those pointed questions.

Captive Insurance Company

If you have high property and casualty insurance needs, you can create another corporation that is essentially in the insurance business by collecting premiums from your primary company and investing those premiums into quality investments. The primary company gets a tax deduction since insurance premiums are an expense, and if the premiums are less than $1.2 million per year, the captive insurance company only has to pay taxes on the investment income. The captive insurance company might also be able to take out a key-person life insurance policy as well. As you can imagine, there a bunch of hoops to jump through and lots of due diligence, but a captive insurance company might prove worthwhile.

Controlled Executive Benefits and Endorsement Split-Dollar

These programs are similar in the sense that life insurance is used to retain key employees by controlling the access to the cash value. The tax deferral or tax savings might not be available with type of arrangement, and depending on how it is setup, the payout to the beneficiary might be taxable as well. This is very complicated, and your garden variety financial planner might not be comfortable with these. Your best bet is to speak directly to an advisor who works for a life insurance company such as Transamerica, Northwestern Mutual, New York Life, etc. Or at the very least get a second opinion.

Again, do you homework and ask around before jumping into a life insurance-based product. They have their place, and they can provide huge tax savings especially during high marginal rate tax years. But not all products and plans are the same.

ExPatriates or ExPat Tax Deferral Planning

For our small business owners or contractors working overseas, there is a consideration when it comes to tax deferred retirement planning. Currently the amount of foreign earned income that can be excluded from ordinary income tax is $101,300 for 2016. So, if you qualify as an expat and your income is less than $101,300, all your income is excluded.

Fast forward, if you elect to defer some of your earnings into a tax deferred retirement account you might be creating a tax liability unnecessarily. In other words, if your income was already being excluded from income tax, why put money into a tax deferred retirement account just to pay tax on the money later when that money was never supposed to be taxed in the first place. Huh? Stay with us.

You make $101,300. You pay $0 in taxes. You put $5,500 in a normal trading account. This $5,500 was never taxed and never will be. You make $10,000 on it because you're smart. You sell the investments and recognized a $10,000 taxable gain all at capital gains rates.

Same situation, but with an IRA-

You make $101,300. You pay $0 in taxes. You put $5,500 in an IRA. This $5,500 is not taxed. You make $10,000 on it because you're smart. You sell the investments, withdraw the money and recognized a $15,500 taxable gain, all at ordinary income tax rates.

There are more devils in the details of course, but you get the general idea. To put money away in a tax deferred retirement account when that income was already going to be excluded generally does not make sense. A Roth IRA in this situation would be more ideal.

Implementing a 401k plan sidesteps this problem. If you are a self-employed expat and you elect S corporation status, you can defer a portion of your salary and the company can make a profit sharing contribution (which reduces business income and subsequent taxes), yet you enjoy the full $101,300 exclusion on your W-2 and K-1 incomes. Save taxes with the exclusion, and defer taxes with the 401k plan. Not a true double-dip, but a good way to use two systems for tax savings simultaneously.

[Rest of this page blank for a nice chapter summary]

Small Business Retirement Planning Recap

There are also several options and combination of options, and we can work with you to settle into the best plans. Here are some jumping off points-

▲ **One Person Show or Husband/Wife Team** – Solo 401k plan with Roth Option is the best bet. Very low cost, efficient contributions, and has a good mix of pre-tax and after-tax contributions to hedge against future income tax rate risk.

Second best option is SEP IRA which allows conversion to Roth IRA each year. But this is usually after the fact, or when you are in crisis management mode and want to save taxes.

▲ **Multiple Employees** – Company-sponsored 401k plan with Roth and Safe Harbor provisions is the best bet. Similar benefits to Solo 401ks. However, Safe Harbor provisions forces the company to make contributions to avoid highly compensated employee (HCE) testing.

Piggyback the profit sharing plan and cash balance plan to the 401k plan to super-size your contributions while retaining over 90% of the plan assets for the owners.

SIMPLE 401ks are not as attractive. While the non-elective company contributions are slightly lower than 401ks, the contribution limits are low in comparison. At $60,000 in salary, a 401k allows for a total plan injection of $32,500 whereas the SIMPLE 401k is only $13,800.

▲ **Multiple Entities** – Company-sponsored 401k plan implemented at the multi-member LLC level and adopted at the subsidiary S Corp entity level. This would be an Affiliated Service Group and be subjected to controlled group testing.

[more blank pages]

Chapter 11
Business Valuations, Sale, Exit Plans

Business Valuation Techniques

Are you considering buying or selling a business? It can be exciting, but the biggest problem is determining a value. If you are Mark Cuban from Shark Tank, you have money to burn and can take risks on pricing mishaps. But if you are like most people, the value of what you are buying or selling becomes a sensitive issue.

Large corporations that are traded on the New York Stock Exchange or are listed with the NASDAQ are easily valued. If you wanted to buy Apple, you would simply buy all the outstanding shares at market price. While that is an over-simplification, small business are way more complicated in terms of valuation.

Here are the basic techniques-

▲ **Market-Based**- business brokers in a certain geographic area have a good feel for what a business is worth based on historical information, trends, and their ability to add value to the business being sold. But are you comfortable taking someone else' word for it? Perhaps.

▲ **Asset-Based**- this technique looks at the market value, book value and liquidation value of the company's assets. These values will all be different of course with liquidating probably being less than book (depending on prior depreciation), and with book being less than market.

▲ **Earnings-Based**- this takes into account past performance of the company from a cash flow and taxable earnings perspective.

The important thing to remember is that these techniques are not independent of each other. Often they are used in conjunctions with each other. For example and as alluded to earlier, a jumping off point is three times net earnings plus book value. So if your business earned $300,000 per year and had $500,000 in assets, you might be able to justify $1.4M.

Control Premium

There is a concept you should be aware called control premium. It can add significant value to your business during a sale. Let's say you own 30% of a market and your competitor who is also buying your business owns 40% of the market. Comparable in size, but when combined the singular company has control of the market at 70%.

The ability to control the market allows a company to perhaps raise prices, or lower prices temporarily to drive out remaining competition or dictate better terms to vendors. Sure some of this is business school theoretical stuff, but glimmers of these issues are observed in real life, every day.

There are other control premium examples that might include location, key employees, clients, etc. So giving a new buyer more control demands a control premium to the value of the business.

Earnings and Cash Flow Based

This is the most common focus for buyers. For service industries such as law, medical, accounting and information technology, the earnings based valuation technique will be used the most. For example, accountants will sell their practice for a factor of 1.1 to 1.5 of gross revenue. How does a factor get determined?

Simple actually, and we'll use an accounting firm for illustration. First, when you are considering the net earnings of any business you need to back out the officer compensation to determine potential earnings. Here is a quick table showing some of the math-

Gross Revenue	500,000
Expenses	325,000
Officer Wage	75,000
Taxable Earnings	100,000
Earnings, Officer Wages	175,000
Profit Percentage	35%
Three Years of 35%	1.05
Gross Revenue x 1.05	525,000
Earnings x 3 Years	525,000

So this table is suggesting that if your business profits are 35% including your compensation, then 3 x 0.35 equals a factor of 1.05. And since service industries such as our accounting firm example have very little assets, the earnings based technique is usually all a seller and buyer need to reach an agreement.

Assets and Market

Aside from earnings and cash flow valuations, some businesses are attractive because of other reasons. Perhaps a target business has a monopolistic government contract. Or perhaps the target business has some key employees that you want to assume and add to your core competencies. Or channel experience. The list goes on. So while cash is nice, and earnings are nice, not everything is easy to put a value on. These softer assets or intrinsic value can actually be a much larger and smarter reason for an acquisition.

Depreciation, Amortization, Personal Expenses

Other considerations when reviewing a seller's financials are non-cash deductions and personal expenses. When a seller is depreciating assets or amortizing purchases, those expenses only affect the seller's financials. So a careful analysis of cash flow versus taxable income must be performed.

Personal expenses include items such as travel, meals, mileage, home office and family-member wages. Let's be frank- business owners have been known to deduct personal expenses through the business. A buyer might not get a straight answer from the seller, but these activities should be reviewed and perhaps added back into the statement of cash flows when evaluating a transaction.

Appraisal

Valuation techniques are just conversation starters. There are CPAs and other experts who do nothing but business valuations and appraisals. And if you purchase a business with a Small Business Administration (SBA) or other bank loan, you will undoubtedly have to an appraisal done on the business you are buying.

Purchase Price Allocation

Generally speaking when you purchase another business, you are only buying the assets of that business. In other words, you are not buying the entity. Why not? Well, the entity could have a lot of skeletons in the closet. Using our accounting firm example above, if the previous owner had made a mistake on a tax return and that mistake led to $100,000 in damages for the client, as the new owner do you want that responsibility or exposure? Nope.

There are circumstances where an asset sale is NOT ideal. At times the entity holds a license that is non-transferrable such as a liquor license or the entity has a contract with the government that took 7 years to bid and be awarded, and is also non-transferrable. But for most transactions, you will be executing an asset sale.

Within that asset sale is allocation of assets. Buyers and sellers have competing interests on price of course, but they also have competing interests on tax consequences. And to add to the complication, based on each party's unique circumstances, a buyer and seller's interests might be in concert with each other. In other words, an asset allocation might provide a favorable tax position for the buyer because of his or her own tax world, while still providing a favorable or at least neutral tax position for the seller. And these issues can affect the purchase price as well.

As business consultants and tax accountants, the Watson CPA Group is very aware of these competing interests and how they interplay with price negotiations. Let us help!

Let's review some basics.

Asset	Priority	Buyer	Seller
Cash	Class I	NA	NA
Investments	Class II	NA	NA
Accounts Receivable*	Class III	NA	Ordinary Income
Inventory, Book Value	Class IV	NA	None
Fixed Assets	Class V	Amortized, Varies	Recapture/Gain
Intangibles	Class VI	Amortized, 15 years	Capital Gain
Goodwill	Class VII	Amortized, 15 years	Capital Gain
Non-Compete	NA	Amortized, 15 years	Ordinary Income
Consulting Agreements	NA	Expensed	Income + SE Tax

* Sellers using an accrual method of accounting would not recognize income for the sale of their Accounts Receivable

The IRS breaks assets into classes, and essentially once you've allocated everything to Class I thru Class VI, whatever is left over is then considered Goodwill. So if the price is $200,000 and all your assets add up to $150,000, then you are also purchasing $50,000 in Goodwill.

Some more notes. Cash and investments are usually kept by the seller in an asset sale. And commonly so is Accounts Receivable- most sellers will say that they earned this income, and it is just a matter of collecting. Buyers are usually accepting since collections can be tough- why pay for an asset that might not fulfill its value. If, however, a seller does transfer his or her Accounts Receivable (AR) to you, that will be considered ordinary income for a seller who is uses the cash method of accounting. Who would have Accounts Receivable yet use a cash method of accounting? Lots. The Watson CPA Group invoices clients but does not recognize income until payment is made. We use the cash method of accounting, and use our AR as a way to maintain the naughty list and the good list.

Ok. Back to the competing interests.

Generally speaking, the buyer wants as much allocation to items that are currently deductible such as a consulting agreement and to assets that have short depreciation schedules. However, there are always circumstances where the buyer might want to defer deductions to later years, or some other unique scenarios. When people ask us this question it takes about 10 seconds to ask the question, about 30 seconds to give the generalizations, and about two hours of consultation, projection and review to ensure allocation is being handled correctly.

The seller typically wants as much of the purchase allocated to assets that enjoy capital gains treatment, rather than to assets that bring ordinary income. Capital gains max out at 23.8% (including the net investment income tax) where as ordinary income could be as high at 39.6%. Again, there are always scenarios that might make sense to flip this around- perhaps there is a net operating loss from previous years that needs to be used before expiration, or some other situation.

Bottom line is that price and asset allocation must be handled carefully. It is commonly used a negotiation tactic, and to properly negotiate you as a buyer or a seller should know what the other side is thinking. That's just smart business.

Recapture of Depreciation

Assets that are eligible for depreciation might have two elements of gain. One is recapture of depreciation and the other is capital gain. Let's say you had $50,000 in furniture that is being sold with the business, and you depreciated it to $10,000. If $65,000 was allocated to furniture, you would have a $40,000 recapture taxed as ordinary income and another $15,000 in capital gains taxed at your capital gains rate. Here is in table format-

Furniture Purchase Price	50,000
Accumulated Depreciation	40,000
Tax Book Value	10,000
Price Allocation to Asset	65,000
Tax Book Value	10,000
Recapture, Ordinary Income	40,000
Remainder, Capital Gains	15,000

Non-Compete Agreements

Even though non-compete agreements are tough to enforce they still show up in business asset sale and purchase agreements. As an aside, you should consider using a non-disclosure agreement in addition to your non-compete agreement. Typically these are bad for both parties from a tax perspective- non-compete agreements or covenants not to compete, whatever you want to call them, at taxed to the seller as ordinary income but then are amortized over 15 years for the buyer. This is one area that both parties have an interest in keeping low (but you should consult an attorney at to actual value of the non-compete agreement, it might have some repercussions from a litigation perspective).

Sales Tax and Assumed Liabilities

Sales tax might need to be collected on the sale assets, and are usually collected by the buyer. Most sellers will want the buyer to simply back out sales tax from the purchase price. So, if a $500,000 deal would incur $10,000 in sales tax, the buyer is essentially paying $510,000 since the seller still wants $500,000 in proceeds. Sales tax will vary by state and by purchase price allocation, and is only due on certain assets. Again, this needs to be vetted out and modeled by experienced tax accounts- we suggest us.

Of course if the transaction is a stock sale as opposed to an asset sale, then sales tax does not usually apply.

Assumed liabilities. Messy. Try not to do it. There are instances where you must, and it can get complicated beyond the scope of this book.

Employment / Consulting Agreements

Transition between owners is critical. A tax and accounting firm can buy another tax and accounting firm, and even though the work is nearly identical, the seller is usually retained to help with client transition. This is true in most businesses, especially those in the service industry.

The value of the employment or consulting agreement is an instant tax deduction to the buyer, but it incurs ordinary income tax PLUS self-employment tax for the seller. Unless that seller was smart, read our book and elected to be treated as an S Corp. Remember, most deals will be an asset sale, so the seller retains the business entity. And if that entity is an S Corp then that income can be sent through the entity and shelter some of the self-employment tax.

Some more thoughts. At times the buyer and seller will use the employment/consulting agreement as quasi-seller financing without calling it seller financing. This can help with debt ratios, and debt service calculations (more on that later) since the bank will want you to be able to service all debt instruments including their own. These agreements at times can bypass some of that scrutiny.

Also, some attorneys do not like these agreements lasting for more than one year. Some cases have been litigated, and purchase contracts have been considered null and void because there was not an effective transfer of ownership because the seller was under an employment / consulting contract. Seems crazy, but true.

There have been instances where a seller was retained through a consulting agreement, and misrepresented the company to customers. Lawsuits have been successfully litigated resulting in damages being awarded based on the behavior and representations of the seller while contracted as a consultant for the buyer. Be careful.

As a buyer you should get in, use the seller during a short transition, and get going. As a seller, you should help your buyer, defer future client interaction to the new owners, and get out. Transition is one of the toughest things to agree upon, execute and find success. Good luck.

Deal Structure

You will probably need an attorney's advice for your purchase agreement, but here are some highlights to get the creative juices flowing.

Revenue Guarantees, Holdbacks

Many times, especially in service oriented businesses, a buyer is purchasing future cash flows. Therefore if revenue drops off during transition and subsequent ownership transfer, the value of acquisition is reduced. A buyer should protect him or herself by including a revenue guarantee from the seller.

The contract should define the period of time, the guarantee amount and the modification of purchase price. In a contract with seller financing, a reduction in loan balance or debt forgiveness would essentially reduce the purchase price. In cash deals, it is smart to keep a portion of the purchase price in the holdback escrow account. A holdback is where funds are held until certain milestones or obligations- very useful for revenue guarantees, warranty work, work in progress, and any other unknowns.

A buyer could protect themselves with a pay-as-you-go plan. Again, this is useful in a service oriented acquisition where revenues collected are then turned over to the seller using a gross revenue factor.

Seller Financing

A buyer wants the seller to have some skin in the game or dog in the fight, or whatever euphemism you like. And, many SBA loans want this as well. It adds motivation for the seller to ensure the buyer's success during transition.

Due Diligence

Due diligence is a big deal, and it varies by the size of the contract. Sellers have been known to frontload projects or simply inflate sales in an attempt to look attractive to suitors. There are two quick ways to discover that a buyer might have a problem which warrants deeper investigation.

First, tax returns should be reviewed. If the most recent tax return's income is substantially higher than the first two in a three-year look back, you might have a seller inflating the numbers. Remember, as a business owner you want to minimize your tax consequence so a tax return can be a good litmus test of a business' income. Second, a quick tally of deposits should get close to the income numbers on a tax return. Yes, a seller could trickle cash deposits into the bank account to inflate numbers. But when you combined these two quick reviews you can get a good idea of how the business performs.

After that, the sky is the limit on the things a buyer should review. Employment contracts, vendor contracts, title searches and encumbrances, technology of the business, etc.

Work in Progress
Who will be responsible to complete projects that straddle the closing of the sale and purchase? What percentage of completions are agreed upon? How will the revenue collected be assigned and used in revenue guarantee calculations? Any prepayments, deposits or retainers?

Similar to work in progress, or WIP as accountants say, is warranty work. How is that handled? These are all questions that need to be broached, discussed and agreed upon.

Lawyer Stuff
Representations and warranties are attorney nomenclature that need to worm their way into a decent contract. Representations are things that you believe to be true or those things that a reasonable person would expect you to represent as true. Warranties are things that you are guaranteeing to be true, which is a much higher standard. Don't fret over this stuff too much, your attorney will hammer it out.

Indemnification, damages and arbitration are some more terms that you'll find in a contract to protect all the parties' interests.

[Rest of this page blank for no good reason]

Non-Compete Agreements

While non-compete agreements or covenants not to compete continue to get litigated with limited success for the buyer. There are three elements that routinely cause these agreement to get tossed- restricted activities being too vague, restricted are being too broad and time period being too long. In addition, a non-compete agreement cannot prevent someone from earning a living in their chosen profession. On the following page is some language that was used in a purchase contract of a service oriented company-

For good and valuable consideration received as part of this Agreement, Seller herein agrees that for Five (5) years after Closing (the "Restricted Period"), Seller shall not engage in any Competitive Activity, being the current activity of the Seller, within a 100 mile radius of Anytown USA (the "Restricted Area"). During the Restricted Period in the Restricted Area, Seller shall not, except insofar as the restrictions are for the benefit of Buyer:

▲ *Canvas, solicit, or accept any business from any present, clients or new clients of Seller, unless actions are in attempt to gain business for Buyer's sole benefit;*

▲ *Give any other person, firm, partnership, or corporation the right to canvas, solicit, or accept any business for any other firms from any present or past clients of Seller;*

▲ *Directly or indirectly request or advise any present or future clients of Seller to withdraw, curtail, or cancel its business with Buyer;*

▲ *Directly and indirectly disclose to any other person, firm, partnership, or corporation the names of past or present clients of Seller;*

▲ *Solicit, induce or attempt to influence any employee, independent contractor or supplier of Buyer to terminate employment or any other relationship with business of Buyer or the prior business of Seller.*

Seller acknowledges that the restrictions contained in the foregoing sections, in view of the nature of the business in which Buyer is engaged, are reasonable and necessary in order to protect the legitimate interests of Buyer, that their enforcement will not impose a hardship on Seller or significantly impair Seller's ability to earn a livelihood and that any violation thereof would result in irreparable injuries to Buyer. Seller therefore acknowledges that, in the event of Seller's violation of any of these restrictions, Buyer shall be entitled to obtain from any court of competent jurisdiction preliminary and permanent injunctive relief as well as damages and an equitable accounting of all earnings, profits and other benefits arising from such violation, which rights shall be cumulative and in addition to any other rights or remedies to which Buyer may be entitled.

Ok. Don't run out, copy and paste this into your contract and think you are good to go. Every deal and every jurisdiction will require tweaks here and there, but you get the general idea. Basically it will be hard for a buyer to prevent a seller from competing for a livelihood, but a buyer can prevent a seller from poaching their previous clients. Talk to an attorney.

Small Business Administration Loans

The SBA does a wonderful job of providing people with loans for startup and business acquisition purposes. The terms are extremely favorable yet the fees can be a bit high (2-4% of loan value). The SBA uses approved lenders such as Wells Fargo to put deals together, and the process can take 12-16 weeks. Yes, they advertise 8-10 weeks, but in our experiences with consulting on other business acquisitions the process is longer.

Common deals are an 80-10-10, where the SBA lends 80%, seller finances 10% and the buyer brings 10% as a down payment. If there is real estate involved, the SBA really shines since they will finance 50% and a local lender can finance 40% in the first position. This is huge- the SBA is kicking in 50% but taking a junior creditor position. Any local bank would love this arrangement since they are guaranteed to get paid first and paid in full on any default.

SBA loans on business acquisitions is 10 years and current rates are in 5% to 6% range, which is fantastically good. SBA loans on real estate (such as office buildings or commercial space) is 20 years with current rates in the 4.5% to 6.0% range. That too is incredible. If the deal involves both business assets and real estate, then the SBA at times will blend the terms based on the prorated loan amounts. For example, if 33% if used for business assets and 67% is used for real estate, the term might be 17 years with an equally blended interest rate.

SBA deals vary across the board, but they are usually good deals if you can stomach the slow, arduous underwriting and processing. As an aside, there is a fast-track program for deals under $150,000.

Entity Structure

As alluded to earlier most business acquisitions will be an asset sale and purchase. Therefore, you'll need an entity to perfect the terms of the contract. LLCs, partnerships, S Corps, C Corps, etc. all have their place and consultation with the Watson CPA Group will be beneficial in determining the best plan.

If your transaction involves real estate, typically we suggest that a holding company owns the real estate and another operating company owns the business assets. Accountants, attorneys and lenders all like this arrangement from all the angles you would expect- taxes, liability and underwriting. Again, we can help.

Debt Service

This is a big deal, and it is often overlooked. We have seen too many business acquisitions fail because the buyer did not get quality advice on debt service. Let's look at two common scenarios that need to be avoided. First is the asset-heavy acquisition-

Fixed Assets	1,000,000
Income x 3 Years	450,000
Purchase Price	1,450,000
Down Payment	145,000
Financed	1,305,000
Payment (15 Years, 5%)	10,320
Annualized Payments	123,838
Annualized Income	150,000

In this scenario, a buyer would need to have a considerable down payment to make the cash flow provide for debt service plus owner compensation. This was a real case we dealt with recently, and the buyer couldn't stomach working for $16,000 per year for 15 years.

In the second scenario, the fixed assets are small but the terms offered by the seller were onerous in terms of loan length-

Fixed Assets	10,000
Income x 3 Years	90,000
Purchase Price	100,000
Down payment	10,000
Financed	90,000
Payment (5 Years, 5%)	1,698
Annualized Payments	20,381
Annualized Income	30,000

This too was a real case. And in this case, the buyer decided that she did not want to take on the business only to clear $9,500 per year. It wasn't worth the work in her opinion.

In both of these situations the acquisition would have paid for itself from a cash flow perspective. Let's say that the owners in both situations were also able to justify working for the incremental leftover cash ($16,000 in the first scenario, and $9,500 in the second scenario). This only looks at cash.

From a tax perspective, it will be even less attractive since a portion of the annualized payments will be principal reduction which is NOT a tax deduction. So, while your net cash might be $16,000 in the first example you might actually pay taxes on a higher number such as $80,000 (especially in the later years). $80,000 at 25% marginal tax rate becomes a $20,000 tax bill for $16,000 in net cash. Now you are upside down by $4,000, and hopefully future growth can pay for it.. hopefully.

Buy-Sell Agreements

As stated earlier, businesses are easy to start, hard to get out. With partnerships, all owners need clauses in the partnership agreement to deal with divorces, death and incapacitation. Corporations, partnerships and sole proprietors might also want to effect ownership transfer or buyout. Easy, right. Yes, easy from an administrative perspective. For example, a divorce clause is straightforward. In the event a partner or shareholder get divorced, the business has the right to purchase the ownership interest of the divorcing owner. Yup, easy.

But wait. What about the money? Let's say the corporation is worth $1.0 million, but only has $200,000 in cash. How does the corporation buy out a 50% owner with $200,000 when his or her share is worth $500,000? Enter the Buy Sell Agreement funded by life insurance and drafted by an attorney, and reviewed by your tax and accounting consultants.

The first requirement is to establish a price. This could be a fixed amount regardless of company health, or it could be a formula such as the 3x net income plus book value. Or to help avoid fighting and heartburn, the agreement could name a third-party business valuation firm or arbitrator. It is a balance between what is fair and what is easy to administer.

Next, the owners or partners would purchase a cash value life insurance policy on each of the other owners or partners. So, if there are three owners, each owner would buy two life insurance policies for a total of six policies. If an owner dies the remaining owners will use the death benefit to pay for the deceased's ownership interests. If the owner departs either through divorce or incapacitation or some other contractual obligation such as removal for cause, the remaining owners will use the cash surrender of the life insurance policy to purchase the departing owner's interest.

Many people are reading this book because they are considering getting into business, and perhaps the Buy Sell Agreement is just silly to even think about. But, as the Watson CPA Group has witnessed numerous times before, small businesses have a unique way of becoming big businesses, and at some point exit strategies must be considered.

Having said that, Buy Sell Agreements are unnecessary in two cases- first, when the company has no value. Second, when the remaining owners or partners could very easily shutdown the old company and start a new one without the deceased or departed owner.

Exit Plans, Succession

Selling your business is tough. What is even tougher is realizing the urgency in transferring the ownership and control to someone else. Handing over the keys come easy for some, and very challenging for others.

Books have been written just on exit and succession planning so it is difficult to cover every angle in our over-arching book. But there are some general concepts to consider.

Most small business owners fret over two things as they get older- what the heck to do with his or her day, and income. The first worry is like nailing Jello to the wall. Do you go into the office to open the mail? Is your only responsibility maintaining client relationships? Are you a mechanic at heart, and still want to tinker with cars but not sign checks?

It is amazing how many owners want to stay on in some capacity, and then realize that the daily grind stinks, they are not needed as much as they envisioned, and how fun not knowing the time or day can be. But at first, the control aspect.. the what will I do with my day aspect is a big challenge. Remember, most small business owners got into business by turning a hobby into a profession, and while it became a job on many levels, at the core it remained a passion. Tough to give up.

Just like Brett Favre- a case where a person needed the game more than the game needed the person. That is tough to accept. But then again, father time is undefeated. So, get over it.

Income is one of the other concerns. If I just sell my business, will I have enough income? It depends on two variables- what you need and how long will you need it. More challenges. More Jello.

So, what does a small business owner do?

Sell Outright

Selling can be nearly impossible. Remember, the United States Board of Tax Appeals defines fair market value as, "The price at which property would change hands between a willing buyer and a willing seller, neither being under any compulsion to buy or sell, and both having reasonable knowledge of the relevant facts."

Face it. Some businesses are much easier to sell, and some are not. Do you have a lot of competition? If you do, that might be good since competitors might be looking to increase market share.

Is your business unique? Makes a boatload of money, but very specialized and isolated with few competitors. Selling these types of business is much more difficult. Sure, you can always find an investor who wants to learn your craft, but that is not as easy as selling your Subway franchise to another Subway franchisee.

These are things that small business owners need to consider.

Key Employees
What about selling the company to one or two or three key employees? Perhaps. This can solve a lot of concerns right away.

First, you know the employees. You trust them. They might even share the same passion you do for the business. You've trained them to do things your way, which might or might not last, but at least you feel more comfortable than an unknown.

You can dictate the transition. So instead of a cliff-type transition where you lock the doors at 5:00PM on a Friday and hand the keys to the new owner at 8:00AM on a Monday, you can slowly slide towards phasing out. But then again, as Def Lepperd once said, "It is better to burn out than to fade away." Just kidding. Perhaps fading away is better.

Income can be generated by guaranteed payments or stock purchase loans. For example, one common way to sell your company to other key employees is have them buy a small percentage from the company. Let's say you have two people. The company sells 5% to each of them, and over time the new owners use their distributions to payback the buy-in.

When the buy-in is complete and a date has been established for transition, the company buys 90% from you. This will probably be financed, but cash certainly works. So, the company owns 90% of the stock, and the remaining controlling interest is now owned by the two key employees. They run the company. You are out, or at least fading away.

You have to be careful, and you will certainly need an attorney for these arrangements. S Corporations cannot have two classes of voting stock, so if you sell 10% to a key employee, he or she is an owner with voting rights from the beginning. He or she will receive a K-1, with taxable income. Depending on the tax consequence, there might need to be a split between the shareholder distribution being used for payback of the buy-in and personal income taxes.

During the buy-in period, termination for cause would require the forfeiture of the shares at a predetermined value. Same with death, divorce and incapacitation. Again, more lawyer stuff.

There truly are a million ways to structure these buy-ins. The Watson CPA Group recently represented a business owner who wanted to setup an account for three key employees. Profits exceeding a predetermined amount was placed into an account that would pay life insurance premiums. An insurable interest existed on each key employee for the company since their services were valuable. And if the key employee separated from the company, the company recovered the cash value of the life insurance policy.

It was intended for this account to grow in value plus the cash surrender which would be a sizeable down payment on the acquisition of the business ten years later. In these deals, valuation technique must be established at the onset.

In another deal, a client of ours did a similar cash account and arrangement with just one of his key employees. There was not a life insurance element. Basically it was a deposit of profit percentage each year for five years. The account could only be used as a down payment for acquisition. Need to be careful how this is structured too so it doesn't appear to be a second class of voting stock.

In both of these deals we represented the business owner. However, had we represented the key employees, we would have asked some basic questions such as how is profit margin determined? Should officer wages, depreciation and amortization be backed out? Does the employee or group of employees get first right of refusal? In other words, what prevents the business owner from selling to someone else? Is there a poison pill to that effect? Is there guaranteed seller financing? If so, what are the terms?

Again, many variations. Many dangers. Seek legal advice. Seek our advice.

[Rest of page intentionally left blank]

Chapter 12
Other S Corporation Thoughts

Rentals Owned by an LLC Fallacy

Should you put a rental in an LLC? Sure. Why not? Everyone else does. The real answer is Perhaps. There are several myths out there regarding the use of an LLC as a shelter from potential lawsuits and litigation, but most concerns stem from tortious liability.

So, what do you do? Securing a decent umbrella policy both at the personal and commercial level is the Watson CPA Group's strong recommendation for liability arising from your acts, errors and omissions. General umbrella policies are $300-$500 per year. The liability floor of many umbrellas is around $500,000 so you might have to raise the liability limits of each rental to meet the floor (so there's no break in coverage).

It appears that many credible lawsuits will sue to the limit of coverage to avoid lengthy and expensive trial litigation. Again, **please consult your attorney for your unique situation**. And no, we don't sell insurance.

Specifically for landlords, keep your rental in proper working order- tight railings, shoveled sidewalks and driveways, cooler hot water temperature settings, newer tempered windows, update smoke detectors, CO2 monitors, etc.

If you think you're clever and quit-claim the title / deed to the LLC after you close on the loan be careful. The lender might catch wind of it through routine title checks that they now perform, and the lender might call the loan. Not good.

Having said all that, it is not a bad idea to have an LLC own your rental property if you can. If you can avoid having to personally sign for the mortgage note through a non-recourse loan, that would be helpful too (lenders usually want a maximum of 60% loan to value). You might also consider having your tenants sign Hold Harmless Agreements. Essentially you are adding layers to your liability onion.

Additionally, if you are investing with partners an LLC with a solid operating agreement might be the only way to properly handle the ownership. A common situation is where two unrelated people invest together and need ways to affect ownership changes. Of course the Watson CPA Group can assist you in creating the LLC.

On small side note- real estate professionals might also be creating a mess with the material participation definitions within a partnership LLC. If you are considering to claim the real estate professional designation, we encourage you to read our recent tax article on the subject-

www.watsoncpagroup.com/realestatepro

Rental Losses with an S-Corp

As mentioned earlier, K-1 income from an S-Corp will be reported on Schedule E of your personal tax return since it is business investment income. If you do not materially participate in the S-Corp's operations, this can be a huge windfall if you are a rental property owner too. How does this play into S-Corps? Here we go-

Let's presume that you have a rental loss of $50,000. Rental income is typically considered passive, meaning that you are not directly earning the income as you would with a job. Passive losses may be deducted from non-passive income such as wages, but there are limits. Passive loss limits for married taxpayers max out at $25,000, and that number decreases as your gross income increases.

Specifically, passive loss reduces $1 for every $2 over $100,000 adjusted gross income and by $150,000 (for married filing joint taxpayers) the passive loss deduction is $0. Bummer. Not all is lost however.

Let's also presume that you are a minority investor in an S-Corp that earned $50,000 and reported the income on a K-1. Let's say you do NOT materially participate in the running of the S-Corp. Without the rental, you would be taxed on $50,000. Without the S-Corp you would only be able to deduct $25,000 worth of passive losses. But with both the rental and the S-Corp, you shelter $50,000 of your K-1 with your rental losses, and pay $0 tax. Cool, huh?

Granted, this is rare- most S-Corp shareholders actively participate and cannot offset their S-Corp income with rental losses. Although there might be some wiggle room with spouse A owning 90% of an S-Corp, for example, that he or she doesn't materially participate in. The same spouse A could then own 100% of the rental properties. This can get convoluted for sure, and careful tax planning must be exercised.

As a side note, it is NOT a good idea to make an S-Corp election on your LLC if it owns rental property. Rental property by definition is passive income (unless you are a real estate professional as defined by the IRS) and therefore not subject to self-employment tax. But if you run your rentals through an S-Corp, you will be required to perform payroll and you'll be paying Social Security and Medicare taxes which are the same as self-employment tax. Don't do it. You'll artificially increase your tax liability by essentially converting passive / unearned income into earned income.

Audit Rates and Risks with an S-Corp

There are audits risks with any business form, and for any taxpayer. Typically taxpayers under $200,000 in income face a 1% audit risk. And S-Corps face a 0.42% audit risk.

The Treasury Inspector General of Tax Administration (TIGTA) recently released figures about S-Corp audits. Over 62% of S-Corp audits resulted in a no-change audit. Good news. However, of those S-Corps with one shareholder and losses in excess of $25,000 for three consecutive years, the IRS had an average adjustment of $92,000 on the shareholder's individual tax return. Wow! Truth be told, most S-Corp audit concerns stem from net profits being paid out as distributions without corresponding salaries, and the associated Social Security and Medicare taxes.

To reiterate, only 0.42% of S-Corps were audited, and of those examinations, a whopping 62% resulted in no change. That's incredible odds. Same odds the Bears have of winning a Superbowl. Go Pack!

Back to audits- S-Corps have become super popular because of the low audit risk and more importantly the savings of self-employment taxes. The IRS is catching on however, and is targeting S-Corps where little to no salary is being paid to the shareholders. And this is easy to do. The IRS connects the dots by back-tracking K-1s to your company's EIN to your company's list of W-2s to the W-2's Social Security numbers back to your K-1. The IRS probably has an app for that.

If your K-1 does not have a corresponding W-2, or if your W-2 income is low compared to your K-1 income you are creeping up on the "let's call this guy" list. In other words, your audit risk is increasing.

As tax professionals we get concerned about S-Corps not paying themselves a reasonable wage for obvious reasons. And while it might appear that any salary will allow you to fly below the IRS radar, we strongly advise against it. The more abuse occurring in S-Corps is only going to attract the attention of Congress, and this quasi-loophole might close.

Read our tax article on audits, the types of audits and what to do with an audit at-

www.watsoncpagroup.com/audits

It's riveting.

And No, we do not and cannot play Audit Lottery. As professional tax preparers and accountants, the Watson CPA Group is bound by things such as standards, ethics and law. Just because audit rates might be low, we cannot take an unreasonable position or allow a client to file a fraudulent tax return.

We hate when the law gets in the way of a creative tax return!

1099 Income as Other Income, No Self-Employment (SE) Taxes

Can a 1099-MISC avoid self-employment taxes? Maybe. IRS Revenue Ruling 58-112 defines a trade or business activity as one that is regular, frequent and continuous. Revenue Rulings (58-112, 55-43 and 55-258) indicate that income from an occasional act or transaction, absent of proof of efforts to continue those acts or transactions on a regular basis, is not income from a trade or business.

Some taxpayers who were able to claim their income as 'other income' and avoid self-employment taxes had to demonstrate that the activity was a one-and-done event (giving a speech for example) or was sporadically done. In other words, the taxpayer cannot hold himself or herself out to the public as engaging in the activity.

If you meet these criteria, your 1099 income is exempt from self-employment taxes. If you attempt to file your tax returns with a 1099 and claim that it is not subjected to self-employment taxes, you have a good chance of getting a letter from the IRS. And No, they are not writing to say they agree. If you believe you are correct and need help fighting this, please let us know.

W-2 or 1099-MISC That Is The Question

Many people are finding themselves in a quandary between being a W-2 employee of a company or working for that same company in a contractor relationship. As a quick aside, the IRS and more importantly local state governments are going after companies who employ people as contractors. In Colorado, an independent contractor must hold himself or herself out to the public as a trade or profession before he or she can be deemed a contractor and NOT an employee.

Most contractor relationships would blow up if scrutinized. But the penalties and interest and fines and mess usually fall on the company and not the contractor / employee.

Check with your local jurisdiction to see how this is defined. You can also do a quick search for contractor versus employee and get hundreds of hits. Our KnowledgeBase Articles will also help at-

www.watsoncpagroup.com/kb/20/

Back to your quandary. Typically it is better to be a contractor than an employee. Your taxes are lower, you have more tax wiggle room so-to-speak, and you usually make more money. Why? When a company employs a person the company has all kinds of extra costs such as benefits, unemployment, workers' compensation, disability, health care potentially, etc. To give you a $1, some companies have to spend $1.40.

To give you this same $1 as a contractor costs them just that, $1.

If you are considering two offers, one as an employee and another as a contractor, contact the Watson CPA Group. We can model these scenarios for you and determine that the best choice is, and help you in the negotiation process.

Recap of S Corps

Here is a quick recap or summary of S Corps, and why you might consider making the election-

▲ Must have an LLC, partnership or C Corp in place

▲ Can save 8% - 10% of net income on taxes, possibly more

▲ Must run payroll and prepare a corporate tax return, no exceptions

▲ Payroll ran quarterly, previous distributions can be reclassified as wages (elegance!)

▲ Pull money out with reimbursements for business expenses (home office, mileage, etc.)

▲ Hefty retirement contributions allowed, reduces income

▲ Health insurance premiums and HSA contributions get dollar for dollar deduction

▲ Pay for your children's college expenses through the S Corp

▲ Can retroactively make the S-Corp election back to Jan 1 2017

▲ Low operational hassles

▲ Approximately **$2,940** in extra accounting costs for tax preparation (corporate and personal), payroll, tax modeling and consultation.

Attention! Sales pitch coming- S Corps are easy, they typically make sense if you are above $35,000 in net income after expenses, and they will improve your financial position in life. Contact us to get started. Did that sound too cheesy? Seriously the right questions must be asked and answered since not all S corporations make sense.

Epilogue

Watson CPA Group Fee Structure

The Watson CPA Group prides itself in being transparent and having a simple fee structure. Most business services and tax returns will fit into the fees described below. Sure, there's always the outlier or the unusual situation, but the following information gives you an idea of our philosophy. We only have time on this earth to sell, and we cannot inventory it. Our fees are an attempt to coincide with expected time spent.

Personal Tax Prep

We competitively offer a simple fee range of $500 to $700 for most personal tax returns. Small biz, rentals and state included.

Small Biz, LLCs, Rentals Tax Prep

Small businesses are commonly reported on your personal tax return on Schedule C. Rental activities are reported on Schedule E. Typical fee range is $500 to $700.

Partnerships, Corps Tax Prep

Fee range is $800 to $1,100 for partnership and corporate tax returns.

Business Formation

We can create a business or corporation for $425 plus the state filing fees. Includes Articles, EIN, Operating Agreement and S Corp election.

S-Corp Election

We can convert your business into an S Corp for $375. Even if you are late. Save on self-employment taxes and implement advantageous executive benefits!

S Corp Costs

People want to know costs, and while this might seem like more shameless self-promotion, you still need to understand what you are getting into. The Watson CPA Group specializes in S corporations which have a small number of shareholders, and often just a one-person show.

Epilogue

Because it is a core competency for us, we have created an S Corp package that includes the following-

	Aspen	Vail	Breck	Keystone
S Corp Reasonable Salary Calculation	Yes	Yes	Yes	Yes
Section 199A Pass-Thru Optimization	Yes	Yes	Yes	Yes
S Corp Payroll Filings and Deposits	Yes	Yes		
Annual Processing (W2s, up to five 1099's)	Yes	Yes		
S Corporation Tax Prep (Form 1120S)	Yes	Yes	Yes	Yes
Individual Tax Prep (Form 1040), One Owner	Yes		Yes	
Estimated Tax Payments	Yes	Yes	Yes	Yes
2018 Tax Planning, Mock Tax Returns	Yes	Yes	Yes	Yes
Unlimited Consultation, PBRs	Yes	Yes	Yes	Yes
First Research Industry Reports	Yes	Yes	Yes	Yes
Small Business Tax Deductions Optimization	Yes	Yes	Yes	Yes
Solo 401k Plan	Yes	Yes	Yes	Yes
IRS Audit Defense	Yes		Yes	
Annual Fee	**$2,940**	**$2,640**	**$2,460**	**$2,160**
Monthly Fee	**$245**	**$220**	**$205**	**$180**

Couple of things to keep in mind- we make very little profits on payroll processing... we offer it as a convenience to our clients. One throat to choke with a single call can be reassuring but if you want to run your payroll, go for it! And... the benefit of the Watson CPA Group preparing both tax returns is that we slide things around depending on income limitations, phaseouts, alternative minimum tax (AMT), etc. Having our arms around both can yield some good tax savings!

Some more things to consider- Since only a partial year remains, our usual annual fee is pro-rated to not charge you for services you didn't use (like payroll and consultation). However, a large chunk of our annual fee is tax preparation which is typically a fixed amount of $1,300 (both corporate and personal). Whether we onboard you in January, July or December, we have to prepare a full year tax return. This increases the monthly fee for the remaining months of 2018 but the monthly fee will later decrease in January of 2019 to reflect the amounts above.

Break-even analysis is based on our annual fee of $2,940. If an S corporation saves you 8% to 10% (on average) in taxes over the garden variety LLC, then $2,940 divided by 8.5% equals $35,000 of net business income after expenses.

You can always find someone to do it for less- we know that. At the same time, we have a vested interest in your success and provide sound tax and business consultation as a part of our service. Here are links to our Periodic Business Review agenda and End of Year Tax Planning that we cover throughout the year so our consultation to you is comprehensive-

www.watsoncpagroup.com/PBR

www.watsoncpagroup.com/EOY

These general fees will cover most situations. However, depending on the number of transactions, accounts and employees, these fees might have to be adjusted to reflect additional complexities. The Watson CPA Group is not out to gouge anyone or do a quick money grab- we want to build relationships by doing things right for a reasonable fee. Check out our fee structure here-

www.watsoncpagroup.com/fee

No more shameless promotion… the book is almost over. Hang in there!

Client Portal, Long Distance Relationships

Since 2007 we have used ShareFile to administer our Client Portal which provides secure, online document exchange. The Client Portal will allow you to securely upload your financial documents to the Watson CPA Group.

Most email servers balk at files over 10MB. The client portal does not have a file size limitation which is great since QuickBooks can be a little chunky.

You can also install a PDF printer allowing you to print anything to a PDF file. Screen shots, online activity, Excel spreadsheets; anything you normally print to paper can be saved as a PDF. This file can then be uploaded to us through the Client Portal. Most operating systems have a PDF printer already installed- if not, please do an internet search for free PDF printers. This is a very handy tool.

All financial statements and any "soft" copies of files that you send us will be placed in your client portal folder. For example, if you fax us some information and then lose your copy, you can download your fax in PDF from your portal folder. How cool is that? We recently had a fire in Colorado Springs, and one of our clients lost everything- but her financial information was safely kept in her client portal.

Long distance is what the Watson CPA Group does. With over 80% of our clients living outside of Colorado Springs, we are comfortable with phone calls, email and Skype. We are also comfortable with preparing financial reports and tax returns in all the states. Our researching tools, and the speed and volume at which data travels nowadays allows us to serve clients' needs everywhere.

Accounting Services
The strongest reason for using a professional accounting service is- you do what you do best with your time. Let us do what we do best with ours. Sure, you trot down to BestBuy and buy the latest and greatest of QuickBooks. But the negative effects of that move can be insidious.

First, QuickBooks makes everyone feel like an accountant. Accounting is a profession, not a hobby. Let's not forget the 5 years of business school plus a killer exam. While it is not necessarily difficult, an accountant will look at things differently than a bookkeeper. We are accountants. We are not bookkeepers. QuickBooks is a garbage in garbage out system- it won't prevent you from depreciating real estate under Section 179 (which is a No-No by the way). QuickBooks won't prevent goofy payroll or balance sheet entries either. But Yes, we use QuickBooks too.

Most importantly, would you rather be closing your next sale or BBQing on a Sunday with buddies, or getting sucked into the world of accounting at the hands of your latest QuickBooks purchase? Focus on growing your business, and we'll focus on reporting it to the IRS while minimizing the tax consequence.

What We Offer With Accounting Services
The Watson CPA Group offers accurate and comprehensive financial reporting with our accounting services. An in-house bookkeeper is good, but another set of objective eyes can prevent errors and possible fraud. Banks, lenders and IRS agents prefer a set of accounting records and financials that have been prepared by a Certified Public Accountant. Remember, these professionals review financial records every day, and they can quick spot accidental inconsistencies and errors. Heck, even PaySimple which offers ACH and credit card processing might require financial reports to judge your credit worthiness.

For our local Colorado Springs accounting clients, on or about the 29th of the preceding month we will send a postcard and an email alerting you of our expected pickup date (between the 6th and 8th). Even with online bank and credit card access, there might be items you need to provide us such as sales reports for sales tax processing, government notices, new employee forms, inventory figures, etc. Face to face interaction might be old school, and while we live in a virtual world we stay true to our roots.

Remember, even if we don't do the data entry, at least consider using us as a backup to your current accounting. This type of insurance can help you sleep at night or thru your kid's talent show.

Lastly, when we dive into your financial world we can then offer healthy and sound business consultation.

Yes We Use QuickBooks

As Chris Rock once said, men don't get married.. men surrender. Same with QuickBooks. For as much as we despise the QuickBooks monstrosity, it's here to stay for a while, and therefore we have surrendered. Having said that, using QuickBooks on your behalf offers some advantages.

Portability is the biggest reason. If you decide to switch accountants or a meteor crashed into our office with laser precision and uncanny timing, you can take your QuickBooks data file to any other accountant. You can also buy QuickBooks, take some webinars and be your own bookkeeper in a pinch. PeachTree, Creative Solutions and other accounting packages are OK, but the portability is suspect.

Online Accounting Software

Online accounting packages or programs are becoming more prolific, and frankly they can do a better job. Xero Accounting, FreshBooks, and Wave Accounting are just a few. Online accounting offers simplicity, whereas QuickBooks is 90% more than most businesses need. Online accounting also allows for collaboration between you, us and your staff (or partners).

Accounting Deliverables, Financials

We perform bank and credit card reconciliations, code your transactions and turn it all into financial reports that are elegant, simple and meaningful. Yes, we said elegant! Profit and loss reports, balance sheets and general ledger entries are the common reports you'll get, but we can customize anything.

There are three levels of assurance provided when creating financial reports; Compilation, Review and Audit. Each level has unique standards as governed by professional organizations such as American Institute of Certified Public Accountants (AICPA) and Generally Accepted Accounting Principles (GAAP). Your financial reports are considered Compilations, and are limited to internal management use only. However, we can perform Reviews and Audits as necessary (yuck!).

Industry Statistics, Comparisons

The Watson CPA Group can also create charts and graphs to determine trends in your sales, or other expense categories that are sensitive to your success. For example, cost of goods sold is critical to those in the fast food industry (quick service restaurant)- how do you compare to yourself in previous months or years, and how do you compare to others in the same business?

Statistical comparisons and trend analysis is a service we provide to each owner to identify action items and areas needing improvement. When factoring the impact of cost of goods sold, labor and rent on business profits, the variations can be dramatic. We will work with you to keep more of your money as you continue to develop your business.

Anyone can crunch numbers. But we crunch numbers AND tell you what they mean, plus offer business consultation and coaching to create a successful future.

Exchanging Documentation

We are flexible in extracting the necessary information from our clients- email, fax, mail, drop-off, pickup, etc. Whatever works best and easiest for you! We are a Colorado Springs accounting firm, but we work with clients throughout the country, in any location. Technology is our friend.

Having said that, most clients give us direct access to their bank accounts (checking accounts and business credit cards) to make the process seamless. Sounds crazy but several banks such as Chase, Wells Fargo, Bank of America, just to name a few, have an **Accountant's Login** option. This allows us to view canceled checks and download statements. We can't move money, write checks, transfer- basically all the bad stuff. Please check with your bank to see if this would be an option for you- it would save you valuable time and resources by not having to provide this information. We get it ourselves!

If this type of access makes you uncomfortable we will work with you to find a solution that fits for everyone. But remember- we truly have better things to do than snoop around your world. We get in. We get out. We move on. All with a helpful smile.

More About the Watson CPA Group

The Watson CPA Group has provided worldwide business consulting, accounting and tax preparation from our Colorado Springs offices since 2007. We use secure client portals to safely exchange financial information, saving you time and resources. In person appointments are nice, better with donuts, but are not required.

With 14 tax and business consultation professionals including 5 CPAs on our team, the Watson CPA Group consults on corporation structures, business coaching, industry analysis, executive benefits, retirement planning, exit strategies and business valuations, income modeling and tax representation. Not all firms can say they offer this approach beyond the nuts and bolts of accounting and tax preparation. Here is some more information on our team-

www.watsoncpagroup.com/team

This depth is an incredible benefit to our clients, including our professional network of knowledgeable Colorado CPAs. And No, we are not the stuffy firm down the street. We are your advocate!

Consultative Approach

The Watson CPA Group is not just a group of tax preparers or number crunchers- anyone can carry the one or balance a checkbook! We are tax and business consultants, and our firm will take you through the cycles of your personal and business lives. Many accountants are only compliance oriented, and while IRS compliance is critical, being proactive is equally important.

Final Words

We hope you enjoy reading this book, and wish you the very best of luck in all your endeavors. If we can be of any assistance, please don't hesitate to reach out to us

Made in the USA
Middletown, DE
17 March 2018